DISRUPT YOU!

Jay Samit

DISRUPT YOU!

**Master Personal
Transformation,
Seize Opportunity,
and Thrive in the
Era of Endless**

Transferable skills chart © NOVA: www.novaworks.org

www.flatironbooks.com

The Library of Congress Cataloging-in-Publication Data is available upon request.

ISBN 978-1-250-05937-6 (hardcover)
ISBN 978-1-250-05939-0 (e-book)

Flatiron books may be purchased for educational, business, or promotional use. For information on bulk purchases, please contact the Macmillan Corporate and Premium Sales Department at 1-800-221-7945, extension 5442, or write to specialmarkets@macmillan.com.

First Edition: July 2015

10 9 8 7 6 5 4 3 2 1

To all those who seek to disrupt the status quo with big ideas.
May this book shorten your journey.

Contents

Foreword

When new users discover LinkedIn, most intuitively grasp that it offers a useful way for individuals to pursue jobs and provides a way for companies to recruit those individuals. But even today, not everyone recognizes—and thus not everyone truly capitalizes on—the larger capabilities that LinkedIn unleashes.

When I first started talking about LinkedIn with Jay Samit in 2006, though, he got it. He understood that LinkedIn is more than an online résumé service and even more than a tightly connected distributed-trust recruiting tool. Jay recognized immediately that LinkedIn is a powerful network-intelligence platform—a way to build relationships, research competitors, learn best practices, surface new workplace trends, and ultimately identify opportunities.

Now that I've read about the unique tactic Jay used to launch his career in the entertainment industry after graduating from UCLA in the early 1980s, I understand better why he grasped the full implications of LinkedIn so quickly. As you will discover when you read the anecdote yourself, Jay was already looking at the world through network-intelligence lenses at a time when most people still thought the only things that networks delivered were new episodes of *Cheers* and *Dallas*.

Embracing innovation has always been a hallmark of Jay's career. Whether creating the market for royalty-free digital stock photography or trying to get major record labels to adopt new digital distribution strategies, Jay has always looked toward technological disruption as a positive force.

Instead of learning one way to do business, then settling into complacence, he has actively sought ways to create new markets; introduce new products, services, and operations; and broaden consumer bases. Instead of closing his eyes to change or simply trying to endure and survive it, he has responded to shifts in the market with foresight and a mandate to make the most out of the new opportunities that disruption creates.

And that's the mind-set all professionals should aspire to now. In this networked era, new technologies introduce change at faster and faster rates. Tightly connected social platforms further accelerate and amplify these technological and economic shifts. Disruption is the order of the day—and it trickles down, reshaping industries, companies, and the careers of individual professionals.

Whatever industry you're in, the technologies that drive it are going to change. Your customers are going to demand new solutions. Your competitors are going to alter their tactics. To stay relevant, you must keep your career in permanent beta. That means committing to a lifetime of learning and professional growth, a lifetime of strategic adaptation.

To successfully navigate today's professional landscape, you must understand the dynamics of disruption. The currents of change shift more quickly and with more force now. If you're not ready for these shifts, they'll clobber you. But as Jay teaches in this book, you can learn to spot them early. You can swim with the currents of change instead of against them. And when you do that, disruption can propel you toward opportunities, creative challenges, and prosperity.

—Reid Hoffman, November 2014

DISRUPT YOU!

Introduction

"Psst . . . What would you do with a million dollars?" the sexy dis-embodied voice would whisper to passersby. After stopping in his tracks and looking around, the surprised pedestrian would see a visual parade of yachts and race cars, mansions and glamorous women in evening gowns dancing across the kiosk's twenty-inch screen. The year was 1984, and California was in dire straits. The country was emerging from a recession, and California's unemployment rate was at an all-time high. Finally, and with much fanfare, it was decided that the troubled state would run a lottery, the revenues of which would generate the sorely needed funds for the state's schools. A multi-million-dollar contract would be awarded to the company that developed the best technology system for selling the new lottery's tickets. My prototype kiosk with built-in motion detectors was going to be my ticket to fame and fortune.

At the time, I was a twenty-four-year-old with a small multimedia company that did special effects and production work for hire. Our specialty was producing video games and interactive training programs on laserdisc. When the lottery was announced, I had a big idea: why not apply my expertise in the arcade video-game business to help the lottery become more interactive and fun? I partnered with Syntech, a lottery machine manufacturer that supplied ticketing hardware to create a player-activated terminal dubbed the PAT 2500. The PAT 2500 would actually talk to potential customers and encourage them to buy tickets. I outfitted the seventy-nine-inch-tall computer kiosks with laserdisc players, motion detectors, and speakers. The kiosk would beckon to anyone who came near it. Using Intel 8031 microprocessors, the kiosk was state-of-the-art. It's hard to imagine this now, but in 1985 this rudimentary contraption was one of the very first commercial machines capable of handling audio and video. At the time, almost no one had a computer in their home or on their desk, and the computers that were used in workplaces were shared by multiple users and had small, monochromatic displays. The PAT 2500 featured a twenty-inch full-color display and capacitive touchscreen. I was convinced that my machine and I were going to revolutionize the way lottery tickets would be bought and sold all over the world. At twenty-four years old, I was sure I had figured out how to become a billionaire.

I was competing for the lucrative California Lottery contract against GTECH, who manufactured a primitive adding-machine-size unit that displayed greenish numbers on a black CRT. There was no comparison. I was sure my time had come. I was the young Turk disrupting the lottery industry! I was to the lottery what Henry Ford's Model T was to horse-buggy makers!

I was wrong.

We weren't awarded the contract. GTECH won the contract, and I was stuck with an amazing kiosk in my garage.[1] I was nothing more than a guy with big ideas; I was intent on changing the world, making a lot of money, and having fun along the way, but after I lost the lottery contract I was broke and dejected.

With no lottery prospects, I spent the night before I was to fly home to Los Angeles from Sacramento tossing and turning. That night, thinking about who I was and how desperate I was to make my mark in the business world, I began what I would later come to call "self-disrupting." I analyzed all the pieces that came together to form my identity. I began to define what unique experiences and knowledge I had that would set me apart from my peers. I thought about the way I made decisions, how I processed and responded to information, how I approached problems. I thought about the way I presented myself to the world and how I communicated my abilities to potential business partners and clients. And I thought about how I was spending my time and energy. If I was going to find opportunities to make a name for myself in the world, I was going to have to change something in my approach. Then I started thinking about my business in those same terms: Where was the value in my lottery machine? How could I put it to use in a different way?

By the time I landed in L.A. the next morning, a subtle shift had taken place. When I arrived at LAX, looking for the cheapest way to get home from the airport, I stopped by the information booth to ask about shuttle times and services. Just my luck: no one was manning the booth, and there was no place in the terminal to find shuttle or bus information. I realized, perhaps as a result of my previous hours of self-questioning, that this problem presented an opportunity. I started to think through my situation from every possible angle: How many of Los Angeles International Airport's fifty million annual visitors shared this problem? How many hours a day were the booths manned, and at what cost? How many languages do visitors speak? Instinctively, I was deconstructing the size and scope of the opportunity while reassembling the strengths only I could bring to solving it. Who else had a prototype for a state-of-the-art interactive kiosk in their garage? Twenty-four hours earlier, I had thought my big idea was interactive lottery kiosks, and now I knew I had been wrong. With one pivot I realized what my next business venture would be: automated airport information booths.

I adapted the PAT 2500 into an airport information system that provided taxi, bus, and shuttle data in eight languages and even added an autodial phone (this was years before people had mobile phones) to connect the traveler with the dispatcher. By just touching the screen, visitors would be welcomed to Los Angeles by a friendly woman who spoke their language and could provide them with accurate information on how to cost-effectively get to more than five hundred local destinations. Within a couple of years my fledgling work-for-hire company had become LAX's sole information service provider, putting in place the systems billions of travelers still rely on today. Just think about the last time you were at the airport: did you interact with a kiosk to print boarding passes, check luggage, or change your seat? The kiosk that disrupted the human ticketing agent was once a failed lottery machine.

I was twenty-four years old, and from the ashes of failure I had risen to launch myself on a path of serial entrepreneurship—a path I've now been on for more than thirty years, and one that's never let me down.

———

That early success was not an accident. It was the logical outcome of the introspective process I first implemented that night after finding out I had lost the lottery kiosk contract. I had always been creative, and I knew I wanted to make a splash in the business and entertainment worlds. I had lots of ideas, but I could never pull the pieces together to make my dreams happen. Like most people, I didn't know how to channel my ideas and energies into positive actions. Frustrated by my lack of progress, I reexamined my assumptions about myself and my personal skills. I came to refer to the intense and introspective process of questioning my beliefs and goals—which has, time and again, led to my biggest business breakthroughs—as self-disruption. Through self-disruption I have come to see that I can accomplish what I once thought impossible. I've discovered that if I am able to express any problem as a series of challenges, I can build a team capable of rising to those challenges. I have realized that businesses—whether they make dog food or software—don't sell products; they sell solutions. Over the course of my career, my method of self-disruption has led me to work quickly and easily across entirely divergent industries—automotive, telecommunications, packaged goods, and quick service restaurants—changing the very nature of those businesses. I went from running a twenty-person startup to being a global officer of an international company with over 160,000 employees. I've collaborated with Fortune 500 companies, foreign governments, and even the Vatican. In one year alone, I took stakes in more than twenty companies around the world (without investing a dime) and generated over $100 million profit. And best of all, I've never worried about job security or where my next big idea will come from, because I can always return to the techniques of self-disruption that have helped me transform myself and my businesses time and again.

> Businesses—whether they make dog food or software—don't sell products; they sell solutions.

Over the past three decades, I've come to see that I'm not alone in the way I question my beliefs and find opportunity. History's successful innovators have always employed aspects of this approach. Gutenberg's ushering in of the Renaissance and the eventual democratization of knowledge wasn't born from the invention of movable type, but rather from the way he deconstructed the value chain of surplus German wine presses, enabling him to invent the printing press. Magician Harry Houdini went from doing multiple performances a day in a dime show to being the most famous entertainer on the planet—not because he was the best prestidigitator, but because he disrupted the way entertainment was mass-marketed. Nearly a century later, Canadian street performer Guy Laliberté would similarly deconstruct the value chain of the circus, disrupt the industry with Cirque du Soleil, dominate Las Vegas showrooms, and become a multibillionaire.

Every successful disruptor employs one or more of these techniques to transform themselves, their businesses, and the world. They look internally, questioning their assumptions about themselves and reevaluating their unique talents. They put themselves on the path to success, even if they didn't know what might lie ahead. And they understand that they cannot fall in love with their ideas, that they must be willing to destroy their concepts and pivot their energies before the market can render their businesses obsolete.

All disruption starts with introspection. The way we understand our internal value chains—how we view ourselves and how we interpret our personal strengths—is at the core of all external success. I have applied these insights to raising over $800 million for startup companies as well as launching new businesses in billion-dollar industries as diverse as telecommunications, music, and ecommerce. I didn't go to the right schools or know the right people, but I did learn how to disrupt my own belief systems in order to reposition myself to take advantage of opportunity and achieve success. And I've done it again and again—achieving resilience and security in an often unstable business landscape.

> 🐦 *All disruption starts with introspection.*

The self-made billionaire in his twenties, an unheard-of possibility a decade ago, now happens with regular frequency. The startup company, with little funding and a small staff, displaces hundred-year-old companies with billions in revenues virtually overnight. The consultant, with no background in technology or operating a business, makes millions of dollars from teaching one course online. The Arab Spring, which peacefully overthrew long-standing governments in Bahrain, Tunisia, and Yemen, is able to successfully force rulers from power without weapons or international support. The tightly interconnected world of the twenty-first century is exploding with new opportunities for personal empowerment and financial independence. What did all of these disruptions have in common? They were led by people who understood how to analyze their internal value chains to pinpoint their unique talents and capabilities and then to analyze the value chains of their industries to find opportunities for disruption.

Sir Richard Branson founded Virgin as a record store, only to discover that the real value was in creating, not just selling, records. The most successful serial disruptor in history, he has created billion-dollar companies in eight different industries.

Lowell "Bud" Paxson deconstructed the value chain of his failing Florida radio station. When no one would advertise on his station, he bought surplus goods and sold them on air instead of running commercials. This idea was so successful that he transformed his local station into the billion-dollar retailing empire now known as the Home Shopping Network.

A century ago, Joyce Clyde Hall was going broke selling penny postcards, until he killed his big idea that people wanted to write home to loved ones. His realization that most people can't write led him to fill out the postcard for them. With the stroke of a pen he created Hallmark and launched the entire greeting card industry.

A few years ago, the website Tune In Hook Up was designed by Chad Hurley, Steve Chen, and Jawed Karim to disrupt the world of online dating. Most dating sites featured still images of prospective partners, but the former PayPal employees thought that showcasing dating videos would be much better. While the dating site was a failure, Hurley, Chen, and Karim realized that people really enjoyed watching the uploaded videos. Abandoning their original dating site concept, the team pivoted and renamed the site YouTube.

The steps for disruption are not taught in college or business school.

Yet every successful entrepreneur's story, and decades of quantitative research, prove the validity of the techniques I describe throughout *Disrupt You!* It makes no difference whether your goal is to make millions of dollars or solve global warming, start a restaurant or a revolution.

For years I have mentored entrepreneurs and aspiring students on how to disrupt. What I've discovered is that these techniques can be applied to virtually any field or endeavor. I truly believe that everyone can achieve personal success. *Disrupt You!* provides readers with instructions for self-disruption as well as the tools for applying the knowledge they gain to disrupt the business and noncommercial worlds. This book is for all those willing to annihilate their assumptions in order to create a reimagined self. It's a guide for those wishing to get more out of their jobs, careers, and lives. It can also be a guide for our world, as disruptors are the only ones capable of dealing with the macro issues affecting society at large and our planet as a whole. *Disrupt You!* reveals a new paradigm for breaking the patterns that limit personal success and growth by sharing actual case studies from dozens of the world's most accomplished disruptors.

Renaissance Florentine philosopher Niccolò Machiavelli said that entrepreneurs are "simply those who understand that there is little difference between obstacle and opportunity and are able to turn both to their advantage." It's this type of thinking that will lead to success in today's world.

You have a choice: pursue your dreams or be hired by someone else to help them fulfill their dreams. The great disruptors constantly reinvent themselves and their careers. They never fear losing their jobs, because they create jobs. They control their own destinies. This book is written to answer two very basic questions: How did they do it? How can I do it? The third question is entirely up to you: Will you do it?

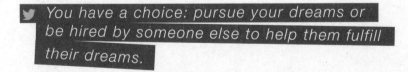

You have a choice: pursue your dreams or be hired by someone else to help them fulfill their dreams.

Chapter One

In Defense of Disruption

The world as we have created it
is a process of our thinking.
It cannot be changed
without changing our thinking.
—Albert Einstein

In first-century Rome, an innovative glassmaker created *vitrum flexile*, flexible glass. Proud of his invention, he requested an audience with Emperor Tiberius. The emperor threw the drinking vessel down on the ground, but, much to his surprise, it did not shatter. At the time, all drinking vessels were made of gold and silver, which tainted wine with a metallic taste. Considering the glassmaker's creation, Tiberius realized it would completely disrupt the Roman economy. If goblets were no longer made of gold and silver, the value of the precious metals would diminish immeasurably. Tiberius asked the glassmaker if anyone else knew the secret formula. When the inventor took a solemn oath that he alone knew how to create *vitrum flexile*, the emperor had the man beheaded.

Today it is not so easy to thwart disruption.

The business headlines will tell you that the world has become a scary place. Advances in 3-D printing that create just-in-time inventory threaten the jobs of 320 million manufacturing workers around the globe.[1] Self-driving cars, trucks, and drones will displace tens of millions more workers. Renewable energy, such as solar photovoltaic cells, which have decreased in cost by more than 85 percent since the year 2000, will shift the geopolitical future of nations whose economies are supported by fossil fuels.[2] According to a recent McKinsey Global

Institute study, the automation of knowledge work will have a $5 trillion to $7 trillion impact on white-collar jobs.[3] Ecommerce and productivity gains in delivering retail goods are expected to further reduce the number of retail stores by as much as 15 percent.[4] What is the real estate value of a mall, factory, or office building when its purpose is made obsolete? America's workforce is now dealing with the realization that even though the recession is over, it has been a jobless recovery. This era of endless innovation has resulted in large multinational corporations shedding more than 2.9 million domestic jobs since the recession, and the pace of change is only accelerating.[5] It seems that whenever reporters, news anchors, pundits, and economists discuss this rapid pace of change, they throw around the word *disruption*—often employing the language of warfare—destruction and disorder. As generations-old companies and once valued brands and businesses are displaced by nimble, efficient new startups, we're led to believe that disruptive new technologies have given the dogs in our dog-eat-dog world a powerful and violent strain of rabies.

The disruption characterizing our current business landscape goes beyond innovation—and there *is* a difference between the two. Take the mighty sword, for example. Men have been fighting with swords for over five thousand years. Early bronze swords were lethally sharp, but, given the weak tensile strength of bronze, they had to be short in length. The innovation of steel and other alloys allowed the sword to grow in length, broadness, and societal importance. Skilled swordsmen became the defenders of kings and kingdoms, and the sword became the symbol of liberty and strength. Innovation therefore consisted of how each new culture and generation improved upon swords, changing how they were forged and how they were wielded in combat. But one of the great Hollywood adventure movies, *Raiders of the Lost Ark,* provides the perfect illustration of how disruption works. When Indiana Jones is challenged to a duel by an Arab swordsman flamboyantly waving his massive scimitar, Indy nonchalantly reaches into his holster, pulls out a revolver, and shoots the swordsman dead. With the presence of the pistol, the sword was made obsolete. Disruption is to existing businesses and business models what Indy's Smith & Wesson was to the sword: it instantly changes the way the world functions and the course of history.

Disruption is almost always led by a technological change. But disruption's impact extends far beyond the technology industries. Eli Whitney's invention of the cotton gin in 1793 did more than just make cotton a profitable crop; it led to a quintupled growth in the number of slaves in the South and sparked the industrial revolution in the North. It catapulted a young nation's economy and hastened the onslaught of the Civil War. Every American's life was affected. History was altered by this one technological breakthrough. A technology or product is disruptive when it creates an entirely new market, consumer base, or user and destroys or displaces the market for the technology it replaced. Email disrupted postal mail, for example, and Wikipedia disrupted the traditional multivolume bound encyclopedia.

Early in my career, I saw firsthand the difference between something that is truly disruptive and something that is merely innovative. When I launched my first company, Jasmine Productions, we were a small twelve-person operation doing small-time graphic and special-effects production work for hire. I was eager for an entry into mainstream Hollywood. At the same time, the Japanese electronics manufacturer Pioneer was also looking for an inroad. Pioneer had acquired control of a new home video format—the laser videodisc—from Philips and MCA (Universal Studios). Branded LaserDisc, the twelve-inch vinyl-record-size platters had audio and video quality vastly superior to that of VHS and Betamax videocassettes, which were then popular with consumers for home video entertainment. The laserdisc player was marketed as a "record player that produces beautiful sound and pictures," which could be enjoyed on your television. Laserdiscs were read by lasers and had no moving parts, as fragile videocassettes did, so the picture and sound quality would not deteriorate over time, nor would the discs jam or tear the way videotape did. Additionally, whereas videotape had to spool linearly through the entire tape to get to a different point, the lasers could instantly go from any point in the video to any other point, thus creating the possibility of "interactive video." Stories could have different outcomes depending on which choice a viewer made. Unlike the linear narratives of movies and television, the laserdisc could combine the interactivity of video games with the production values of film. I was convinced this would revolutionize all forms of entertainment, and I wanted to lead this revolution.

Pioneer Electronics needed developers to create consumer titles for this emerging field. The technology was so superior to videotape that I couldn't see how it could fail. I joined up with other filmmakers to work on *Time Frame,* the first interactive laserdisc title produced for the home, which Pioneer was going to distribute under its newly minted DiscoVision label. I felt like a rock star signed to a music label. We had dozens of ideas for interactive laserdiscs for kids and adults to enjoy. We planned to produce hit after hit. IBM and the Japanese electronics manufacturers had spent hundreds of millions of dollars inventing this new medium, and I was lucky enough to get in on the ground floor. I was going to be the king of the laserdisc and forever change home entertainment. I was sure the laserdisc would replace videocassettes the way television replaced radio after World War II.

Unfortunately, after the first Christmas season, it became clear that because home consumers couldn't use laserdiscs to record their favorite television shows, the way they had been doing with videocassettes, consumers saw the value of laserdiscs as being very limited. Our first major sales season was a bust. We knew we were going nowhere fast. The laserdisc's only redeeming legacy was that its core technologies would become the basis for the more successful optical disc formats that followed over the coming decades: the CD and the DVD. As quickly as I had imagined how big the interactive video home market and my personal fortune were going to be, the sales never materialized, and Pioneer abandoned home entertainment. How could we have been so wrong?

I learned then that there is a difference between failing and failure. Failing is trying something that you learn doesn't work. Failure is throwing in the towel and giving up. I refused to be a failure. As Winston Churchill once said, "Success is stumbling from failure to failure with no loss of enthusiasm."

> I learned then that there is a difference between failing and failure. Failing is trying something that you learn doesn't work.

I realized that the laserdisc hadn't transformed home entertainment because the only new thing it offered customers was an improved experience. The laserdisc sought to compete on the playing field already established by the VCR. The VCR disrupted television viewing for an entire generation; laserdiscs were just an incremental improvement in visual quality. Laserdiscs were sold in the same sales channels, by the same salespeople, to the same consumer as videocassettes.

For a product or a process to be truly disruptive, it must create a new market and transform an existing business model. This realization launched my thirty-year study of disruption. True disruption alters a market or system forever. The DVR, for example, didn't just change how we watch television; it upended the entire advertising-supported television business model of the previous fifty years.

> 🐦 *True disruption alters a market or system forever.*

But just as early man progressed from the Stone Age to the Bronze Age to the Iron Age, each disruptive technology will itself eventually be disrupted. One hundred fifty years ago, the invention of the gramophone was disruptive. Because of the gramophone, mankind's love of music became a mass media industry (a market was created), and for the first time in history, artists and musicians were able to amass great wealth from their craft (a new business model was launched). The gramophone meant that experiencing the musical talent of Enrico Caruso, the greatest tenor of his generation, was no longer restricted to just a few affluent patrons of opera. Common citizens developed a passion for music and could suddenly afford a library of popular recordings. Records were so popular with the masses that blues singer Bessie Smith became a millionaire in the 1920s. Eventually, through incremental improvements in recording and playback, the compact disc was born. The CD became the crowning technological innovation of the music industry, but it did not force any significant changes to the multibillion-dollar business model. Artists still signed with labels, labels still produced and released albums, and consumers purchased the entire thing on a CD, just as they had once purchased a record.

The $40 billion music industry was born of one invention—the gramophone—and comfortably relied on one business model for more than a century of profits. Then disruption came from another technology: the Internet. Disruptive digital services such as Napster, iTunes, and Spotify killed the mighty album, creating a market for single downloads; eviscerated the music labels' revenue model; and shot the industry dead. One can argue about the inherent value of each incremental innovation in business, but the impact of disruption is undeniable and unmistakable. In the wake of digital disruption, EMI—the hundred-year-old company that invented electric recording, the company that signed Caruso, the Beatles, and thousands of other artists—simply ceased to exist.

In the twenty-first century, billion-dollar industries can be disrupted and waylaid virtually overnight—no sector of commerce or government is immune to the threat.

For the record companies and recording artists disrupted by digital downloads and MP3s, for the postal workers and direct-mail businesses disrupted by email, for the newspaper and publishing executives disrupted by new advertising models like Craigslist and delivery platforms like ebooks and desktop self-publishing, disruption brings with it a sense of doom and gloom. We think of these businesses contracting and jobs being lost. But the truth is, wherever a business has been disrupted, volume is released. Massive opportunity is created and major shifts in economic wealth follow. Disruption creates opportunity. The railroads created railroad barons. The automobile created oil tycoons. Silicon Valley has created thousands of dot-com millionaires. Most people are surprised to learn that the richest man in Los Angeles is not a Hollywood celebrity, but a doctor who made over $7 billion by developing disruptive pharmaceuticals.[6] Identify the right trend or create the right startup, and billions of dollars could be yours. Anyone has the power to disrupt, and everyone has the opportunity to benefit from disruption. There has never been a time in history when upward mobility has been so equitably disbursed.

> There has never been a time in history when upward mobility has been so equitably disbursed.

Yes, the pace of disruption has increased exponentially, thanks to a confluence of disruptive technologies that change how we work, communicate, travel, learn, and age. A century ago, having a few thousand customers for your product made you nationally known to America's seventy-six million citizens. Now, over six billion potential consumers are just one click away from becoming customers. Cloud computing, wearable technology, 3-D printing, and the Internet of Things may just be abstract concepts to you today, but the impact they will have on your career and fortune is inevitable. There are fortunes to be made by identifying and exploiting the smallest aspects of these seismic shifts in technology and business organizations. Executives at Gulf Oil didn't have to know how to design or manufacture automobiles in order to recognize the growing demand for gasoline in 1913; they just had to satisfy the consumer's needs, so they created the first drive-in gas station. Today the world spends $2.5 trillion consuming petroleum,[7] and oil companies account for five of the world's top ten revenue-producing companies.[8] To financially benefit from technology changes, you don't need an engineering degree or an M.B.A. To survive and thrive in the era of endless innovation, you merely need to think like a disruptor.

FORGET THEORIES OF DISRUPTION

Since Clayton Christensen coined the phrase "disruptive innovation" in his 1997 book *The Innovator's Dilemma*, scores of academics and management consultants have studied a range of industries and companies in order to identify and classify various forms of disruption. Christensen asserts that there is a firm distinction between sustaining technologies and disruptive ones—think of the improving gas mileage of cars over the past thirty years as a series of sustaining technologies. But an electric car that doesn't require gasoline: that would be disruptive technology. At first, disruptive technologies pose no threat to the entrenched technology because of poor performance. In the case of the first generation of electric cars, the mileage may be great, but the battery can't get the vehicle from Los Angeles to Las Vegas. If Tesla, on the other hand, were to launch a $30,000 car with a thousand-mile range, then it would be game over for the combustion engine.

Following in Christensen's footsteps, an entire cottage industry of innovation experts have developed their own jargon for identifying and labeling disruptions. There are now more theories of disruption out there than we can count. Some focus on the most profitable high end of an existing market, while others examine how disruption works by encroaching on the low end.[9] One theory holds that disruption starts at the fringe of existing markets by addressing unmet needs of new customers.[10] Yet another focuses on price as its market force.[11] My favorite piece of modern management jargon is the technology S curve, which shows on a graph that new inventions grow slowly in the market, then have an explosive growth period, before gradually tapering off as they mature over time.[12] In other words, things start off small, get big, and then die off. My personal belief is that the technology S curve could be used to graph anything from the life cycle of the hard-drive industry to the life cycle of an oak tree. Every living thing grows and eventually dies. Everything. Knowing the S curve of the dinosaurs doesn't help us understand why they disappeared or how mankind can avoid extinction. Neither can plotting the S curve of your product or company better prepare you for the inevitable. The management science of disruption has now reached its own maturation stage, as evidenced by the fact that the University of Southern California, where I am an adjunct professor, even offers an undergraduate degree in disruption! But the problem with all the theoretical approaches is that they are like the blood-spatter science used by Showtime's Dexter Morgan: great for revealing what killed the victim, but worthless for predicting who will be slaughtered next.

I prefer to leave the past to historians, anthropologists, and archaeologists. I believe most people want to know how they and their businesses are going to survive. And the truly motivated and bold want to know how they can thrive by becoming agents of change. The methodologies outlined in *Disrupt You!* are powerful because they are predictive and equip anyone to become a disruptor.

I've had the luck and privilege of being at the center of some of the most disruptive trends of the past thirty years. From the birth of the personal computer and the launching of the commercial Internet to the creation of ecommerce, digital media, and smartphones, I have had a front-row seat, working alongside some amazing Davids who have upended some multi-billion-dollar Goliaths. Several times my colleagues and I partnered with the very companies our disruptions would eventually destroy. Disruption causes vast sums of money to flow from existing businesses and business models to new entrants. *Disrupt You!* is about entering the fray.

> 🐦 Disruption causes vast sums of money to flow from existing businesses and business models to new entrants.

When I was in my twenties and the personal computer industry was in its infancy, all the best and brightest minds I knew were imagining new uses for the home computer. PCs could balance checkbooks, word-process, make newsletters, play video games, format movie scripts, and be used for a host of other applications where typewriters couldn't compete. Everyone saw that the PC had limitless potential, but no one had yet made significant money from this hobbyist endeavor. Just as every engineer today has an idea for a new smartphone app, scores of software companies were forming to compete for the potential billions this new disruptive industry promised. These new companies created software, circuit chips, motherboards, and myriad hardware components. Each firm was staking its fortunes on pushing the technical limits of what the primitive PCs could accomplish. Every day, new innovations and companies sprouted up like dandelions in summer.

While technological developments create the opportunity for disruption, one doesn't have to be a master of the new technology to reap the benefits. The young entrepreneurs of the 1990s were so desperate to find a way to cash in by improving upon the new technology—or trying to invent new gadgets and gizmos for the new technology to utilize—that they were investing in computer systems that cost more than the cars they drove. But which fledgling startup of the era was the first to sell for over $100 million? It wasn't a software company. It wasn't a hardware firm, either. In fact, my friend Billy Myers didn't even know how to use a computer. But he was a born entrepreneur who recognized an opportunity created by disruption when he saw it. While other entrepreneurs were busy investing in complex computer systems, eager to create the newest, latest, greatest technological breakthroughs, Billy took a step back and analyzed what was happening around him. What he saw was people buying a $2,000 item for their home. His epiphany was dirt simple: something as expensive and valuable as a computer needed a dustcover. Who wouldn't spend $10 to protect a $2,000 investment? Billy began making plastic dustcovers for monitors and central processing units (CPUs). He made dustcovers for keyboards and external hard drives. When he noticed people storing their software on dozens of little floppy disks, he made plastic cases and plastic file drawers. Consumers are using a mouse? Then they must have a plastic mouse pad. Billy was the first to identify and create a personal-computer accessories market, and he eventually sold his company, Micro-Computer Accessories, to Rubbermaid for a fortune.

Billy's success wasn't born of inventing anything new; it was the result of his seeing opportunity created by disruptive technology and then seizing that opportunity. While Kaypro, Eagle, Franklin, Magnuson, Osborne, and dozens of other computer companies spent millions in their fight to capture a piece of the exploding PC market, one outsider identified where the most value could be captured the fastest in this new industry. (Decades later, when Apple unveiled the iPhone and launched a second generation of app developers scurrying to cash in, I smiled and watched as each customer lined up at the Apple Store to purchase a new expensive phone and, with it, a $30 plastic case. Most app companies spend millions of dollars competing for downloads and App Store placement, only to lose money and fail. Meanwhile, the iPhone accessories market quickly grew to a $16 billion business.)

Billy's story of producing and selling dustcovers, disk cases, and mouse pads at the dawn of the era of the personal computer is a perfect illustration of a beloved phrase of both sailors and coders: K.I.S.S.— *keep it simple, stupid*. While Billy was selling computer accessories, I realized I didn't have the staff or funds to out-engineer the big guys. So I took a page from Billy's book and looked for an opportunity in a part of the market others had overlooked. My goal was to capture as much value in the shortest amount of time possible. I wanted to generate profits that could fuel expansion into more costly product sectors.

In layman's terms, I wanted to get in the game, make some money with a simple product, and then reinvest my profits into better, more complex products. I also wanted to focus on a niche that had high margins with little existing competition. I was twenty-eight years old, and I had been running my work-for-hire technology production company for nearly seven years. I decided that the new technology of the CD-ROM offered me the opportunity I was looking for. I partnered with IBM— then the nation's leader in computer sales—and licensed my product for IBM to ship and sell globally. My very first product, the Jasmine 6-Pack, came bundled with all IBM ActionMedia II PCs, sold for $1,500, and had a manufacturing cost of only $12. So where did I find opportunity for a 12,500-percent-profit-margin product that no one else had seen? Stock photography.

> 🐦 *Capture as much value as possible in the shortest time possible.*

When computers went from having monochromatic screens with phosphorus-green text to featuring full-color, TV-like displays, I knew it wasn't going to be long before users were going to want to see and use real photos on those screens. I realized that corporate brochures, newsletters, training software, and educational software all would require thousands of photographs of people, places, and things that could be incorporated into their products. I had worked at an advertising agency during college, so I was able to identify a need that most engineers wouldn't have seen. As we will see in the next chapter, being successful as a disruptor is about applying your unique experience and viewpoint to find opportunity.

My company's new product focused not as much on how personal computers were disrupting technology as on how they were disrupting existing, non-technology-related business models. At the time, whenever anyone needed a photo for something they were publishing, they had only two choices: hire a photographer or contact a stock photography agency. So if you needed a photograph of an elephant, either you could fly a nature photographer overseas and wait several weeks to get your image or you could call a stock photography agency. As primitive as it sounds, you would call the agency on the telephone and tell them you needed a photograph of an elephant by a river. The agency would overnight you a few dozen slides to choose from. The single-use licensing fee to use the image could range from a few hundred to a few thousand dollars. The process was slow, manual, inefficient, and very, very expensive. My solution was simple.

I contacted stock agencies that didn't understand or didn't care about the PC. I quickly made a deal with PhotoBank for the rights to digitize 750,000 images from all around the globe. In addition to fantastic nature and travel imagery, PhotoBank had a huge collection of photographs of people doing every conceivable job or social activity. I licensed the images and put three hundred at a time, organized by theme or topic, on CD-ROM discs, agreeing to pay PhotoBank a royalty for each CD-ROM I sold. There were two unique aspects to my business model. First, anyone purchasing my software could use any or all of the three hundred images on the disc royalty-free. Companies that bought my CD-ROMs could save tens of thousands of dollars a year and would have the legal right to use the images over and over again. Second, since I couldn't fit the three hundred images onto a single disc at the highest possible resolution (i.e., the quality needed for magazine printing), my product wouldn't cannibalize the stock agency's existing business. Magazines and other professional print organizations would still have to go through the stock agency to get the high-resolution images. My customers were individual users and small businesses that wanted to put pictures in brochures, in school papers, or on fliers they were creating on their new word processors.

By becoming an IBM business partner, my company enabled its product to appear in IBM's trade show booths and brochures, and we gained access to their thousands of customers. IBM opened doors for us, and my company experienced explosive growth for our products. With this steady revenue stream, we were later able to expand into other software products such as games and education. When the technology evolved and computers began playing sound and video, I started licensing music and video libraries to extend the wave without having to substantially change my initial business model. My startup became an established and recognized leader in the field. We had broad distribution and controlled valuable shelf space at retail. Building on our initial success and first-mover advantage, Jasmine Multimedia Publishing eventually produced over three hundred CD-ROMs, ranging from video games to office productivity tools. And as soon as I realized that the advent of the Web meant the death of packaged software, I sold my company before *we* were disrupted—and focused all my energies on how I could use the Internet to disrupt other industries.

THE DISRUPTOR'S PATH TO SUCCESS

This success was not the result of my having invented a new technology. Instead, I used an existing technology to disrupt a different business. This, in the turbulent times of ceaseless technological transformation, is the secret to thriving as a disruptor.

A business or product can be understood as the sum of its value-adding links. Traditionally, these links are thought of as research and development; design; production; marketing and sales; and distribution. Each of these disparate links contributes different value to the business as a whole. All products begin with research and development. R & D defines what need the product fulfills and what functions it must possess. The product must then be designed and produced within the financial and material constraints available to the company. Marketing and sales focus on how to create and fulfill demand for the product. And lastly, distribution deals with the logistical issues of getting the product to consumers. Each link must be solid and sustainable if a product is to succeed, and each link can be disrupted by new entrants that are able to fulfill the same functions in a more efficient manner. A business is at risk for disruption when one or more of these links can be replaced by a technology or product that delivers improved services or additional value to a new market in a more efficient way. Let's take the obvious example of mail. E-mail was able to disrupt the distribution link in the value chain of postal mail by enabling people to send messages to one another instantly and directly, rendering the postal service unnecessary in almost all matters of daily communication.

But to thrive in the era of disruption, you don't have to invent anything new. There's no need to discover something the world has never seen before. Rather, there are riches to be found simply by capturing the value released through others' disruptive breakthroughs. While email disrupted the distribution link in the value chain of postal mail, countless businesses have seen tremendous growth and profitability by using email to market, sell, design, and even produce other products. In other words, a disruption in one link in the value chain creates opportunity in other links.

> 🐦 *There are riches to be found simply by capturing the value released through others' disruptive breakthroughs.*

Anyone who takes advantage of the opportunities created by disruption, anyone who refuses to be intimidated by technological innovation, anyone who finds ways to continually reinvent themselves so that their unique assets will never become obsolete—these are the people I consider disruptors.

Success as a disruptor is about capturing the value that is released through disruption. Every business will be disrupted sooner or later by technology. From the family restaurant that doesn't know how to interact with OpenTable, Yelp, or Groupon to the mortgage broker made redundant by online loan originators such as Quicken, you can either embrace the disruptor's journey or become roadkill. In today's business world, if you are not moving forward, you're falling behind.

The pace of change continues to accelerate, and therefore new opportunities abound. New entrants will replace old corporations that have survived on the momentum of milking every last dime out of established products instead of accepting the realities of cannibalization and championing disruption. As Kodak executive Larry Matteson said before the century-old company filed for bankruptcy, "Wise businesspeople concluded that it was best not to hurry to switch from making seventy cents on the dollar on film to maybe five cents at most in digital."

My first business success was in publishing CD-ROMs. It would have been easy to define myself as a CD-ROM publisher, but if I had, then when that industry disappeared, my career would have gone with it. Instead I see myself as a serial disruptor. I'm constantly looking for ways to apply new technological advancements to revolutionize how we work, learn, and play. I've run businesses in ecommerce, digital media distribution, social advertising, mobile apps, and crowdfunding. I've made a career out of capitalizing on the opportunities made available through disruptive technologies. I pride myself on knowing how to adapt when the rules of the game are changed; I refuse to be merely a pawn moved around the board.

Though I spent the majority of my career as a startup entrepreneur, in each of my three "corporate" gigs (as senior management at Universal Studios, EMI, and Sony), I was brought in specifically as an *intrapreneur*. An intrapreneur disrupts from within the corporation, rather than waiting for the company to be attacked by external forces. At Universal Studios in the mid-1990s, I was tasked with finding ways to leverage the newly created World Wide Web to see if it could help market movies, sell music, book theme-park vacations, and generate new revenue streams. In the early aughts, I was president of EMI recorded music, where I had the dual challenge of combating the wave of Internet piracy launched by Napster and its descendants while migrating our revenue streams to digital downloads and streaming services. I was then hired by Sony—a company that for decades had been a leading innovator—to create a digital ecosystem for all the company's disparate divisions: music, film, video, books, personal electronics, PlayStation, television, and computers.

When one is fully empowered, being an intrapreneur is the best job in the world. You have all the speed and agility of a startup, turbocharged with the financial and marketing muscle of a global corporation. You also get to pick your own team (which is so critical for building a successful business) and can afford to hire the best in the world. In each of my corporate gigs, I built new divisions to go after emerging market opportunities. Sometimes we were able to influence the overall corporate culture; other times we were treated like an ugly stepchild with Ebola.

All three of my corporate stints allowed me to be a part of major industry during a time of great disruption. Unable to chart its own destiny as an independent entertainment company, Universal Studios has changed hands six times since the 1990s. EMI was acquired by a private equity firm for the record-setting price of $4.7 billion,[13] only to be cut up and sold piecemeal four years later.[14] Sony, unwilling or unable to adapt to a changing digital landscape, lost nearly 90 percent of its value when the company went from a market capitalization over $100 billion in 2000 to $18 billion in 2012.[15] I have been both the victor and the vanquished. I have successfully disrupted markets dominated by IBM, Microsoft, Apple, and Google, and I have been disrupted by two college students in a dorm room. The lessons I learned from my rung on the corporate ladder influence *Disrupt You!* as much as what I learned from running startups. The truth is that corporate employees can no longer be immune to the entrepreneurial spirit. Incremental innovation is like walking on quicksand: it will keep you very busy but won't get you very far. Building disruptive organizations must be infused into the DNA of every successful twenty-first-century corporation.

One of my favorite expressions is "Security robs ambition." The majority of people are not willing to risk what they have built for the opportunity to have something better. Many professionals (including most of the middle-aged lawyers I know) have grown tired of their career but feel ensnared by their safe salary and comfortable routine. It is no coincidence that we refer to our accumulation of material goods as "trappings." The longer you stay at a job you don't like, the more money you will earn and the less likely you'll be to leave to pursue your dreams. But the choice is always yours. Ask yourself, Would you rather work forty hours a week at a job you hate or eighty hours a week doing work you love?

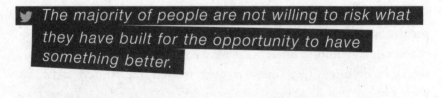

The majority of people are not willing to risk what they have built for the opportunity to have something better.

Would you rather work forty hours a week at a job you hate or eighty hours a week doing work you love?

Most people were raised to believe in the so-called forty-forty life plan. Back in the era of stable corporations and fully funded pensions, employees worked forty hours a week for forty years and then retired. In the era of 401(k) plans and no pensions, working forty hours a week for forty years is not a formula for success. Twenty-three million Americans aged sixty or over are considered "financially insecure," and one-third of senior households have no money left over each month or are in debt after meeting essential expenses.[16] Worst of all, if one sees oneself as having achieved only a narrow band of experience at one company or in one field, what happens if that field goes away? While you are lamenting your "safe" position in life, someone else may be disrupting your entire industry and putting the company you work for out of business. Think your big corporate job is safe from disruption? Only seventy-one companies from the original Fortune 500 list published in 1954 remain on the list.[17] Only 14 percent of the largest, most successful companies survived long enough for an employee to work his or her whole career at one company and retire.[18] Security doesn't rob ambition; the *illusion* of security robs ambition.

> 🐦 Security doesn't rob ambition; the illusion of security robs ambition.

D *isrupt You!* examines how anyone can adopt a disruptor's mindset and set themselves on a disruptor's path to success—whether that means starting your own business, proving your value at the company where you're already employed, or rebranding yourself for career transformation. We will look at how successful disruptors identify opportunities created by disruptions in the value chains of other businesses, find big ideas, and know when to pivot their energies and adjust their business models. Finally, *Disrupt You!* explores the ways various businesses and social organizations have recently been disrupted and predicts which links in their value chains are ripe for future disruption.

According to *USA Today*, 50 percent of today's college students want to be entrepreneurs.[19] In addition to students, countless other workers dream of being their own bosses, creating their own small businesses, or even just making more money. Dozens of business incubators are sprouting up all around America. In 1980, there were only twelve incubators in the entire nation; today there are over 1,250, and that number is estimated to grow by 10 percent per year.[20] As I travel around the country speaking at incubators, I encounter first-time entrepreneurs thirsty for practical advice on how to transform their industries and make constructive change. Even in these tough economic times, many Americans quit their jobs last year because they wanted more from their lives than a paycheck.[21] They want to make a difference. *Disrupt You!* isn't just for startup entrepreneurs or corporate employees; it is for everyone looking for a promotion, a raise, or a way to get more satisfaction out of their lives.

Chapter Two

Become a Disruptor

Everyone thinks of changing the world,
but no one thinks of changing himself.
—Leo Tolstoy

Being a disruptor is simply a state of mind. It is the ability to look for opportunity in every obstacle, to respond to every setback as a new beginning. It is being in the silver-lining business. Every successful person who has skillfully transformed a business or social organization started with a personal problem and then noticed how many other people shared the same problem. What sets disruptors apart from other people who merely experience problems is that disruptors see themselves and their worlds differently. That unique viewpoint enables them to become agents of change—and to reap the rewards. Disruption isn't about what happens to you; it's about how you respond to what happens to you.

> Disruption isn't about what happens to you; it's about how you respond to what happens to you.

Every road warrior has experienced the misery of missing a connecting flight and feeling helplessly stranded at some faraway airport. But when this happened to legendary entrepreneur Sir Richard Branson, he responded differently. In 1979, when the twenty-nine-year-old music executive missed his flight to Puerto Rico from the British Virgin Islands, he looked around the airport and added up in his head how many other travelers were also stranded. He quickly chartered a plane and wrote on a blackboard VIRGIN AIRWAYS $39. Everyone got to where they wanted to go. But Sir Richard and his fiancée, Joan, got to fly for free. For Sir Richard, starting what would become a billion-dollar airline really was as easy as missing a flight. Disruptors recognize that the problems they're facing are probably happening to others as well.

While still in college, Jenn Hyman watched as her frustrated sister Becky experienced a dilemma familiar to nearly all women: having "a closet full of clothes but nothing to wear." Becky's desire to look fabulous for a friend's wedding couldn't be fulfilled on her modest salary. She wanted to wear a high-end designer dress from Hervé Léger or Proenza Schouler, even if just for one night. That's when Jenn came up with a simple disruptive idea: what if there was a dream closet where women could rent the latest designer fashions, affording them a new dress for every occasion? Jenn partnered with her Harvard Business School classmate Jenny Fleiss, and Rent the Runway was born. "Our intention is to disrupt every single part of what retail has meant historically," Jenn remarked recently in a *Forbes* interview.[1] And disrupt they have. With nearly $55 million in venture capital funding, Rent the Runway now employs more than two hundred people, ships dresses and accessories to women around the world, and is challenging the way New York's top designers and department stores do business.[2]

While Jenn and Jenny were launching their empire, most American college students were drowning in debt. American college graduates now owe over $1 trillion in student loans.[3] An entire generation is carrying the burden of a mortgage without the advantages of owning a home. Attorney Gene Wade looked at this massive problem and created a simple but disruptive solution: an affordable online degree. Unlike other digital schools, Wade's UniversityNow provides students with an all-you-can-eat model for as little as $2,600 a year.[4] The bargain pricing includes all books and tuition for fully accredited degrees ranging from undergraduate degrees to M.B.A.'s. "I became an education entrepreneur because the current system does not have the capacity to serve people with unique higher-education needs," Wade says. With over $42 million in venture funding, UniversityNow is well

JAY SAMIT

positioned to disrupt the business of higher education and free future generations from unmanageable debt.[5] Wade is a man on a mission, with big, bold dreams.

What Sir Richard Branson, Jenn Hyman and Jenny Fleiss, and Gene Wade have in common is the mind-set of the disruptor. Rather than observing a problem and sitting back and waiting for others to solve it, they jumped in headfirst, seeing massive problems as massive opportunities. To adopt the mind-set of a disruptor, you must first disrupt yourself.

THE ART OF SELF-DISRUPTION

In the previous chapter, we saw how disruption occurs when a link in the value chain is entirely transformed by the introduction of a new technology or product—one that creates a new market demand and forces an overhaul of the previous business model. I suggested that a disruptor is not necessarily the inventor of a revolutionary new product, but can be anyone who seizes the opportunities created at other points in the value chain of a business when one link has been disrupted. In this chapter, we will explore how you can analyze and disrupt the links in your personal value chain to unlock your potential and prime yourself to seize opportunity.

"The mind is everything. What you think, you become," Buddha wrote two millennia ago. Your self is nothing more than what you believe it to be. You must remove all the internal and external definitions of *self* that limit your progress in life.

Self-disruption is not a comfortable or easy process. It requires you to get out of your comfort zone. As trite as it sounds, think of the painful and time-consuming metamorphosis a caterpillar must endure in order to emerge as a brilliant butterfly. Self-disruption is akin to undergoing major surgery, but you are the one holding the scalpel. A search for "self-help" on Amazon yields over 400,000 volumes on getting out of your own way, achieving your dreams, and re-creating your life from the inside out. I am sure each of these books is filled with lessons on healing your emotional self and building self-esteem. I am not a psychologist, and I am the last person on earth who should give advice about eternal happiness or spiritual awakening. But I am an expert on deconstructing a set of assumptions so as to disrupt a problem and thereby create new opportunity.

> 🐦 *Self-disruption is akin to undergoing major surgery, but you are the one holding the scalpel.*

Just as every company has a value chain that defines a business's success, we can think of our own identities as being formed by our internal value chains. Our internal value chains make us who we are; they guide the way we function in the world. Our research and development center takes input from our environment and perceives it as either an obstacle or an opportunity. The brain, our design-and-production center, dictates actions in response to our perceptions. We market and sell ourselves in the ways we present ourselves to the world, which are based on what we see as our personal strengths or limitations. We distribute ourselves in the ways we choose to spend our time and where we focus our energies. When viewed from this framework, the process of self-transformation becomes approachable: you need only analyze each link in your internal value chain and find the single link that's holding you back. Then make changes to that link to disrupt yourself.

DISRUPTING YOUR RESEARCH AND DEVELOPMENT LINKS

In 1948, UCLA psychologist Bertram Forer proved how malleable human self-perception could be with a famous experiment. Dr. Forer instructed his class to complete a very detailed personality assessment test. He then provided each student with a unique personality analysis based on his or her answers. The students were asked to rate the accuracy of the analysis against their own self-perception. Forer's test has been administered to thousands of students for more than half a century, and it continues to average a 4.26 accuracy rating from participants, on a scale of 1 to 5. With an accuracy rate better than 85 percent, it is perhaps the most meticulous measuring tool for human personality traits ever constructed. There is just one problem with Forer's test: it is a hoax. Every student, regardless of how they answer the questions on the assessment test, is provided with this identical analysis:

You have a great need for other people to like and admire you. You have a tendency to be critical of yourself. You have a great deal of unused capacity which you have not turned to your advantage. While you have some personality weaknesses, you are generally able to compensate for them. Disciplined and self-controlled outside, you tend to be worrisome and insecure inside. At times you have serious doubts as to whether you have made the right decision or done the right thing. You prefer a certain amount of change and variety and become dissatisfied when hemmed in by restrictions and limitations. You pride yourself as an independent thinker and do not accept others' statements without satisfactory proof. You have found it unwise to be too frank in revealing yourself to others. At times you are extroverted, affable, sociable, while at other times you are introverted, wary, reserved. Some of your aspirations tend to be pretty unrealistic. Security is one of your major goals in life.

No matter how participants answered the questions, Forer gave them all the same feedback, saying he was analyzing their unique personalities—and 85 percent of the time, participants said that Forer's assessment described them accurately.[6] If our identity is so easily influenced by external sources, then we must have the ability to alter our mind-set. Think about how Forer's personality test might apply to you. The external voices in our lives become the research and development links in the value chain that makes us who we are. When in your life have you started to believe those voices? What have they told you about yourself? How are they holding you back?

I was not supposed to be successful when I grew up. (Just ask any of my relatives.) As a small child, I had difficulty learning to speak and read. When I entered elementary school, they divided all the students in my class into three reading groups: the Eagles, the Hawks, and the Mud Hens. I was a natural-born Mud Hen. Even at five years old, you know when the teacher is putting you in the loser group. Eagles soar, while Mud Hens sit in the corner and play with clay. I couldn't learn like the other children and was convinced by teachers that I was stupid.

Years later, after some testing, my parents and teachers would discover that I was dyslexic.

When I was a child in the 1960s, dyslexia was not viewed as a gift; it was a learning disorder. Schools either put dyslexic students in special education classes or moved us to the back of the classroom. Labeling students as *different* sets them down a path of believing that they are less than their peers. Everyone can relate to being different at one time or another in school. We have all been told repeatedly what talents we're lacking. *You're bad at math. You can't read a map. You have no artistic ability. You will never understand how to run a business.* Repeated frequently enough by parents, teachers, and role models, these opinions become internalized by children. Over time, most people accept the limitations conferred on them by society.

Luckily for me, the sixties were a time of new and experimental education theories. The United States was racing to the moon, and academia was breaking with the past. The era of rote memorization was giving way to individual self-expression. Teachers began trying new things in the classroom. Students like me were given the choice to write an essay or draw a picture. Take a spelling test or gather a bagful of things that started with the "sm" sound, such as Smurfs or smiles. I put Saran Wrap over the head of my sister's Barbie doll for "smother" and got both a gold star and a trip to the school psychologist.

I managed to make it through elementary school masking my learning "disorder" by developing creative work-arounds to compensate for my inability to do things the way everyone else did. I'd rather give a show-and-tell talk in front of the whole class than write a report. Given the choice of working on an assignment by myself or creating a team project, I would always opt for the team, where I could delegate the tasks I wasn't good at. Not able to compete on a level academic playing field, I learned to invent new ways of circumventing the system to mask my inability to read or write at the level of my peers. By fifth grade I had adapted my world to fit my skills and was getting straight As. In retrospect, working around the established system to survive was the ideal training ground for an autonomous disruptor. I was disrupting my traditional education from a very young age.

Turns out I wasn't the only dyslexic disruptor. Steve Jobs, Albert

Einstein, Thomas Edison, Alexander Graham Bell, Sir Richard Branson, Leonardo da Vinci, Michael Faraday, Henry Ford, Ted Turner, and Walt Disney were all dyslexic. They all complained of being bored in school and were thought by educators to be unmotivated. So many great disruptors across so many divergent fields are dyslexics that it can't be statistically accounted for as a coincidence. In the military, George Washington and General George S. Patton, two of the most creative strategists on the battlefield, were dyslexics. Status-quo-challenging artists such as Pablo Picasso and Andy Warhol "suffered" from this gift as well.[7] Could there actually be an advantage to thinking this way?

Steve Jobs, in his brilliant commencement address to Stanford University's class of 2005, reflected on his academic challenges in college. Jobs knew he wanted to achieve something great when he set out on his life path, but he didn't know what steps would lead him to success.

> Of course it was impossible to connect the dots looking forward when I was in college. But it was very, very clear looking backwards ten years later. Again, you can't connect the dots looking forward; you can only connect them looking backwards. So you have to trust that the dots will somehow connect in your future. You have to trust in something—your gut, destiny, life, karma, whatever. This approach has never let me down, and it has made all the difference in my life.[8]

Like most dyslexics, Jobs was bored in class. He dropped out of Reed College after a semester. But rather than go home, Steve dropped in on classes he thought might capture his imagination. One was a course in calligraphy. Years later, when designing the Macintosh computer, he drew on that experience to create the first personal computer with multiple typefaces. When graphic artists gravitated to the Mac, Jobs realized that his fledgling company had found its first niche market. Desktop publishing was born, and Windows PCs soon followed suit. Jobs audited one random college class, and the entire role of computers in society was transformed.

In recent studies on identical twins at the Center for Regenerative

Therapies Dresden, behavioral geneticists concluded that the personal interactions twins had with their environment actually remapped their brains. A feedback loop develops as new behavior is positively reinforced, and in the end, two identical twins can develop radically different personalities. The child who makes more sounds gets spoken to more frequently. Over time, this child will develop more verbal connections in his brain as a result of the positive reinforcement he receives from his environment. The study found that the twin who gets less attention grows up to be introverted and less verbal.[9] On a daily basis, we adapt in response to our environment.

When Mohandas Gandhi was studying law in London, his ideas were not widely followed or accepted. Upon returning to India, Gandhi changed his environment and lived among the people, and only then did his new self-perception emerge. In his book for entrepreneurs, *The Start-up of You,* LinkedIn cofounder and super angel investor Reid Hoffman put it this way: "Identity doesn't get found. It emerges."[10]

From a very young age, we are taught to believe that we have immutable limitations. Parents, teachers, and coaches praise or criticize us. With IQ tests and school entrance exams, we are judged and scored. As adults, we might have a career counselor administer the Myers-Briggs Type Indicator questionnaire to tell us what kinds of careers we are best suited for.

Life experience is often a continuous research and development funnel that narrows our goals and results in our limiting the opportunities we think are open to us. We temper our ambitions based on the feedback we receive from those around us. Are you an extrovert or an introvert? Do you rely on intuition or rational thinking to make decisions? The unfortunate reality is that what holds most people back is actually their own beliefs that they are not good enough or deserving enough to be successful.

So much of the research and development we do on ourselves begins very early in life. We design our persona based on the feedback we get at home and at school. Students who are told they are smart actually do better in school. Kids who are told they are gifted at sports actually grow up to become better athletes. This phenomenon has been proved over and over again in clinical studies; Columbia University sociologist

Robert K. Merton called it the Matthew Effect, after the biblical passage, "For unto everyone that hath shall be given, and he shall have abundance. But from him that hath not shall be taken away even that which he hath."[11] In other words, you get what you believe you deserve.

🐦 *You get what you believe you deserve.*

In his bestselling book *Outliers*, Malcolm Gladwell recounts Canadian psychologist Roger Barnsley's study of professional hockey players. As statistically impossible as it seems, the most successful athletes in the National Hockey League were most likely to have been born between January and March. The reason was the Matthew Effect.

"It has nothing to do with astrology, nor is there anything magical about the first three months of the year," Gladwell writes. "It's simply that in Canada the eligibility cutoff for age-class hockey is January 1. A boy who turns ten on January 2, then, could be playing alongside someone who doesn't turn ten until the end of the year—and at that age, in preadolescence, a twelve-month gap in age represents an enormous difference in physical maturity."[12]

So the older, larger children excelled at hockey, and their parents and coaches reinforced this by telling them that they were good at hockey. Getting praised for being good at something made the sport more enjoyable to the children. The more approval the children received, the more they enjoyed the game, the more time they spent practicing, and the better they got. This positive reinforcement was not only internalized into the children's identities but hardwired into their brains. The children developed superior hockey minds. The slight biological advantage that they had when they first hit the ice at age ten propelled these players toward mastery and a profession in hockey. When children born in January through March turned pro, they joined a league dominated by players sharing their first quarter birthdays. We become what we believe we are.

The same is true for how women perceive their roles in society and the workplace. If girls are called bossy whenever they are assertive, are they less likely to develop into outgoing adults? In Sheryl Sandberg's book on women and the workplace, *Lean In*, she points out that "we cannot change what we are not aware of, and once we are aware, we cannot help but change."[13]

DISRUPTING YOUR DESIGN AND PRODUCTION LINKS

Dr. Sally Shaywitz, who teaches at the Yale University School of Medicine and is codirector of the Yale Center for Dyslexia & Creativity, has devoted her career to studying dyslexia. Her research provides a scientific basis for reclassifying dyslexia as a learning gift instead of the malady I was raised to believe it was. Dyslexic brains are physiologically hardwired to solve problems differently. Using fMRI scanners, Shaywitz has identified in dyslexic readers "a neural signature for dyslexia" that is a disruption of the two neural systems in the brain's posterior. Dr. Shaywitz's research shows that dyslexic brains are actually wired differently.

"Brain imaging now provides visible evidence of the reality of dyslexia," writes Shaywitz. "Dyslexia is no longer a hidden disability."[14]

Dyslexics tend to see problems in their totality; we actually process problems outside of a linear set of steps and draw conclusions from unrelated associations. Dyslexics' ability to see the big picture enables them to swiftly analyze a business's points of potential value. For example, Ted Turner was able to see value others couldn't in the old MGM film library and launched new revenue streams in the emerging world of cable television. Dr. Shaywitz refers to the higher critical thinking and creativity associated with dyslexia as a "Sea of Strengths." How fascinating that dyslexic Steve Jobs's most effective advertising campaign for Apple was "Think Different."

Virgin Group founder and chairman Sir Richard Branson personally credits dyslexia as his "greatest strength."

"Back when I was in school, few people understood dyslexia and what to do for it," Branson explains. "On one of my last days at school, the headmaster said I would either end up in prison or become a millionaire. That was quite a startling prediction, but in some respects he was right on both counts!"[15]

Common traits in the sea of strengths that the dyslexic entrepreneur brings to the business world are critical thinking, out-of-the-box problem solving, tenacity, and higher intelligence. A groundbreaking study of the links between entrepreneurs and dyslexia conducted by the Cass Business School, in London, found that 35 percent of U.S. business owners surveyed identified themselves as dyslexic.[16] The study, led by Cass professor of entrepreneurship Julie Logan, identified that dyslexics were more likely to delegate authority and excel in oral communication. Much as I did in school, most dyslexics compensated for weakness in one area by building strengths in another. "We found that dyslexics who succeed had overcome an awful lot in their lives by developing compensatory skills," according to Cass. "If you tell your friends and acquaintances that you plan to start a business, you'll hear over and over, 'It won't work. It can't be done.' But dyslexics are extraordinarily creative about maneuvering their way around problems."[17]

The way our brains process and respond to information can be thought of as the design and production links in our internal value chains. Just as a business can transform itself by changing the way it designs and produces its products, you can remap your neural networks to actually think differently. You have the power to alter the physical hard-wiring of the connections in your brain. How you choose to think changes how the brain processes information. For example, recent studies have shown that positive thinking is more than a motivational tool; it actually adapts our physiology.[18]

It is possible to rewire your brain to comprehend and problem-solve as if you were dyslexic. Don't let yourself dwell on problem solving as a series of discrete steps. Train yourself to look outside the given variables and see the big picture. Don't try to see the steps to solving a problem; first visualize the solution and then work backward to determine what you will have to do or build to get to that solution. By thinking this way, you will discover the shortest path, the minimum steps required, and identify all the missing pieces to solve the puzzle. An entire industry has developed around teaching people and institutions to think holistically like this. London-based Innovation Arts is a consultancy that uses "visual facilitation" to change the way corporate teams communicate, design, and develop new products and ideas, with clients ranging from British Telecom to financial services firm Swiss Re.

Professional athletes practice the same moves over and over again to develop muscle memory. "I have been visualizing myself every night for the past four years standing on the podium having the gold placed around my neck," said Megan Jendrick, a two-time Olympic gold-medal-winning swimmer, when asked about how she performs so consistently.[19] An athlete's body instantly knows how to react to any given situation, because they have rehearsed it and drilled it into being. Visualizing success is no different.

Cognitive neuroscientist Antti Revonsuo has dedicated his career to studying the role of dreams in humans. His lab work at the University of Turku, in Finland, and the University of Skövde, in Sweden, has shown that the part of the brain called the amygdala is most active when we are in the REM stage of sleeping. The amygdala controls our emotions, and this explains why our dreams feel so emotionally real to us. We are actually scared when being chased in a dream. Our brain does not distinguish between reality and a dream when we are sleeping. Revonsuo also discovered that the part of our brain that controls our limbs' motor functions (climbing, running, bracing for a fall) is engaged during REM.[20] The brain is teaching the body how to react, even though our arms and legs are not moving. Revonsuo concluded that we dream in order to rehearse real-world behavior. Our dreams condition us to respond much the way the athlete conditions her body.

> Our dreams condition us to respond much the way the athlete conditions her body.

By taking just five minutes each morning to visualize success, you train your brain to accept that you are capable of handling success. By visualizing each step of your journey, you are actually getting your mind prepared to handle the opportunity.

"The mind is really so incredible," says former California governor Arnold Schwarzenegger. "Before I won my first Mr. Universe title, I walked around the tournament like I owned it. I had won it so many times in my mind, the title was already mine. Then when I moved on to the movies I used the same technique. I visualized daily being a successful actor and earning big money."[21]

The second benefit of starting your day with visualization is how good it will make you feel. A negative mind will never find success. I have never heard a positive idea come from a person in a negative state. As you will discover in later chapters, success is merely turning obstacles into opportunities: the bigger the obstacle, the greater your potential for success. In World War II, the German Blitzkrieg ("lightning war") was a seemingly unstoppable ground-and-air assault. The Nazis launched columns of panzer tanks to quickly dominate Poland, the Netherlands, Belgium, and France. After the Allied forces landed at Normandy, few in our military had any idea how to defend against the dreaded Blitzkrieg. At the time, General Dwight D. Eisenhower proclaimed to his generals, "The present situation is to be regarded as opportunity for us and not disaster."[22] With that spirit in mind, the Allies realized that the Blitzkrieg left the sides of the advancing column's flanks exposed, sending fifty thousand German troops into a trap. Eisenhower visualized the victory in his mind and then shared his vision with those under his command. This one positive approach to an obstacle turned the Battle of the Bulge into a major victory.

> A negative mind will never find success. I have never heard a positive idea come from a person in a negative state.

Think of the way you approach problems and react to the world around you as the design and production links in your internal value chain. Where can you find opportunities in your life to design and produce different responses? How would incorporating visualization or changing the way you think transform the way you live?

DISRUPTING YOUR MARKETING AND SALES LINKS

Not knowing what to do with me when I was a toddler, my mother forged the date on my birth certificate so that I could be sent off to school an entire year early. Throughout elementary school, I was the smallest and least coordinated. I was awful at sports and was always the last kid picked to join teams. I learned to hate athletics and completely avoided anything having to do with physical activity. I became what I believed. Even today, I am one of the few adults I know who doesn't follow or watch any professional sports. I had internalized the belief that I couldn't succeed at sports and therefore adapted my goals to conform to the world's view of my identity.

But when I turned forty, I decided to confront my self-identity of being uncoordinated and horrible at sports. Thanks to a doctor's note that got me out of PE class starting in the seventh grade, I hadn't participated in any athletic activities since I was twelve. I was an obese, two-hundred-pound middle-aged guy who was out of breath after walking up a short flight of stairs. As I raced around the world through airports huffing and puffing, I realized I had become a heart attack waiting to happen. Thinking about this in terms of my internal value chain, I saw that my marketing and sales links were ripe for disruption. I was presenting myself to the world as an out-of-shape, intimidated middle-aged man. That needed to change.

I sought out a mentor. Working in my department at the time was Kenny Johnson Jr., who was training for the U.S. Olympic wrestling team. I asked Kenny for a list of exercises and repetitions that could get me into shape. I committed to doing the routine twice a week. The first day it took me three hours, and I was so wiped out that I had to lie down for the rest of the day. Within three weeks, the same routine took just forty-five minutes. The second month, I added in two miles on the treadmill once a week. After six months, I weighed 165 pounds, could do two dozen pull-ups, and was able to run four miles.

With a new sense of identity, and having overcome the limitations ingrained in me since I was four years old, I decided to pursue a fantasy goal of mine: I learned how to trapeze. I was nearly twice the age of most of the other aerial performers, but I soared through the air with twice the sense of joy. I had disrupted the marketing and sales links in my internal value chain, and I changed my body by changing my mind.

Mark Zupan, a former professional athlete, similarly refused to be defined by what others saw as limitations. After a car crash confined him to a wheelchair, the former football and soccer player focused his energy on wheelchair rugby. "Breaking my neck was the best thing that ever happened to me," Zupan says. "I have an Olympic medal. I've been to so many countries I would never have been, met so many people I would never have met. I've done more in the chair . . . than a whole hell of a lot of people who aren't in chairs."[23] The way we market and sell ourselves should not be determined by what others perceive of us. Our lives and careers are determined by our acceptance or rejection of our perceived limitations.

DISRUPTING YOUR DISTRIBUTION LINK

Sara Blakely wanted to be a lawyer, but she failed the LSAT test required to get into law school. Reflecting on that experience years later, she said, "I think failure is nothing more than life's way of nudging you that you are off course."[24]

Blakely took a sales job in Florida to pay the bills, but she knew that if she was going to achieve success, she would have to focus her real energy in a different way. Required to wear panty hose at her job, she hated how the seamed foot looked in open-toed shoes. She cut off the toes and realized that the toeless panty hose could be marketed as a new product. Though she wasn't trained as a fashion designer, prototype maker, or sales executive, she was determined to bring her product to market. Blakely went to hosiery mills and major retailers, and at both places her business card was ripped up in her face. Not having the funds to hire a lawyer to patent her creation, she went to Barnes & Noble and bought a book on how to write your own patents. She tirelessly devoted all of her free time to building her company, which eventually made her a billionaire and made Spanx a world-renowned brand name. Her advice to others going through the self-disruptor process: "Don't be intimidated by what you don't know. That can be your greatest strength and ensure that you do things differently from everyone else."[25]

The last link in the internal value chain is distribution, which can be thought of as how we choose to spend our time and where we direct our focus. Think about the way you spend your days and nights. Are you devoting the time and energy necessary to achieve your dreams, or do you find yourself channel-surfing on the couch every night after work?

One of the most common excuses people give for not pursuing their goals is lack of time. "If only I had the time to study a new field or learn a new profession" is the lament of every dissatisfied person strug-gling to juggle work and family. But the most successful people have the same twenty-four hours in a day that you do. The only difference is that they take control of their time. Think about where you can find ad-ditional time. What daily indulgences might you be willing to give up in pursuit of your dreams? Why not take the next step and enroll your-self in "Traffic University," like my friend Ed Gartenberg did. Com-mitted to lifelong learning, Ed listens to audiobooks in his car. He drives an average of twenty-five thousand miles a year commuting to downtown Los Angeles from the San Fernando Valley suburbs. With rush hour traffic averaging twenty miles an hour, Ed spends more than twice as much time each year learning than the average full-time col-lege student spends in the classroom. Not only is Ed continuing to learn and achieve his goals, but he's transformed the frustration of gridlock into a mobile sanctuary of knowledge. Each morning, he looks forward to his commute and has built up such a vast knowledge of his-tory at Traffic U that he has made plans to pursue an actual university Ph.D. in history when he retires from his law practice at age sixty-seven.

> 🐦 *The most successful people have the same twenty-four hours in a day that you do.*

Taking a page out of Ed's Traffic University, I realized that I wasted over three hundred hours a year in the air flying. Now, instead of dreading the lost time in flight, I've begun to look forward to my time in the sky, where no one can interrupt me with emails, texts, or calls.

But "if you want something done," comedienne Lucille Ball used to say, "ask a busy person to do it. The more things you do, the more you can do."[26] A dream with a deadline is a goal.

> 🐦 *A dream with a deadline is a goal.*

Your energy is a valuable resource: distribute it wisely.

> 🐦 *Your energy is a valuable resource: distribute it wisely.*

Think about yourself in terms of your personal value chain. The research and development links are all the various ways you interpret the world around you. Where do you thrive best—in an office environment or in a more independent and creative setting? What type of people do you work with best? What do you believe about yourself that might not be true? How can those self-assumptions be annihilated? Seeing environmental influences as nothing more than links in the chain that make you who you are, you are empowered to make the changes necessary to become who you want to be.

The next links in the chain are production and design. What emotions and actions are produced when you're confronted by a challenge or problem? Do you feel frustrated or defeated, or can you change the way you think so that you can tackle problems with an open mind, thinking holistically? How do you react in stressful situations like getting a new boss at work? Do you worry that you'll have to prove yourself all over again to keep your job, or do you view it as an opportunity to get the promotion you think you deserve? The environmental stimuli are the same, but your reaction and resulting actions are completely different, depending on your mind-set.

So much of self-disruption is making deliberate choices in your life instead of running on autopilot. We've all walked into a large conference or meeting without knowing a soul in the room. The fight-or-flight response from your autonomic nervous system pumps you full of adrenaline, causing your heart and respiratory rate to increase. Consciously take yourself off autopilot. It is not ten thousand years ago—no Neanderthal is going to kill you. Realizing that everyone feels the same way you do, why not turn this into an opportunity to greet others and make them feel welcome and safe? By following this approach to all your challenges, you will quickly see that success comes not from circumstances beyond your control, but from the way you respond to those circumstances.

Disrupting the next link in your personal value chain involves analyzing how you market and sell your potential. Not your skills or accomplishments, but your limitless potential. Most people, when applying for a job or raising money for their startup, focus their energies on explaining what they have achieved in the past. Success is all about championing and defining the future. As Henry Ford was fond of saying, "Whether you think you can or think you can't—you're right."

Finally, think about how you distribute your time and energy. Are you in a position where you have to spend hours doing things you hate? Could you devote more time to educating yourself so that you can pursue the job of your dreams? Could you find a way to use your time more efficiently? Or could you even just make the changes necessary to devote more of your energy to tasks you enjoy? What would happen if you changed the way you spent your day so completely—would it enable you to really follow your dreams?

Disrupting your internal value chain is the same as breaking down a car engine in order to rebuild it into a race car. You can't win a race without a winning mind-set. You have everything you need to thrive; you just have to plan for the race of your life. Each person's journey and process is unique. The key to adopting a disruptor's mind-set is to honestly assess your internal value chain to overcome every obstacle in the way. Annihilate all the assumptions that put limitations on your dreams and your expectations for yourself. Question what you've always been told are your strengths and weaknesses. Train yourself to think differently. Market your potential. Distribute your energy wisely and efficiently. As four-time Academy Award–winning actress Katharine Hepburn famously stated, "We are taught you must blame your father, your sisters, your brothers, the school, the teachers—but never blame yourself. It's never your fault. But it's always your fault, because if you wanted to change, you're the one who has got to change."

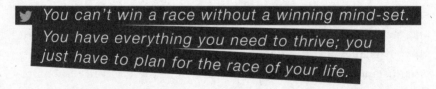

You can't win a race without a winning mind-set. You have everything you need to thrive; you just have to plan for the race of your life.

Chapter Three

The Disruptor's Map

Map out your future—but do it in pencil.
The road ahead is as long as you make it.
Make it worth the trip.
—Jon Bon Jovi

The previous chapter demonstrated how you can analyze your internal value chain to adopt the mind-set of a disruptor. By pinpointing weaknesses and vulnerabilities in the various links that form our identities, we empower ourselves to make the changes necessary to thrive. We have determined that success in the era of disruption comes from finding and exploiting opportunities created by the entrant of a new technology or product. But today's most successful disruptors didn't just sit around waiting for opportunity to knock. No, they went out and created it. All of the innovators I know created opportunity for themselves by seeing their lives and their paths to success as journeys. I'm not saying they had everything planned out, but almost everyone I interviewed for this book had a starting point and an end goal in mind. They didn't wait to understand what all of the steps along the way would look like, but they did try to draw some sort of map for themselves before they embarked. I have often said that if I knew everything I know about business today back when I started my first company at twenty-one, I would never have started it. Accepting that the odds are against you is the same as accepting defeat before you begin. Once you've decided to pursue your dreams, you'll need some guiding directions. Whether you want to think of it as creating a disruptor's map, writing a mission statement, or putting together a personal business plan, I encourage you to create a document by responding—in writing—to the prompts detailed in this chapter.

> 🐦 *Accepting that the odds are against you is the same as accepting defeat before you begin.*

TURN YOUR ASPIRATIONS INTO INSPIRATIONS

Remember how easy it was as a child to daydream about your future? You could easily see yourself as an astronaut, rock star, or firefighter. Perhaps you saw a movie or read a novel that instantly transformed your dreams. What boy didn't want to run off and enlist in the air force after watching *Top Gun*? What girl watching *Broadcast News* hasn't dreamed of being a powerful network news producer in Washington, D.C.?

In 1987, a struggling, unknown twenty-five-year-old comedian named Jim Carrey looked up at the Hollywood sign and wrote himself a check for $10 million. A dream turns into a plan the moment you assign a deadline to it. Carrey filled in the date on the check as Thanksgiving 1995. He began his disruptor's journey by giving himself a specific timeline to accomplish his goals. Once you have a date, you can work backward in your mind, listing the steps needed to achieve your goal. Amazingly, Carrey made his goal happen a year ahead of schedule. In 1994, for his starring role as Lloyd Christmas in *Dumb and Dumber*, Carrey was paid $10 million.

While we can't all be movie stars, we can visualize our futures. What do you really want to accomplish? What steps will it take to complete your journey? Over a hundred years ago, an Illinois farmer named Wallace Wattles wrote a bestselling book about visualization titled *The Science of Getting Rich*.

"Live in the new house; wear the fine clothes; ride in the automobile; go on the journey, and confidently plan for greater journeys," Wattles wrote. "Think and speak of all the things you have asked for in terms of actual present ownership. Imagine an environment, and a financial condition exactly as you want them, and live all the time in that imaginary environment and financial condition."[1]

Wattles's point is that you can't achieve dreams you don't have. You wouldn't invest in a company that didn't have a business plan, would you? Where is the company going? What are its goals? Does it have the resources it needs to succeed? Why not demand the same things of yourself? You can always change businesses, but you have only one life. If you don't know where you want to be in five years, how do you expect to get there? As life coach Tony Gaskins so wisely says, "If you don't build your dream, someone will hire you to help build theirs."

> If you don't know where you want to be in five years, how do you expect to get there?

I grew up in a row house in Philadelphia, where I had little exposure to and thus no concept of what wealth was or how rich people lived. Then one day I became fixated on a man with pet polar bears.

My father was a public school math teacher living a pretty standard urban life until the Soviets launched *Sputnik* in 1957. This act of Communist superiority spurred the United States government to create the Defense Advanced Research Projects Agency (DARPA). With the fate of the free world at stake, DARPA had nearly unlimited funds and access to America's best research universities, with one mission: to restore America's technological lead. It was because of DARPA that computers first became networked, creating a hypertext system that eventually became the Internet.

But back in 1957, America, at the height of the Cold War, when millions of homeowners were building fallout shelters in case of nuclear attacks and schoolchildren were being trained to get under their desks to "duck and cover," *Sputnik* galvanized the American public into action.

Washington realized that a lot more engineers were needed to beat the red menace. With a wave of hysteria from an anxious public, the federal government began funneling nearly limitless amounts of money into mathematics, science, and engineering education programs. All good and patriotic American high school math teachers were called upon to go back to college to get advanced degrees. My twenty-nine-year-old father realized: if the government was going to pay for him to go back to school during his summer break from teaching, why not go to the farthest place they would send him and turn these summers of higher learning into family vacations? So began my favorite part of my childhood: our cross-country road trips and the man with the polar bears.

As my father worked on his master's degree at Arizona State University, my sister and I lived in the dorms on campus. It was there, as a young boy, that I had my first interaction with computers. At the end of the summer, before we had to return to our real lives in Philadelphia, my dad would take us to see the sights all across America and fill my head with a world greater than my imagination. I loved Disneyland, SeaWorld, and the national parks, but the place that profoundly changed my view of the world was Hearst Castle.

For those who haven't been to La Cuesta Encantada (the Enchanted Hill), as newspaper tycoon William Randolph Hearst named it, Hearst Castle is an over-the-top, opulent, sixty-thousand-square-foot house set atop 250,000 acres of rolling hills—including fourteen miles of private coastline—in San Simeon, California. Built over twenty-eight years, the castle has fifty-six bedrooms, sixty-one bathrooms, nineteen sitting rooms, indoor and outdoor swimming pools, tennis courts, a movie theater, an airfield, and the world's largest private zoo.

As a small child, I couldn't appreciate the antiquities Hearst had assembled from all over the world. Solid gold faucets and twenty-foot-long dining tables didn't register with me, either. But on a sweltering California summer day, when our tour guide explained that, in addition to the cattle and zebras roaming around the property, Hearst had men truck ice up the mountain every day to keep the polar bears cool, I was mesmerized. That was wealth. That was the thing dreams were made of.

So when my parents told me that if I got all As in school I could someday build my own castle like Hearst's, I believed them. I remember spending the next year drawing out the floor plan of my castle on graph paper and magically getting straight As on all my report cards. I wanted to be successful and began visualizing my future. I didn't need to know how I was going to get there, but I knew what I wanted to achieve. My dreams may have changed as I matured, but I still have a picture of Hearst Castle on my office wall.

Bestselling author and motivational speaker Norman Vincent Peale has written volumes on the importance of attitude. "Formulate and stamp indelibly on your mind a mental picture of yourself as succeeding. Hold this picture tenaciously. Never permit it to fade. Your mind will seek to develop the picture . . . Do not build up obstacles in your imagination."[2]

Before you head off on your commute each morning, find a quiet place and retreat to it. Put away the phone and close out the present world. Fifteen minutes each morning will change the outcome of your entire day. Close your eyes and imagine the world you want. What do you aspire to do? Visualize living that life. Visualize every detail and engage all your senses. Hear the waves crashing outside the beach house you want to own. Smell the salty sea air. The more you focus on being in the world you want to create for yourself, the more powerful the results. As Antti Revonsuo discovered by studying subjects while in the dream state of sleep, your subconscious cannot emotionally distinguish between what is real and what you feel is real. Starting each day with a positive mind-set is the most important step in your journey to discovering opportunity.

> 🐦 *Starting each day with a positive mind-set is the most important step in your journey to discovering opportunity.*

Financial guru and talk show host Suze Orman didn't start off life rich. After failing in the restaurant business, and with no formal finance training, Orman started working on Wall Street. In her books, she has recounted how she felt intimidated and unworthy, but she visualized a better life for herself. Orman's most famous self-perception-changing affirmation is "I will have more money than I will ever need."[3]

As you spend more time consistently visualizing your future, a pattern will develop. You will begin to focus on those things most important to you. Let these aspirations inspire you, and write them down. What are you passionate about? What is missing from your life? Start writing down your dreams and begin turning them into goals. That is the essence of a personal road map or life path.

ASK YOURSELF, WHERE DO I WANT TO GO ALONG THE WAY?

You've thought about what you're aspiring to; now think about what else you want to find along the way. Do you want a family? Are you willing to delay one part of your life to pursue another aspect with more focus? "The purpose of life is a life of purpose," author and billiards guru Robert Byrne wrote.[4] What matters most to you? How you embody and achieve these core values will determine how you measure your success. Try writing these values down on a piece of paper. Be as detailed as you can. Include your personal and professional goals.

Next, list your priorities in terms of relationships and time commitments. How much personal, spiritual, and family time do you require? *All work and no play* is unsustainable as a life plan. You can truly have it all, just not all at the same time. The more realistic you are about how you are going to prioritize your goals in life, the more in charge of your future you will be. For women, balancing goals against a ticking biological clock makes this step all the more important. Try to be honest and complete—the more detail you put into your plan, the more resources you will have to achieve it.

> 🐦 *You can truly have it all, just not all at the same time.*

Being an active and involved father was as important to me as building my business. I found the balance I needed in my life by running my company out of my home until my boys were old enough to go to school. We made a game out of the boys being super-quiet whenever I got a business call. Once they were old enough, I would involve them in my software publishing projects so that they understood what Daddy did all day. As it turned out, at nine years old my eldest had a real talent for proofreading packaging and enjoyed finding mistakes that all of us "grown-ups" missed. I knew what I wanted out of life and set my priorities accordingly.

While on maternity leave in 2010, first-time mother Kristy Lewis came up with the idea of creating a healthier microwave popcorn. Balancing motherhood and launching a business, she started Quinn Popcorn (named after her newborn son), which is now available at over a thousand retail locations. "The first year was really challenging. I was working 24 hours a day. But if you have a mission, you make it work," Lewis said.[5]

Comedian David Brenner was at the top of his career when divorce threw him into a bitter custody battle for his son Cole. Though Brenner was the most frequent guest on *The Tonight Show* in the 1970s and '80s, a judge declared that he would be considered an absentee father if he was away from home for more than fifty nights a year. Brenner's dream to be a great father was more important than being America's top comic, so he stopped appearing on Johnny Carson's show in order to keep custody of his son. We all have choices to make with our lives and our careers. The disruptor's map helps you focus on taking control of those choices.

Achieving work-life balance is about defining your goals and expressing them on your disruptor's map. What are the things outside your career you wish to achieve or experience? Plan for space and time on your map to pursue your passions. How much time do you need to set aside for family and friends? We all get so caught up in our own lives that we miss out on the lives of those dearest to us. Plan for ways to get more enjoyment into your life and you *will* get more joy out of it.

> Plan for ways to get more enjoyment into your life and you will get more joy out of it.

PACK YOUR DISRUPTOR'S SUITCASE

Whether you are going away for a vacation or an important business trip, you pack a bag filled with the things you will need. You can't enjoy Hawaii without a bathing suit, and it is pretty hard to give a PowerPoint presentation without your laptop. A career is just a longer trip with a whole lot more baggage. Set off unprepared and you shouldn't be surprised when you don't achieve your goals. Today you need to recognize which things might be essential for you to arrive at your ultimate destination. You must bring urgency to packing your disruptor's suitcase.

> A career is just a longer trip with a whole lot more baggage.

As you've been thinking about what you aspire to and considering your other priorities, you haven't had to take into account the resources you'll need to achieve those results. As with a business plan that assumes the need for additional team members and skill sets to build a company, your disruptor's journey will require external help. What training, mentors, and capital will you need? As you would do with any competing product, research other individuals in your industry and find out how they got the resources they needed to succeed. In most cases, you will discover a world full of people waiting to help you achieve your goals.

Even the work you do and where you do it can be a resource. When accepting a job, always ask yourself two questions: Will this position move me closer to achieving my goal? How long will I stay at this job before moving on? The answer to the second question should be determined by how much you can learn and grow at that particular job. A job at a small startup, for example, may give you the opportunity to try your hand at a wider range of tasks than you could in a more regimented position at a larger company. By testing and pushing your limits at the startup, you may discover personal strengths and skills that you didn't know you possessed. On the other hand, overreaching will highlight areas where you need additional training and experience to succeed. Choose wisely and with purpose.

When a job no longer offers you the opportunity for personal growth, then it is time to move on. Remember that there is a big difference between giving up and knowing when you have had enough. If your daily routine is monotonous, and weeks roll into years, you will find your dreams slipping away. If you can't afford the risk of quitting, try transferring internally within your company or look for another position in your field. If you work in a larger corporation, speak with someone in human resources about the type of skills you would like to develop, and you may just find out that the company is willing to pay for you to take courses or earn an additional degree in exchange for staying with the company. I can assure you that when you reach the midpoint of your working years, you will have more regrets about the things you didn't try than the ones you tried and didn't succeed at.

I have spent my life going into new industries and fields with little understanding of their inner workings and not knowing any of their key influencers. In each case, my success was not achieved alone. When I was recruited by EMI president and CEO Ken Berry to bring the hundred-year-old British record company into the digital age, I knew nothing about running a music label. I remember exactly what Ken said to me on my first day: "I have eleven thousand people who know the music business. What I don't have is a future." Over the next few years, every time I hit a brick wall or had an idea that might or might not work, Ken made the time to mentor me. Together we transformed the company and the music industry by pioneering new business models in digital downloads, music subscriptions, and streaming Internet radio. I didn't travel the road alone, and I can assure you that you won't, either.

Mentors are invaluable—and often crucial—to a disruptor's success. Mentors are also surprisingly easy to find. By reading blogs for your industry, you will quickly discover the luminaries you aspire to emulate. Send them an email. Reach out and ask for advice. Don't write, "Will you be my mentor?" Rather, try something like "I was thinking about starting a company that does X and wanted to know your thoughts." Value people's time when they give it, and thank them when it proves helpful. Even in the twenty-first century, nothing is as powerful or personal as sending a handwritten thank-you note. (The most significant person in my life, my wife, I met through a simple thank-you note.) With persistence and a little luck, you will find a mentor who can guide you through your career and could help accelerate its pace.

"The fastest way to change yourself is to hang out with people who are already the way you want to be," billionaire Reid Hoffman suggests.[6] Role models are a key factor in developing a successful persona. Success *can* actually rub off on you. How do you meet role models? You can start by going to more conferences and gatherings in your field. Get to know the industry leaders. Use LinkedIn and other online tools to reach out to people you admire. Finding the right mentor can provide you with both personal validation and professional growth.

I have a friend who wrote a cold-call letter to one of America's most famous business leaders. She explained that, having won some money on the game show *Jeopardy,* she could afford to work for him as his assistant for one dollar. He must have been impressed by her no-nonsense approach, because he hired her and launched her career as one of the most connected people in the business world. Twenty years later, she sits on many boards and advises the next generation of billionaires. For those without the resources to work for free, paying internships can open the door to endless opportunities. Oprah Winfrey learned the ropes as an intern at the CBS affiliate in Nashville, and designer Tom Ford got his start interning for Chloé. George Hu started as an intern at Salesforce.com and now is the chief operating officer of the $33 billion public company.

The adage that the master appears when the student is ready to learn is true only if you make the effort to seek out advice. Every successful person would love to share his or her knowledge with the next generation. It validates the mentor's accomplishments and gives them a sense of continuing value. Today I mentor college students and first-time entrepreneurs as a way of paying forward all the countless times others have aided me. I enjoy joining their boards, helping them raise capital, and even beta-testing their apps.

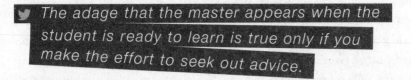

The adage that the master appears when the student is ready to learn is true only if you make the effort to seek out advice.

ACKNOWLEDGE THAT TIME WAITS FOR NO ONE

You are not going to live forever. Hospice workers say that the number-one regret they hear from dying patients is that they wish they had been courageous enough to live true to themselves and had not been guided by the expectations of others.[7] Life is short—so what is stopping you? To really achieve everything you set out to accomplish, you must set deadlines. Work backward from each deadline and develop incremental steps. What are the pieces that make up the whole goal? Bill Murray's character in the movie *What About Bob?* says it brilliantly when he repeats to himself the need to take "baby steps."

Achieving goals is also about delaying the instant gratification that comes so easily in our always-on lifestyle. Delaying marriage, children, or vacations to build a career or a company is about living a few years of your life in a way most people won't so that you can spend the rest of your life living at a level most people can't. The easiest way to set priorities is by working backward from a future goal. I am often asked by young entrepreneurs if now is a good time to start a business. My answer is always the same: "A year ago was the best time to start your business. The second-best time is now."

> Live a few years of your life in a way most people won't so that you can spend the rest of your life living at a level most people can't.

Proving that you are never too old to disrupt is my business partner Doug Netter. At ninety-two, Netter (along with Steven Latham and I) sold the first multiscreen interactive game show to a major television network, in 2012. Doug has been working in Hollywood longer than most executives have been on this planet, but ever since I worked with him to pioneer new technology on *Babylon 5* in the 1990s, he has always strived to innovate television. With this game show we wanted to finally change the way people interacted with traditional television. The tagline for *Bet You Know* is "Instead of watching from home, you can be winning from home." Though the show never made it past the pilot stage, Doug remains a constant inspiration, demonstrating that you really can change any industry if you just keep moving forward and that *never* is the right time to quit.

Every successful disruptor I know refused to sit back and wait. They didn't worry about the time being right or the conditions being perfect; they just dived right in. Do you want to be left standing on the shore?

F ailing to plan is planning to fail," bestselling time management author Alan Lakein cleverly wrote.[8] The author of *How to Get Control of Your Time and Your Life* adds, "Planning is bringing the future into the present so that you can do something about it now."[9] If you've been responding to these prompts, you now have your disruptor's map.

Committing your aspirations, priorities, resources, and deadlines to paper gives you a personal business plan to measure your progress against. The difference between successful and unsuccessful people is that successful ones know that the most unprofitable thing ever manufactured is an excuse.

 The difference between successful and unsuccessful people is, the first know the most unprofitable thing to manufacture is an excuse.

Chapter Four

Building a Brand of One

Who am I, anyway? Am I my résumé?
—*"I Hope I Get It," A Chorus Line*

When I read online that HealthAddress had just been acquired, I knew that meant my friend Kelly Lefkowitz would once again be out of work. We've all been there. You just lost your job and are fearful that the phone will never ring again. You wonder if you'll ever find a job worthy of your talents or even one in your field. When we're in that situation, we like to blame the economy, the competition, or that unappreciative moronic supervisor, but in the end it always comes back to blaming ourselves. It doesn't matter the cause; getting sacked feels like a kick in the gut. Whether you are downsized because of a merger or your company closes its doors, there is nothing more disruptive to your life than becoming unemployed. Being out of work and looking for a new job happens to my friend Kelly more often than it does to other people. Kelly's reward as a brilliant chief financial officer for building a financially sound company is being let go when the firm is sold to a major corporation. Kelly has the unfortunate habit of firing himself.

When he and I met for lunch to brainstorm what he would do next, Kelly had been in finance for more than twenty years. Many middle-aged workers fear that all those years of experience are now used against them when looking for a new job. Are they too old or too expensive? I encouraged Kelly to take this opportunity to disrupt himself. We deconstructed his training and experience, his strengths and expertise. We explored the ways he presents himself and how he spends his time. Kelly has worked with dozens of startups and written over a hundred business plans. He had guided inexperienced CEOs through the whole process of fund-raising. He isn't just a finance guy; he is one of the most experienced strategic-planning experts in the startup space. By thinking of his professional self as the total value of each interlocking link in the chain, Kelly saw how he could transition into his next professional position. He realized that the link in his personal value chain that was ripest for disruption was distribution: every company seeking capital could use his unique talents, but very few could afford him full-time. Why not create a business that would provide his services and those of interim CFOs to fast-growing young companies for only the brief amount of time they most need the financial help? Kelly created the company Strat/Assist and has never looked back.

This chapter will explore the ways disruptors think about their professional selves and how they approach the business world, pinpointing opportunities for disruption to help build their careers. It will also describe how recent disruptions in our business landscape have transformed the way people can promote themselves and their companies.

To succeed in business, one must see oneself as a brand: a brand of one. The links in your personal value chain constitute your unique brand. The research and development links are defined by your education, your previous work experience, and the sources you pursue to find a job in the first place. The work you do—its quality and content—makes up the design and production links. The way you present yourself professionally constitutes the marketing and sales links in your personal value chain. And where you work, with whom you work, and where you devote your professional energies determine your distribution link. Think about your professional value as the combination of these links in the chain. If you are struggling to get a job, or if you are ready to make a career transition, all you need to do is target the link ripest for disruption.

DISRUPT THE RECRUITMENT VALUE CHAIN

For most people, finding the perfect job seems like a fantasy. It can seem as if we never hear about dream jobs until they are filled or that potential employers don't even know we exist. Sites like LinkedIn and Monster.com can't always solve this mismatch of supply and demand.

If anything, the sheer volume of job boards and online résumés has made most applicants feel like tiny needles in the largest of haystacks. But in today's volatile business world, carving out the right career path is essential to attaining your goals—especially if you're looking to start your own business.

The truth is, by thinking of where you look to try to get a job as being a link in the value chain, you can see clearly how value is created and how disrupting that process becomes a straightforward and manageable task. A generation ago, when I first graduated from UCLA, the U.S. economy was in shambles, and virtually no recruiters came to campus. I knew I wanted a job in the entertainment industry, but I didn't have any connections, and I never heard about who was hiring until after the position had been filled. Oftentimes, the best opportunities were filled without ever having been advertised. Looking at this situation from a value chain perspective, I realized that the real value to be captured would be in finding out who would be hiring *before* any job descriptions were posted. Instinctively I knew I needed to create a competitive advantage. I figured that if I had first crack at job openings, I had the best chance of getting hired. But how could I find out before my competitors who would be willing to hire someone with my qualifications?

The answer was simple: take out a help-wanted ad in the *Hollywood Reporter* describing a fantasy position that matched my qualifications. This out-of-the-box approach yielded three key pieces of data. First, the résumés that people submitted in response to my ad showed me the competitive landscape of employable talent. Before the Internet, getting any kind of data like this was a real challenge. This helped me answer questions like: How do I rewrite and reimagine my résumé to be more competitive and stand out? Do I have skills that I hadn't displayed in the proper manner that others had highlighted on their résumés? With this reconnaissance I was able to craft the perfect entry-level résumé.

Second, the majority of people applying for my "dream job" were currently employed somewhere else. These people were not just employed anywhere; they were in jobs that they believed would be the perfect stepping stone to getting my dream job. Logic dictated that if I worked at those places, I would be that much closer to achieving my dream job, too.

Finally, running that ad identified which employers had employees with one foot out the door. Whatever their reasons, the people who responded to my ad wanted to leave their present positions and work somewhere else. Now I had a list of companies that would most likely be experiencing turnover and potentially hiring someone at my level in the near future. All I had to do was make sure that my new, improved résumé was in their human resources directors' hands immediately—before those current employees had even left. One of the very first places that received my revised résumé called me immediately for an interview, and my career was launched.

Today, most jobs are not listed in the newspaper, and online job postings don't always tell you the name of the employer. So how does my thirty-year-old example work in the digital age? The same value chain for human capital still exists, and it is just as easily disrupted.

In 2010, Alec Brownstein was just another copywriter working at the bottom of a large New York advertising agency. It's not that Alec hated his job, but he dreamed of working at a really creative shop with the most innovative creative directors on Madison Avenue. He knew who these creative executives were, but not how to meet them or get on their radar. While googling around to see the latest work by these industry luminaries, Brownstein noticed that no sponsored links were attached to the searches for their names. Sponsored links are the ads that appear on the top of every search results page. Brownstein saw an opportunity.

"Everyone googles themselves," Brownstein explains, "even if they don't admit it. I wanted to invade that secret, egotistical moment when [they] were most vulnerable."

As the only bidder for the names of top creative directors, Brownstein could secure the top search placements for fifteen cents per click. Whenever a creative director's name was searched, the following appeared next to the results: "Hey, [creative director's name]: Goooogling [sic] yourself is a lot of fun. Hiring me is fun, too," with a link to Brownstein's website. His ingeniously simple plan worked.

Eighty percent of the creative directors took the bait and called Alec.

Brownstein received job offers from two superstar creative directors, Scott Vitrone and Ian Reichenthal. Total cost for disrupting one of the world's most creative industries: $6. The effect on Brownstein's career: priceless. That wasn't the only bonus from his investment. In a field that rewards creativity, Alec Brownstein also won a Clio—the advertising industry's most prestigious award—in the self-promotion category.

"Don't be afraid to put yourself out there in an interesting way," Brownstein advises. "The people who you want to work for can't hire you any less than they already are. So shoot for the moon."[1]

The most creative approach a prospective hire ever took to get my attention happened when I was president of a division at Universal Studios. The applicant rightly assumed that everyone, even senior executives, likes presents. One day I received a large box in the mail. Inside were the two oddest items I could imagine: a metal spaghetti colander and a bag of candied dates. Intrigued, I read the note: "My apologies for the mix-up. I asked my assistant to get me dates on your calendar and she misunderstood. Can we meet next week?" I figured anyone who could get me to laugh was worth meeting. You can't get the dream job in your field unless you get noticed. Differentiation in the job market is just another variant on my axiom "Be the best at what you do or the only one doing it."

> 🐦 "Be the best at what you do or the only one doing it."

RELAUNCHING YOUR BRAND

But what happens when you get the dream job, you create a great career, and your entire industry gets disrupted? Worse, if you see yourself as having achieved only a narrow band of experience at one company, or in one industry, and that field goes away, is your career therefore over? Case in point: the music industry at the turn of the twenty-first century.

As I will later recall in detail, in 1999, when nineteen-year-old Shawn Fanning walked into my office at Capitol Records, I knew the world of the record label would never be the same and that the music labels were the canaries in the mineshaft of digital intellectual property. Thanks to their technology, Napster, which Fanning developed with Sean Parker, millions of consumers could steal any song they wanted and play it on any device. Overnight, the music industry's value chain was shattered. Developing songs, discovering and nurturing new talent, designing marketing campaigns, producing music videos, getting airplay on radio or on MTV, making sure new releases got proper placement on retailers' shelves—none of this mattered if no one was buying the albums. U.S. music sales plummeted, from $14.6 billion in 1999 to $6.3 billion in 2009.[2] Perhaps the former head of Yahoo Music, Dave Goldberg, said it best: "The digital music business has been a war of attrition."[3]

The implosion of the music industry meant that tens of thousands of record label employees lost their jobs. When I was global president of digital at EMI, we had to consolidate and close labels, cut our artist roster, and let go of employees all over the world. The company that had grown out of Emile Berliner's first marketing of disc records in 1889, the world's largest independent music company, which had signed Queen and Pink Floyd, would be cut up and sold for its catalog within a decade.

People who had crafted very specific skills in the music business were forced to enter a new job market that wasn't looking for record executives. For these people, career disruption forced self-disruption. Take record label marketing executives as an example. Some of the greatest marketers in the world worked at record labels. Unlike the marketers for Coke or Jim Beam, who get to build off of brand-name recognition that has developed over many decades and millions of dollars in advertising spent, a record label isn't marketing "Capitol Records" or "Blue Note." Instead, marketers at labels have to take an unknown bunch of kids making music in a garage and turn them into a household name around the globe. These creative thinkers have to achieve this miracle over and over again, with limited budgets and with a "product" that can talk back to you and say no if the artist doesn't like the marketing campaign.

This constant introduction of new acts by the labels meant that these marketing teams had mastered a number of highly desirable skill sets that had absolutely nothing to do with music. Everything from creating a band's image (branding) to generating buzz (earned media) to getting on the shelves (point-of-sale merchandising) are experiences and skills applicable to every product sold in the world. With so many music marketers losing their careers, this expertise was now available to other product categories that needed marketing innovation.

For example, in 2011, the global market for mobile phone accessories was estimated at $34 billion.[4] Most items either were sold alongside mobile phones or could be used by other devices and therefore just migrated into the category from portable audio. Earbuds and headphones were, for the most part, undifferentiated accessories. If better branding could be brought to this category of six billion consumers, the potential for profits could be massive.

What if all the tools and creative marketing used for hit bands were applied to headphones? It stands to reason that this approach should be successful, since the end consumer is the same music aficionado. Beats by Dr. Dre, the brainchild of Dre and Interscope chairman Jimmy Iovine, did just that. They hired ex–music label executives to build branding and buzz for the headphones by associating with artists and athletes. Celebrity endorsement on this scale causes pull-through at retail. Consumers go into retail stores and ask for the Beats product by name, which in turn has retailers clamoring for the products. The startup enjoyed massive distribution at retail and sold over $350 million worth of headphones in 2011.[5] The following year, the brand used typical music-label-style guerilla marketing to hijack attention at the London Olympic Games (where official sponsors spent upward of $100 million plus media to participate) without spending a dime. Beats' marketing department sidestepped all the International Olympic Committee's rules by sending the Olympic athletes free headphones. When the global television audience tuned in to see swimmer Michael Phelps (and virtually every other swimmer) sporting Beats headphones before jumping into the water at the Aquatics Centre, it was the brilliant work of ex–music label execs that was on display. Billions of "stolen" TV impressions were purloined by people who had rebooted their careers. For the music label execs who had been put out of work, all it took was a little self-disruption. They disrupted the production links in their internal value chains, thinking critically about their skills and past experiences and applying them to something other than a band or a record label. When people ask me for advice when they're looking to make a career transition, I always tell them to think about *what* they did in their job, not just what company or product they did it *for*.

In addition to thinking about your true skill set, it's critical to continually refresh the research and development link in your internal value chain. In the twenty-first century, lifelong learning is no longer a luxury but a necessity for employment. Would you go to a fifty-year-old doctor who hadn't learned anything new since he graduated from medical school in 1988? Of the hundred most prescribed medications in the United States, everything from Nexium to Tamiflu, all one hundred would have been invented since your doctor finished her residency.[6]

> 🐦 *Lifelong learning is no longer a luxury but a necessity for employment.*

"We're beginning to recognize that it may not make sense to work at just one job for your entire life, retire for a few years, and then die. Instead, we're more likely to take a cyclic approach to life education, work, and leisure and mix these up throughout our lifetimes. People are going back to school at 45, 65, even 80," Maddy Dychtwald writes in her book *Cycles: How We Will Live, Work, and Buy*. "People are having second, third, fourth, even fifth careers."[7]

DIFFERENTIATE YOUR BRAND

Why would an employer hire you if your skills are out of date? And if you're starting your own business, is your knowledge up to date with today's market conditions? Distance learning and online courses have made staying current easier than ever. Most classes can be taken at any time that fits your personal schedule. Many software manufacturers offer courses online at little or no cost that include completion certificates you can reference on your CV. Anyone can claim Photoshop experience on their résumé, but don't you think prospective employers would rather hire someone who is Adobe-certified?

It is also important to think about how your professional education is reflected in the marketing link of your personal value chain. Many certification programs allow those who complete the training to leverage the power of the brand's logos on their business cards or websites. One of my earliest business cards proudly displayed the "IBM Business Partner" logo as a differentiator. An added benefit of taking these courses is that corporate recruiters looking for new talent to hire often scan professional registries of program graduates.

Learning new skills contributes value to the research and development link of your personal value chain, but how you communicate those skills constitutes your marketing and sales link. Getting noticed and differentiating yourself from your colleagues is half the battle. Crafting the right language to describe your accomplishments is also crucial. Most applications are scanned by recruiters for only a matter of seconds. With your entire career at stake, every word needs to be carefully chosen to "sell" your unique story.

The most important tool you have on a résumé is language. Action verbs convey energy and excitement about your accomplishments and communicate your drive. They bring to life past activities and make every experience sound specific and useful. The following list of terms was originally created in the heart of Silicon Valley by NOVA, an employment and training agency that provides educational programing to address the workforce needs of companies in the area.[8] Try rewriting your résumé and incorporating these terms to communicate your work experience and expertise. Think of how your résumé communicates who you are, what you can do, and how those skills make you valuable and unique.

> The most important tool you have on a résumé is language.

Your Transferable Skills

FINANCE

Accounting	Balancing	Developing	Reconciling
Adjusting	Bookkeeping	Estimating	Record-keeping
Administering	Budgeting	Forecasting	Researching
Allocating	Calculating	Managing	Resolving
Analyzing	Computing	Planning	Solving
Appraising	Consolidating	Preparing	
Auditing	Depositing	Projecting	

CREATIVE

Abstracting	Discriminating	Instituting	Playing
Acting	Dramatizing	Integrating	Revitalizing
Conceptualizing	Drawing	Introducing	Sculpting
Constructing	Establishing	Inventing	Shaping
Creating	Fashioning	Memorizing	Sharing
Customizing	Founding	Originating	Singing
Designing	Generating	Painting	Synthesizing
Developing	Illustrating	Perceiving	Visualizing
Directing	Imagining	Performing	Writing
Discovering	Innovating	Planning	

TECHNICAL/MANUAL

Assembling	Drilling	Making	Repairing
Bending	Driving	Manipulating	Setting up
Binding	Engineering	Moving	Shipping
Building	Fabricating	Operating machinery	Solving
Calculating	Feeding	Operating tools	Sorting
Controlling	Fixing	Overhauling	Tending
Cutting	Grinding	Packing	Testing
Delivering	Handling	Programming	Typing
Designing	Installing	Pulling	Weighing
Devising	Lifting	Punching	
Diagnosing	Maintaining	Remodeling	

DETAIL/CLERICAL

Approving	Dispatching	Inspecting	Responding
Arranging	Dispensing	Inventorying	Retaining
Cataloguing	Distributing	Logging	Retrieving
Checking	Enforcing	Monitoring	Tabulating
Classifying	Executing	Operating	Screening
Collating	Extracting	Organizing	Specifying
Collecting	Facilitating	Preparing	Systematizing
Comparing	Filing	Processing	Transcribing
Compiling	Following through	Proof-reading	Validating
Copying	Generating	Purchasing	
Detecting	Implementing	Recording	

RESEARCH

Analyzing	Examining	Interpreting	Researching
Ascertaining	Experimenting	Interviewing	Summarizing
Clarifying	Extracting	Investigating	Surveying
Collecting	Extrapolating	Isolating	Synthesizing
Critiquing	Gathering	Organizing	Systematizing
Deciding	Identifying	Reading	Troubleshooting
Diagnosing	Inspecting	Receiving	Writing

HELPING

Adjusting	Demonstrating	Leading	Rendering
Assessing	Diagnosing	Listening	Representing
Attending	Directing	Mentoring	Servicing
Caring	Educating	Motivating	Speaking
Clarifying	Expediting	Observing	Understanding
Classifying	Facilitating	Referring	
Coaching	Familiarizing	Rehabilitating	
Counseling	Guiding	Relating	

Your Transferable Skills (continued)

TEACHING

Adapting	Demonstrating	Goal setting	Motivating
Adopting	Demystifying	Guiding	Performing
Advising	Developing	Influencing	Persuading
Briefing	Educating	Informing	Presenting
Clarifying	Enabling	Initiating	Stimulating
Coaching	Encouraging	Inspiring	Teaching
Communicating	Evaluating	Instructing	Training
Coordinating	Explaining	Inventing	Tutoring
Deciding	Facilitating	Lecturing	Valuing

MANAGEMENT

Addressing	Controlling	Increasing	Problem solving
Administering	Coordinating	Initiating	Producing
Analyzing	Delegating	Inspiring	Recommending
Anticipating	Developing	Managing	Reviewing
Appraising	Directing	Mentoring	Scheduling
Assessing	Evaluating	Motivating	Strengthening
Assigning	Executing	Organizing	Supervising
Attaining	Expanding	Overseeing	Team building
Chairing	Firing	Piloting	Troubleshooting
Charting	Generating	Planning	
Consolidating	Hiring	Policy making	
Contracting	Improving	Prioritizing	

COMMUNICATION

Addressing	Directing	Learning	Reading
Arbitrating	Drafting	Lecturing	Reasoning
Arranging	Editing	Listening	Reconciling
Authorizing	Enlisting	Mediating	Recruiting
Collaborating	Facilitating	Moderating	Selling
Convincing	Formulating	Motivating	Translating
Corresponding	Helping	Obtaining	Writing
Counseling	Influencing	Persuading	
Creating	Interpreting	Promoting	
Developing	Leading	Publicizing	

I was not always aware of the importance of personal branding. In fact, I spent a good part of my career believing that my work should speak for itself. It doesn't. How we market and sell ourselves comes into play long before we get the opportunity to prove ourselves through our work. My shortcomings in personal branding were pointed out to me in my very first week at EMI, by Virgin Music Group's vice chairwoman, Nancy Berry.

I was raised to believe that in business, men wore suits and ties to important meetings. When I started at EMI, my first time in the C-suite, I was about to fly around the world to meet all of the label heads across the United States, Europe, and Asia, and of course I planned to wear my best suits and ties. I was an international executive, and I wanted to look the part. I had been hired to transform the music industry, and I took the responsibility very seriously. But what I failed to grasp was that this was the world's largest music company, not a bank—everyone around me was wearing T-shirts and jeans. Lucky for me, my first meeting was in Los Angeles with the head of Virgin Records.

I sat in Nancy's Beverly Hills office, the scent of candles wafting in the air, wearing a pinstriped suit and power tie, trying to explain my vision for the future of the music industry to a barefoot vice chairwoman. She graciously listened. But I could tell that my message wasn't registering. Then Nancy asked me a very poignant question that caught me off guard: How was I going to get musicians, their managers, and label executives to follow my lead into this new digital age if no one could relate to me? I looked like a corporate lawyer, not a record guy with a passion for the future of music. I was coming into their world and looked as out of place as an Amish farmer at a Jay-Z concert. Just as she had done with many a developing music act over the years, Nancy did what she does best: she helped me create my brand. She helped me craft a new image before I embarked on my world tour of the company's thirty labels.

I grew a goatee, traded in the suits for an all-black wardrobe, and developed a look that was consistent with the message I was marketing: music evolved. As superficial as it may sound, the clothes do make the man. The first impression I made was critical because I was going to be asking everyone I met all around the world to change how they were running their business. They needed to believe that I understood their world before they would be willing to learn about the new digital world I was pitching. Thanks to Nancy, the message now matched the packaging, and I was able to get everyone on board to achieve the goals I had set for the company.

Sometimes rebranding is as simple as rethinking how you distribute your professional energies. Eileen Gittins, a Silicon Valley CEO, was in her forties and burned out after the dot-com crash of 2000. Looking for more balance and joy, she threw her energy into the hobby of photography. Gittins spent a year photographing people she had worked with and hand-developing each print. Thinking of her brand as more of an artist than a tech executive, Gittins went looking for a site where she could upload her images and print a quality book. Finding none, she combined her passion, her new brand, and her past to create Blurb. Today Blurb ships over two million books a year and has shipped them to seventy-five countries.[9]

The most profound rebranding I have ever witnessed was that of a convicted felon with cancer whose doctors had given him eighteen months to live. In the 1980s, Michael Milken was the most powerful man on Wall Street. A smart, driven trader whom Drexel Burnham once paid $550 million, Milken changed American corporate finance and was the embodiment of Gordon Gekko's "Greed is good." But his excess and success came to a screeching halt in 1989 when the government filed a ninety-eight-count indictment against him. After he served his time in prison, few people ever expected a second act for Milken.

Days after getting out, in 1993, Milken was diagnosed with prostate cancer and informed that he had less than two years to live. He changed his priorities and his brand. Not knowing how much time he had left, Milken put all his energies into helping others. He worked with charities and established the Prostate Cancer Foundation. He helped educational companies get funding and founded the Milken Institute, a think tank that's dedicated to "Changing the World in Innovative Ways." Milken's annual Global Conference attracts global business leaders, heads of state, and NGO directors, all working together to solve the problems facing our world. Michael Milken's rebranding is complete, and his impact has been far greater than anyone could ever have imagined it would be when he was at the height of his Wall Street junk bond trading days, decades ago.

Today, having disrupted myself and changed jobs several times since those early days at EMI, I am back at work in the corporate world of suits. Disrupting your style and brand is about evolving. In the end, failure comes when you stop. Or, as 50 Cent so aptly put it, "get rich or die tryin'."

PERSONAL PROMOTION

Personal branding is especially challenging. You may work at many jobs in your life, but you have only one career. Even if you change directions, as Gittins and Milken did, you need to believe in the core values that make you believe in yourself. If the race against diminishing capital defines the startup company, the race against time defines the brand of one. Instead of reliving past mistakes and beating yourself up for what you could or should have done in the past, look at ways to pivot in the future. Look at your career as a constant race against a ticking clock.

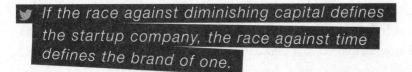

> If the race against diminishing capital defines the startup company, the race against time defines the brand of one.

One of the best ways to leverage and promote your brand of one is through public speaking. I realize that to many, getting up in front of a roomful of strangers may be a bit intimidating, but public speaking is undoubtedly the most effective way to cold-call hundreds of people at the same time.

Every industry has conferences in need of speakers. You don't have to be famous; you just have to be persistent. Send emails out to event planners, outlining in a paragraph what you plan on presenting and why it will be of value to that particular audience. Ninety percent of the time they are happy to find someone to fill a time slot. If you're nervous in front of a large crowd, ask to speak before a local business breakfast meeting or ask to guest-lecture a class at a local university in order to gain confidence. Many national organizations coordinate regional conferences so that you can travel the country giving the same talk at several gatherings of the same group.

The more unique your topic, the less competition you will have. One of the first major speeches I gave, when I was in my twenties, was to the National Association of Chiefs of Police convention. I know nothing about law enforcement, but I did know what impact the Internet was going to have on cyber crime. I was the first computer geek they had ever booked, and the speech resulted in consulting work. What are you uniquely qualified to discuss? How can you be the change of pace the event planner is looking for? The more original the topic, the more in demand you will be. One of the most interesting and unique speakers I have ever heard, Michio Kaku, is a theoretical physicist who makes the most incomprehensible science relevant and engaging.

I was speaking in Mumbai last year to a crowd of nearly a thousand Indian media executives. In a country of over one billion people, I didn't know a single person. After that thirty-minute speech, I was inundated by people handing me their cards, scheduling meetings, and emailing me with requests to work together. Within a month's time I had a network of contacts across the subcontinent and was doing business with one of India's largest tech companies. From Seoul to Rome, Toronto to Moscow, I have walked into darkened rooms filled with strangers and walked out with business associates and lifelong friends.

As we were building ooVoo into the number-one app in the world for teens, I needed to find a way to get the key decision makers at top youth brands to advertise with us. Most major brands work through advertising agencies, so getting to the actual brand's chief marketing officer is a formidable task. The conference I needed to speak at was the PTTOW! (Plan to Take on the World) youth marketing conference, run by Roman Tsunder. I had attended in the past and knew the room would be filled with dozens of potential clients. At many larger conferences, speaking slots are reserved for paid sponsors. So when all else fails, if the audience is paramount to your company's success, don't be afraid to pay to play. As soon as I finished my talk, Target's CMO, Jeff Jones, walked up to me and said that he really wanted to speak with me. His fourteen-year-old daughter was a big user of ooVoo and had told him I was "the guy to meet" at the conference. Target spends over $1 billion a year on advertising.[10] It doesn't get any better than that.

As powerful as public speaking is as a tool for marketing you or your company, I know it is not for everyone. If you are the kind of person who, if given the choice at a funeral, would rather be in the casket than deliver the eulogy, then there is a way to communicate with millions without uttering a word in public: social media.

Blogging, tweeting, and posting give you a controlled environment in which to "speak" with your audience. With a laptop and Internet connectivity, you have the ability to reach everyone in your industry anytime and from anywhere. Every field has popular websites that encourage comments and third-party submissions. A few trade publications and influential newspapers no longer control the media. By being authentic with your voice and sharing your expertise, you'll enable two things to happen. First, your name will start to become familiar in your field. That popularity will help you develop a Twitter or LinkedIn following. All of those followers are potential sources of new business and collaboration. The more you post, the more followers you develop, the higher your Klout Score grows—and the more business you generate. The second benefit of generating all of this "branded" content is that your name appears more frequently in search results.

> With a laptop and Internet connectivity, you have the ability to reach everyone in your industry anytime and from anywhere.

Let's face it: you use Google to find the information and things you need in life. Well, so does everyone else. A decade ago, you would have had to hire a major public relations firm and hope to eventually get a story written about you in *The Wall Street Journal* or *The New York Times* to grow awareness of your work. Today, Google is the great equalizer. When someone is searching for information, they are just as likely to stumble upon your blog as an article in *The Times*. Thanks to search engines, you have the same reach as any other publisher in the world.

The more you post, the greater your chances of being discovered by someone searching for your expertise. Your words allow you to define your reality and disrupt your industry. Your words can have the same weight and authority as those coming from giant media organizations. As author Seth Godin declares in *Linchpin,* "Expertise gives you enough insight to reinvent what everyone else assumes is the truth."[11]

> Your words allow you to define your reality and disrupt your industry.

A young entrepreneur named Stacey Ferreira, whom I met on Ken Rutkowski's *Business Rockstars* radio show, used Twitter to launch her startup MySocialCloud.com. The idea was simple: create a company that stores all of your passwords securely in the cloud. An avid Twitter user, she saw a tweet one day from Sir Richard Branson, inviting anyone who donated $2,000 to his particular charity to an exclusive cocktail party in Florida. Still underage, the nineteen-year-old New York University dropout responded to Sir Richard's tweet, asking if she could attend even if she wasn't twenty-one. Branson, who had started his billion-dollar empire as a teen entrepreneur, responded that if she made the donation, he would take care of it and meet her in Miami. Ferreira borrowed the donation from her parents and flew to meet Branson. Impressed by her, and her vision for the company, he invested $1 million in MySocialCloud shortly after their first meeting.[12] Social media pays . . . though rarely so quickly!

Posting and writing is also a great way to get noticed internally at a large company. After he graduated from Princeton in 2008, my son Danny's first job was as an assistant at United Talent Agency. Everyone starts at the bottom at Hollywood agencies, and differentiating yourself from the pack can take years. With Twitter less than a year old at the time, Danny saw how the new communication medium, if used properly, could be a benefit to the agency's stars. So he took it upon himself to write a guide for UTA talent on best practices for Twitter. The guide spread through the agency and to its high-profile clients. UTA continued its reputation as one of the most forward-thinking agencies, and Danny was able to differentiate himself from the other assistants.

While posting or writing a blog is a great start, the key to building a brand of one is having your name endorsed by more established brands. This is where the disruption of print media again works to your advantage. Major publications such as *Forbes* and *The Huffington Post* don't have the writing staffs needed to address all of the topics they cover. Industry trades are more shorthanded than ever. These publishers are all eager for free content to publish. More stories generate more readers and more revenue. Having the same story you would have posted on your blog appear instead as an article on *The Huffington Post* makes you a columnist. Pete Cashmore, founder of the blog *Mashable* and technology columnist for CNN, has used this technique to become one of the most influential digerati online and in the process built himself a multi-million-dollar media empire that he started with just his computer in his room at age nineteen.

Whether because of ambition or circumstance, every career gets disrupted. The era of the gold watch and guaranteed pension is no more. No multinational company or industry is safe from disruption. But the very same tools that are changing the corporate landscape can be harnessed to provide you with more opportunity for growth and success than has ever been available to the individual. To succeed, you must build your brand of one. And by staying actively aware of your personal brand and the tools available to quickly give yourself a reboot, you will always have the ability to change yourself, your industry, and your world.

> *Whether because of ambition or circumstance, every career gets disrupted.*

Chapter Five

Disruptors at Work and the Value of Intrapreneurship

"They don't have intelligence. They have what I call 'thintelligence.' They see the immediate situation. They think narrowly and they call it 'being focused.' They don't see the surround. They don't see the consequences. That's how you get an island like this. From thintelligent thinking."
—Dr. Ian Malcom in Michael Crichton's
Jurassic Park

There's a great action sequence in the film *Jurassic Park III* in which Sam Neill and William H. Macy are in the island's jungle trapped between a ferocious *Tyrannosaurus rex* and an equally aggressive *Spinosaurus*. The tiny human interlopers have no possible way to fight off the clearly dominant *Spinosaurus* and survive. But the *Spinosaurus* is too busy defending his turf against the *T. rex* to bother with the weak little humans. To the small-brained, physically massive *Spinosaurus*, the combative *T. rex* presents a bigger threat to his survival. Dinosaurs fight other dinosaurs. The insignificant human interlopers can be dealt with later. By doing what he has always done best, the *Spinosaurus* destroys the *T. rex,* snaps his neck, and roars victoriously. Meanwhile, the humans hang on long enough to fly in mercenaries with high-tech weaponry and emerge victorious. This primordial scene is the perfect allegory for why under-resourced startups not only survive but also continually disrupt the dominant players in the market. Great big dinosaurs will always be too busy competing against other big dinosaurs to pay attention to the disruptor. There was a moment in the evolution of every great disruptive company when the dominant market leaders could have crushed (or bought out) their future competition, but they inevitably focused on the wrong competitors.

In the previous chapters, we have examined what it means to be a disruptor, how you can adopt a disruptor's mind-set, and how disruptors leverage their unique viewpoints to find jobs and promote themselves. In this chapter, we will explore how disruptors can influence organizations from the inside. The secret to survival in today's ever-changing business world is recognizing whether you and your company are the disruptors or the dinosaurs. If you are competing against a disruptor, take a long, hard look in the mirror. You might have just become the dinosaur. It happened to me once.

ON BEING DISRUPTED

When I was still working at Universal Studios, I was scheduled to have a meeting with EMI Music CEO Ken Berry at the Capitol Records building in Hollywood. When I arrived, Ken's assistant informed me that the meeting would have to be rescheduled, as Ken had to leave for the airport and fly to London for a board meeting. I knew it would take months to get this meeting rescheduled. When Ken came out of his office to personally apologize to me, I seized the opportunity and offered to have the meeting during his limo ride to LAX. He agreed, and we hopped in the car. Thanks to the Los Angeles traffic, I had more time in the car with the busy CEO than we would have had if we'd met as planned in his office. We had an in-depth conversation about the challenges facing the music industry and EMI's unique opportunity as the world's largest independent music label. Unlike Universal, Sony, and Warner, EMI didn't need to worry about how its digital music strategy would affect its television, video, or feature film divisions. EMI was a stand-alone record label and didn't have any other business interests outside music.

When we arrived at the airport, Ken suggested that we get together again the next time he was in Los Angeles. I knew this would be my once-in-a-lifetime chance to transform a $40 billion industry, but I also knew I would have to, once again, disrupt myself in order to take advantage of it. I had to transform myself from a digital production guy into someone who understood the world of music. Universal Studios, with all its varied divisions, ranging from theme parks to feature films, hadn't yet grasped how the Internet was going to transform its business, because only music was being affected. But for EMI, for which music was the sole revenue source, confronting the threat of the Internet was a matter of survival. I wanted to go to EMI and turn the threats of the Internet into opportunities for growth. While Mr. Berry was on his ten-hour flight, I wrote out my ideas for EMI and outlined a step-by-step plan for growing the company's bottom line by partnering with digital startups instead of trying to compete with them. Before Ken's plane touched down in London, I had e-mailed him my twenty-page treatise, and I was hired the very same day. Thus began one of my early experiences in intrapreneurship.

When I joined EMI as global head of digital distribution, in 1999, I was excited by the challenge of transforming the recorded-music industry. Although my title evoked the idea of digital, my position was unique, because no music label, not even EMI, was actually distributing music digitally in 1999. The music majors—Sony, Warner Bros., Universal, BMG, and EMI—viewed the digital downloads as a threat to the industry that had to be stopped. Labels thought they were in the CD business. I thought we should be in the business of monetizing music regardless of format, packaging, or retail channel. We saw digital as an opportunity to create new revenue streams. As a matter of fact, EMI wasn't even looking for a global head of digital, or even a strategy for dealing with the coming digital age, until I pitched the idea to them.

I had convinced Ken that we had no time to waste. Once I started at EMI, I quickly got the word out in the press and the industry that EMI would partner with any startup around the world that had a new, better way to monetize music. Instead of the old business model of charging companies huge advances to license our music catalog, EMI would take equity in these nascent companies. If the new venture worked, we would make money two ways: through the sale of music and through the sale of stock in the successful ventures. If the dot-com companies failed, we lost nothing. It was a win-win strategy.

I was still aware that people stealing and trading MP3 files online would put us out of business, but I didn't yet have a clue about how to stop them. You don't have to know where the road ends to start on your journey. You just have to know the direction in which you want to travel. I was willing to try anything, as our sales of CDs were starting to slide in a big way. With the full backing of EMI's board, my mantra was simple: make buying digital music easier and stealing a lot harder. I was open to any harebrained idea that entrepreneurs wanted to try. We had nothing to lose, because the alternative was to sit there like ostriches with our heads in the sand and watch while our business was stolen out from under us.

Every company has its fiefdoms, and EMI was no different. An intrapreneur is someone who starts a new division within a structure that is otherwise designed to maintain the status quo. If I was monetizing music in a new way, that meant I was potentially taking away a revenue stream from another label or division. Successful intrapreneurs make internal enemies a lot faster than they make progress. The goal for the intrapreneur is to show measurable results before those who are about to be dethroned destroy you.

At EMI, my team and I inked deals for digital streaming radio, digital jukeboxes, custom CDs manufactured on request, music subscriptions, and even digital music in greeting cards and singing toys. If you walked into my office with a new idea, my job was to test its validity. We tried them all. In my first year with EMI, we took stakes in more than forty companies and generated over $100 million in incremental revenue. While $100 million felt like a lot of money, it wasn't even hitting the charts in the overall U.S. recorded-music industry, which sold $14.6 billion worth of music that year.[1] But as fast as I was trying to move EMI digitally, the physical recorded-music market was devolving even faster.

In the spring of 1999, Shawn Fanning and Sean Parker started Napster in Fanning's dorm room. Napster was the first organized peer-to-peer file-sharing service on the Internet. Fanning's concept of harnessing the underutilized power of consumers' personal computers to create a global distribution system was revolutionary. There is no question that Fanning and Parker are brilliant disruptors. Anyone, anywhere, could "share" (steal) music from any computer that had downloaded the Napster software. Millions of songs were uploaded, and hundreds of millions of tracks were downloaded. Everything that had ever been recorded was available on Napster, without any artist, songwriter, or music label getting paid. Napster's impact on consumers and the music industry was instantaneous and massive. Napster single-handedly disrupted a century-old, multi-billion-dollar industry.

One day in 2000, Sean Parker and Napster vice president Bill Bales came to see me at my office atop the Capitol Records building. I knew that the services Napster offered were illegal, but I thought perhaps we could find a way to harness the technology into a legitimate business. I listened to their plans and their bravado. They didn't have a business model for making any money, but they were convinced that they would eventually own the music labels. I suggested that we find a way to make money together. "Let's create an experiment," I suggested. "Come back with a business model we can try." They never returned.

Years later, I learned that outside my office doors, Bales said, "I don't think we're going to have to make deals with the labels. We think there's going to be enough people using Napster that they'll change copyright law."[2]

Bill Bales wasn't alone in his thinking. One of Napster's earliest investors, venture capitalist John Hummer, bragged to *Fortune* magazine he was "the record companies' worst nightmare."[3] On that point Hummer was right. Stealing music through peer-to-peer services grew so rampant that between 2000 and 2004 the music labels laid off over five thousand employees, and they never recovered.[4] Within a decade, the $14.6 billion U.S. recorded-music business had shrunk to less than half its size.[5]

In October 2000, while I was still the head of digital distribution at EMI, we successfully sued Napster for violating copyright law. Napster was forced to fold, but it was a Pyrrhic victory. The music industry had wasted valuable years fighting the Internet and refusing to adapt to a new business model. While the established dinosaurs fought one another, our customers' needs were ignored. The customer will always find a way to get what he wants, even if the traditional supplier won't comply. For example, when Amazon first approached us about wanting to sell physical CDs online, not a single music company would sell to them, for fear of competing with traditional sales channels—the brick-and-mortar stores. When my division at EMI broke rank with the other music labels and agreed to let Amazon sell our CDs online, we instantly saw EMI sales and market share increase. Today the music retailers the labels tried to protect are all gone, and Amazon is the world's biggest music retailer. The music industry eventually evolved, but not all of the companies survived the evolution. After 114 years in business, on November 12, 2011, EMI, the label that had created the recorded-music industry and signed everyone from Frank Sinatra to the Beatles to Garth Brooks, was sold by creditors like scrap to Universal Music and Sony.

> The customer will always find a way to get what he wants, even if the traditional supplier won't comply.

All my efforts to launch new ways to monetize music couldn't offset the fundamental shift in label economics. We had been disrupted. The change happened so swiftly to the music industry that only those companies that could cover the losses through other revenue streams, such as movies or electronics, managed to survive. The hard truth that I learned as an intrapreneur was to be fearless when you know survival is at stake. Anything less is corporate suicide. The business world is littered with the fossils of companies that failed to evolve. Disrupt or be disrupted. There is no middle ground.

> The business world is littered with the fossils of companies that failed to evolve. Disrupt or be disrupted. There is no middle ground.

DISRUPTING THE DINOSAURS

Like the dinosaurs, the giant corporations that once dominated the business world grew from market conditions that were favorable to them in a prior era in their evolution. Sears, Blockbuster, and Motorola once crushed the competition. Polaroid, Tower Records, and Levitz Furniture were once lauded as innovators. The factors that contributed to these companies' dominant positions created a myopic view of future market opportunities. Each saw the innovation they brought to the market as the end state of advancement, instead of just a milestone on an endless journey of progress. Polaroid's instant photography was more advanced and faster than film, but no match for digital. Tower introduced a deep catalog, but it could never be as deep and endless as a digital service such as iTunes. Levitz had the largest showrooms in their day, only to be later eclipsed by the practice known as "showrooming," the act of going into a brick-and-mortar store for the sole purpose of deciding which product to purchase online. Most CEOs see the future as a continuation of the path that got them to the C-suite and not as an ever-evolving jungle.

When Microsoft CEO Steve Ballmer infamously said in 2007 that Apple's iPhone was "the most expensive phone in the world and it doesn't appeal to business customers because it doesn't have a keyboard, which makes it not a very good email machine," he clearly didn't envision a world where consumers would download a hundred billion mobile apps each year.[6] He also didn't envision a world disrupted by YouTube, where one and a half million viewers would watch the clip of him laughing at the iPhone from their iPhones.

According to Vijay Govindarajan, coauthor of *The Other Side of Innovation*, there are three classic traps of corporate success. The first is a resource trap, in which companies overinvest in antiquated systems while ignoring new opportunities. The second is management's psychological trap, in which lengthy planning cycles deprioritize anything that isn't core to past success. Corporate planning cycles are a classic example of generals fighting the last war over again instead of preparing for what might lie ahead. The last trap is a failure to plan for an evolving future.[7] Based in Rochester, New York, Eastman Kodak has become known for exemplifying "Rochester mentality," and it is the classic example of this cycle. Kodak centered all of its management, research, and manufacturing in one city and focused on building bigger factories in the upstate New York town. After founder George Eastman died in 1932, every subsequent senior manager has been promoted from within the company. Kodak always measured its success against other film manufacturers. At its peak, the company employed 40 percent of Rochester's total private-sector workforce. With no outside influences in the C-suite, any moves into digital picture technology were deprioritized and viewed as dead-end projects. Being assigned to the Kodak digital technology team was tantamount to career suicide.[8]

🐦 *Corporate planning cycles are a classic example of generals fighting the last war over again instead of preparing for what might lie ahead.*

Kodak management failed to forge partnerships with other manufacturers to create a new digital ecosystem. Kodak had the brand name, marketing budget, and dominant market share to own the future of photography. But by being proprietary with its products and geographically isolated from other centers of innovation, Kodak failed. In 2012, after 124 years in business, Kodak was forced to file for Chapter 11 bankruptcy protection.[9]

Similarly, in the early aughts, Sony, once the global consumer electronics leader, was faced with building a new ecosystem in the era of digital content distribution. Where each Sony division was accustomed to building a unique product for their market—computers, portable audio, televisions, gaming systems, and so on—the digital distribution of content would now require all of these disparate devices to communicate with one another. Expecting devices to achieve what siloed executives hadn't been able to do was a formidable problem. Sony executives in Japan, all of whom had been hired straight out of college and worked their entire careers within the company, saw their competition as cross-town rivals Toshiba, Panasonic, Sanyo, Fujitsu, and Mitsubishi. Apple, Google, Amazon, and Microsoft, which were disrupting how consumers discovered, purchased, and consumed media, weren't even on the minds of Sony's product managers. Rochester mentality was translated into Tokyo think. I was brought into Sony by Sir Howard Stringer to change all of that. Once again, my job as an intrapreneur was to cut across silos and build a cross-platform digital ecosystem so that Sony could compete in the digital age. I was charged with launching a digital music/movie/game/book service and working with the various manufacturing divisions to create hardware that would support digital commerce.

While I had absolute support from Sony's global leadership, it was death by a thousand cuts at the company's various fiefdoms. Sony Walkman, for decades the leader in portable audio, refused to make a hard-drive device to compete with Apple's iPod. Instead, Walkman insisted on reintroducing the failed MiniDisc to America. Sony Play-Station, which was launching the cutting-edge portable PSP player, didn't want digital movies or music on their device, because it might cannibalize consumer spending on video games. Sony Pictures didn't want to give up control of its movies on the Internet and lobbied for a competing digital service. Sony's ebook division insisted on launching its hardware without any book publisher support. As I fought unsuccessfully to explain the changing landscapes to my Tokyo colleagues, I would often joke that I knew where the Japanese flag came from: "it was me banging my head against a wall."

"Business organizations are not built for innovation," Govindarajan writes. "They are built for efficiency."[10]

At almost all large corporations, senior management is rewarded for achieving more of the same, and company leaders risk personal career extinction when they venture too far off course. Corporate boards look at their existing competitors as the biggest threat to their immediate quarterly market share and growth. This is the "thintelligence" Michael Crichton describes in *Jurassic Park*. All planning is centered on beating the existing competition, and little time is devoted to reinventing their industry or the structure of their businesses. The majority of resources go to maintaining a multinational company's ranking in the existing ecosystem. Very little attention is paid to initiatives that could cannibalize current revenue streams.

A small division introducing a Kodak digital camera would have threatened to eat into the sales of the more powerful Kodak film division, which accounts for the majority of the company's profits. Even if, continuing our example, that digital camera caught on with consumers, the executive running the group would have committed corporate suicide by antagonizing a powerful internal dinosaur. At large corporations, even when a new startup or idea enters their turf, it is rarely seen as a threat, because initial sales are insignificant. When Steve Jobs launched the iPod in 2001, he had trouble getting retail distribution for his product, while Sony Walkmans were sold in over fourteen thousand locations in the United States. Sony's retail dominance was one of the reasons Apple was forced to go it alone and launch the Apple Store, also in 2001. Then, out of nowhere, just like the *Jurassic Park* humans who built advanced weaponry, the tiny interloper who'd invaded the giant's turf smote the mighty Japanese dinosaur.

In our Darwinian world, every corporate and governmental leader is focused primarily on survival. Digital Darwinism is only accelerating the pace of corporate extinction, and the biggest are often the first to die. As far back as 1965, Intel cofounder Gordon Moore predicted that computing power would double every two years as the number of transistors on integrated circuit boards increased.[11] Moore's Law still holds true in the twenty-first century. The exponential growth of computing power and the rise of technological singularity threaten to disrupt every industry on an ever-increasing rate of frequency. As more and more of our physical world is replaced with virtual solutions, more companies are going extinct. How easy is it for the disruptor to topple a giant dinosaur? Two decades ago, the average tenure for a public-company CEO was ten years. Now, according to a 2012 research report written by consulting firm Challenger, Gray & Christmas, the average lifespan in the corner office is down to five and a half years.[12] For chief marketing officers, it's a mere forty-three months, according to executive recruitment firm Spencer Stuart.[13]

Such high career mortality rates discourage taking risks and only accelerate a corporation's demise. Make a bold move and your career could be over. Play it safe and you continue to get fantastic compensation—at least for as long as your company lives. Senior management at today's public corporations are less interested in the long-term survival of their companies than in hitting this quarter's numbers and making their personal bonuses. In 2014, Wharton finance professor Alex Edmans published a paper entitled "Equity Vesting and Managerial Myopia," which analyzed federally mandated corporate disclosure forms to study the impact of senior management's incentive packages on behavior at two thousand public companies. The results show that as vesting dates for executives approach, CEOs tend to pump up a firm's earnings (and thus its stock price) by cutting investments in research and development, advertising, and capital expenditures.[14]

> Corporate managers are less interested in the long-term survival of their companies than in hitting this quarter's numbers and making their personal bonuses.

In one of my corporate positions, the board was so desperate to make its numbers that it offered triple compensation to any division heads who hit their stretch goals. I put a picture of the CFO on my office wall, next to a charity-style thermometer with the heading "Make Tony Smile." Each week, I filled in the thermometer with my team until we beat our numbers. Did we make the best long-term decisions for the company? No. But we went for the spoils offered to us. The more pressure there is on companies at the top, the less likely they are to launch new initiatives that may take years to become profitable. But this short-sightedness is a gigantic financial opportunity for the disruptor. Disruptors have the benefit of operating in senior management's blind spot.

DISRUPTING FROM WITHIN

In 1995, when my company Jasmine Multimedia Publishing was one of the premier CD-ROM publishers in the business, we thought the world was ours and that it was never going to change. Our bestselling titles were on retailer shelves everywhere. My company's competitive advantage wasn't just making hit video games and edutainment titles; it was knowing how to get our products distributed to store shelves around the world. But unbeknownst to me at the time, the brick-and-mortar retail delivery of software was going to be disrupted forever by a college student named Marc Andreessen and his friends at the University of Illinois.

In 1993, Andreessen first made the Internet accessible to the masses with the creation of a program named Mosaic. Mosaic put a graphic user interface on the Internet and took the World Wide Web mainstream. Microsoft, the largest technology company at the time, licensed the Mosaic technology and renamed it Internet Explorer. Consumers would now be able to access anything, anytime, from anywhere. No longer would consumers have to drive to a store to buy packaged software; programs could be downloaded instantly with just the click of a mouse. I soon realized that all the relationships I had cultivated with store buyers and distributors would now be worthless. All the vendors that manufactured our packaging and compact discs would be irrelevant. Our regional distributors were the first to feel the impact. Computer retailers were the next to suffer. Internally, we knew that our business would have to become more B2C than B2B. We faced a new challenge of having consumers discover our products in the virtual world. The value chain of supply-side distribution and brick-and-mortar retailer had been fundamentally shattered. I knew this meant that software stores would be doomed and that, as the Internet allowed for faster connectivity, books, music, and movies would soon follow. Most of my competitors would be out of business within the next few years. With my company's sales declining, I realized I had to do something different to survive.

Rather than laments on how my industry had been blindsided, only one thought went through my mind: the Web was going to be the biggest disruption of a value chain that I would witness in my life, and I wanted a ticket onto this new superhighway. It was clearly a time to self-disrupt again. Quickly, I tried to deconstruct my skill set and unique value to focus on the best course of attack. I rewrote my disruptor's map. Step one: sell Jasmine.

In analyzing Jasmine Multimedia Publishing's value chain, I realized that the real value to our titles was created in the copyrights, not in the sales or distribution of our products. With a few signatures on a stack of contracts, I sold my firstborn (company) and took a job at Universal Studios as vice president of new media. Jasmine had been core to my identity for so long that I didn't know how I would fare in my new position. I was now part of a giant Hollywood studio and in on the ground floor of setting up a gaming and new media division for this major entertainment company. The year was 1995, Jerry and David's Guide to the World Wide Web had just changed its name to Yahoo!, and I was tasked with figuring out how the Web would impact Universal's feature films, music, television, and theme parks. Our tiny group moved into Tom Selleck's old *Magnum, P.I.* office and eagerly set off to bring all these divisions into the twenty-first century.

Once I got over the excitement of being on a Hollywood lot and driving around in my golf cart, I quickly came to see that large corporations are not set up to embrace disruption. First, our new media division was charged with creating digital products and revenue streams based on only Universal Studios intellectual properties (such as *Frankenstein, Xena: Warrior Princess,* and *Jurassic Park*), but all the rights and assets associated with this content were controlled by other divisions within the company. There was no financial incentive for their divisions or executives to work with us, and plenty of downside if we interfered with others' sensitive relationships with Hollywood talent, agents, managers, or third-party rights holders. Silos and fiefdoms. All the advantages I had imagined would exist at a large company were quickly revealed to require Faustian bargains. Since I was part of a large studio, I couldn't use competitors' movies and intellectual property online, but the leaders of my sister divisions at Universal didn't want me to interfere with their business units by using our own movies and television shows. A century's worth of our owned content was just out of reach of our new division because of a system that had been built up over time to suppress internal disruption.

My second challenge was that in 1996, in the minds of Universal Studios' senior management, "new media" meant CD-ROMs and games. Entertainment businesses just weren't making money online yet. Having spent a decade creating over three hundred different consumer CD-ROM games and titles, I had been brought in as a CD-ROM publisher to produce more of what I had been making, even though the World Wide Web was calling. "New media," it turned out, was an oxymoron. Studio execs didn't want me exploring new revenue streams. They wanted me to focus on what I had already shown to be profitable years before. I had sold my company because I knew the world of physical media was coming to an end, but I couldn't explain that to an entertainment behemoth still making billions from CDs and DVDs. Paul Rioux, a veteran executive of the video game industry, led our division. Paul had headed both Mattel Electronics and Sega in the pioneering days of video games, and his mandate, like mine, was to build a packaged-goods video game division for Universal Studios. What I discovered was that the trick to disrupting from within an organization is to get what you want by giving the company what it *thinks* it wants.

If my job was to make video games, and my passion was to be working on the Internet, then the only possible solution was to make video games for the Internet. But how could I prove my unproven business model without getting fired? Building a team to design, engineer, and market Internet games would take years, and no public company had the appetite for such financial risk. We had neither the staff nor the budget to develop multi-million-dollar online games.

The only online games that existed in the mid-nineties were role-playing games known as MUDs. Multiuser dungeons were real-time multiplayer text-based games usually existing in fantasy worlds populated by dragons and wizards. In essence, they were the chat version of *Dungeons & Dragons*. While these were the nerdiest of nerd games, some MUDs had hundreds of thousands of players. The leader in the space was Simutronics, which made the *GemStone* and *DragonRealms* games. They had spent years creating these online franchises from the earliest days of *Dungeons & Dragons* on the Internet, and they knew

how to adapt them to the much friendlier Web. Simutronics had cultivated the largest gaming audience and had massive distribution through
America Online, then the nation's largest Internet service provider
(ISP). I may have been at a large media company, but I didn't have a
chance at competing head-on with the industry leader. But sometimes success comes from cooperating and competing: coopetition.

I decided to introduce a brand extension. I had brands that would attract gamers, but not the staff or time to build games from the ground
up. I contacted Neil Harris of Simutronics with the idea of having
them license two of Universal's most popular action-adventure television shows for online game play. By adapting their existing game engine, Simutronics would get a new game for a fraction of the price of
developing from scratch, and Universal New Media would get an instant revenue stream risk-free. The result was the hit game *Hercules &
Xena: Alliance of Heroes*, based on *Hercules: The Legendary Journeys* and
Xena: Warrior Princess.

"Universal is excited to take two of the top television properties of all
time and marry them with popular online gaming to create, with
Simutronics, the next generation in multi-player gaming," Rioux
stated in a press release that announced the launch of the product.[15]
The fact that the game was online was lost on most of Universal's senior
management at the time. But the real disruption—that we had moved
the studio into online digital entertainment—was noticed by every gaming company around the world. The brand extension was a quick way for
me to prove that money could be made on the Internet—then still in
its unproven infancy as a medium. With my boss now endorsing an Internet product, all I needed to do next was convince him to let me do
something beyond gaming online.

It is hard to explain to those who didn't live through this era that no
one in Hollywood believed there was money to be made online. The
Internet was just emerging as a medium, and online advertising was
just beginning to be tested by brands. There was no Hotmail or Gmail,
no Skype or Facebook, no Twitter or Instagram, no YouTube or Google.

But there was one generation flocking in droves to this new medium:
college students were quickly embracing the Web as they left home

and their parents' AOL email accounts. These students were forging their own identities online. There was obvious opportunity (remember, this is six years before Facebook) to create a site where college students could have free email (years before Hotmail or Gmail), personal Web pages, free Voice over Internet Protocol (VoIP) telephony, text chat, classified ads, job postings, news, and sports. But as obvious as this massive opportunity was to me, it had nothing to do with Universal Studios' core business. Sure, building a large online community of young people would be great for marketing our movies, television shows, and music, but the idea of social media hadn't been imagined yet. Still, I was determined to find a way to move my career, and the studio, online.

I went back to my disruptor's playbook and examined what contributed value to Universal's core businesses. It turned out that the twentieth anniversary of Universal's highest-grossing comedy was coming up, and it fit my vision for an irreverent online college community like a glove. I would build a social media site for America's five million full-time college students and name it Animalhouse.com.

Animalhouse.com would change how people engaged with the Universal Studios brand by putting one of its properties online and turning it into a social community. My team and I wanted to create an unofficial virtual world where young adults could freely post and share. We enthusiastically explained our vision to my boss and the rest of the new media department, and we were met with a rousing response of corporate indifference. No one got it. It wasn't a game. If it was free, how was Universal going to make any money? Why would an entertainment company spend millions of dollars to build a Web community? What brand would ever advertise on the Internet? As much as the home video division liked the idea of getting some free publicity from the new media group, no one at Universal was going to fund my project.

I have to admit that when I was younger, whenever older executives didn't see my vision, I would always blame them because they didn't "get it." This was a time when most senior executives in Hollywood still dictated their emails to their assistants and few of them had computers on their desks or in their homes. Now that I am on the wrong side of forty, I realize that the problem I faced back then wasn't senior management's *not getting it,* but rather my inability to communicate my vision in a context that they could comprehend. For all disruptors, this is the most important lesson anyone can learn. It is not incumbent on the world to conform to your vision of change. It is up to you to explain the future in terms that those living in the past and present can follow. If you can't overcome this fundamental communication challenge, you will never raise your capital, assemble your team, or build your customer base. An average idea enthusiastically embraced will go further than a genius idea no one gets.

> The world won't conform to your vision. It is up to you to explain the future in terms that those living in the past and present can follow.

> An average idea enthusiastically embraced will go further than a genius idea no one gets.

In the early 1990s, I was one of the few people at Universal Studios living in a digital world, and I needed to bring busy studio executives into it along with me. I should have presented my idea not as an online community, but as a onetime media buy that would yield years of access to our consumer audience. I could have sold this as simply a way to market our current theatrical or home video releases. But I didn't do that. I thought my idea was brilliant and obvious. I received the response disruptors face all too often: I was told no to funding the project. Animalhouse.com was over before it started.

"Over? Nothing is over until we decide it is!" John Belushi's character, Bluto, declares in the movie. "Was it over when the Germans bombed Pearl Harbor? Hell no!" With Bluto as my inspiration, I decided to reframe the problem rather than throw in the towel. My boss didn't say I couldn't build Animalhouse.com; he just said that Universal wouldn't pay for me to build it.

That was when I realized the most obvious of all lessons in business: You can do whatever you want in life, as long as you can find someone else who is willing to pay for it. I made a list of every company and industry that could benefit from Animalhouse.com. Virtually all branding for life, from the beer you drink to the car you drive, happens by the time you are twenty-five. Youth brands would want to get in on the ground floor of Animalhouse. My old development partner Microsoft had just launched its Site Builder Network and surely would want the publicity of working with a major entertainment company such as Universal Studios. Banks and credit card companies were eager to get college students to set up new accounts with them on campus. Hyundai, the Korean manufacturing giant, was about to expand its footprint in America for the first time, with low-cost vehicles aimed at the youth market. Internet advertising pioneer DoubleClick was preparing for its IPO on Nasdaq and would benefit from such a high-profile project. The list went on and on. Piece by piece, I stitched together the funding. Microsoft and Hyundai contributed the most. MasterCard, MBNA, Tommy Hilfiger, Seagram, and Pepsi all jumped at the chance to have category exclusivity for the new project. Richard Rosenblatt's iMall provided the ecommerce, and Ross Levinsohn at CBS Sportsline provided our sports news. Kevin Wall, then running Box-Top Interactive, led the design, and *Ren & Stimpy* creator John Kricfalusi illustrated the site's mascot. Live events on the site were streamed by Mark Cuban's startup AudioNet (later renamed Broadcast.com). It was an amazing collection of talent. Young entrepreneurs saw the future potential of this medium and weren't afraid to jump in full-throttle. It was a collective, forward-thinking group determined to define this new medium. There are two types of people in this world: those who look for opportunity and those who make it happen. I surrounded myself with the latter. There were no Web designers or front-end developers back then. We were all making it up as we went along. I just ran interference with the corporate suits and let all these future luminaries do what they did best. Creating Animalhouse.com was one of the most exciting times of my life and taught me many lessons about disruption, design, and digital distribution—yet I was operating from within a large corporation. This is why intrapreneurship can be so transformative.

> There are two types of people in this world: those who look for opportunity and those who make it happen.

Within six months of its launch, Animalhouse.com had over one million registered college students at nearly 2,500 universities using the site. Universal, which hadn't paid a penny of the social site's development, was making money through advertising and issuing college students their first credit cards. I was promoted to president and put on the steering committee for the entire studio. I was enjoying all of this success because I hadn't listened to my bosses and had refused to let a lack of funding stop me. The experience emboldened me to never let a lack of funding stop me from following my dreams.

In addition to proving the value of intrapreneurship, working on Animalhouse.com taught me firsthand the concept of working with other people's money (OPM). With OPM, every project is doable, and one's return on investment (ROI) is more easily achieved. If your employer doesn't put a penny into your project—other than paying for your time—the ROI should be astronomical. The Animalhouse.com project satisfied different needs for each company involved, and everyone's careers benefited. A few years after Animalhouse.com, Kevin Wall sold his company, BoxTop Interactive, and invested some of the proceeds in another college startup named The Facebook. After I moved on to EMI, Animalhouse.com was sold to a group of investors. But without the support of the studio or the passion of its founders, the fledgling social network soon fizzled out.

The fact of the matter is that today's public-company CEO would rather overpay through acquisition for a new startup than explain to shareholders and Wall Street the years of losses it will take to enter the same market through innovation. Losing money year after year on something unproven is more of a risk than most CEOs are willing to bet their careers on. Amazon CEO Jeff Bezos is a rare exception to this rule. For more than twenty years he has taken the long-term-investment approach over short-term profits. Amazon's success and Bezos's $32 billion fortune are testament that vision pays off. Unfortunately, most public CEOs are more worried about quarterly analyst reports. German enterprise software giant SAP is a perfect example of this trend. SAP's $4.3 billion acquisition of Ariba in 2012 was an admission that the ERP (enterprise resource planning) giant had to abandon its own software for that of a younger, disruptive competitor.[16] SAP's ePurchasing software products were unable to dominate the cloud-based Software as a Service (SaaS) industry and had many products that overlapped with Ariba's.

This shortsighted approach to overpay today for future top-line growth is why there's so much opportunity to profit from breaking existing value chains. CEOs will gladly overpay for your company if the acquisition enables them to keep their jobs. This is why so many acquisitions end up adding no value to the acquirer. The CEO is not risking his or her career with the purchase of a company; on the contrary, the CEO is buying another chance to keep his or her job. First-time CEO Marissa Mayer acquired thirty-seven companies in her first twenty months leading Yahoo![17] Yahoo!'s market cap was in a tailspin, so the quick fix was to try to buy her way out. What will surprise many people who don't deal with high tech is that virtually all the companies Yahoo! purchased were losing money.

> CEOs will gladly overpay for your company if the acquisition enables them to keep their jobs.

Contrary to popular belief, most of the millionaires in Silicon Valley did not get rich by building profitable businesses, but rather by selling the *potential* of their new enterprises to established industry giants. Read that last sentence again. Thousands of millionaires and dozens of billionaires built their personal fortunes without ever making a profit. They all got rich selling money-losing companies. As Tumblr founder

David Karp said so eloquently upon selling his pre-revenue company to Yahoo! for $800 million, "Fuck yeah."[18]

> 🐦 *Most millionaires in Silicon Valley did not get rich by building profitable businesses but by selling the potential of their new enterprises.*

Tumblr aggregated young Internet users that Yahoo! had failed to reach and was independent at a time when Mayer, as Yahoo!'s new CEO, needed a quick solution to her slipping numbers. The value of Tumblr wasn't in its revenue potential; it was in its unique visitors per month. Mayer was betting that Yahoo! could unlock that value. The task is the same for disruptors working in large corporations who are hoping to establish their value and accelerate their careers. These internal agents for change can leverage their understanding of the corporate value chain to find an idea that solves a problem for the company at large and get rewarded for their actions.

Chapter Six

In Search of the Zombie Idea

You can kill a man but you can't kill an idea.
—Medgar Evers

In 1982, I was a twenty-one-year-old UCLA graduate looking to make my mark on the world. In the midst of a terrible recession and an energy crisis that destroyed the U.S. automobile industry, jobs were few and far between, so I knew I needed to have a unique skill or to find a field that was growing. As I searched for work, an old codger from Texas who had made a fortune in scrap metal gave me a piece of advice that continues to serve me well all these years later: "Be the best at what you do," he said, "or the only one doing it."

Everyone will tell you that uniqueness and authenticity are two of the most important traits in business. But when you are coming straight out of college, without a work history or specific skill set, "unique" doesn't translate to valuable or employable. Because the original IBM personal computer, model 5150, had just been introduced to the home market, I reasoned that knowing how to use a PC would be just the differentiator I needed to get a job. Using up virtually all of my savings from working at an advertising agency during college, I bought the world's first "portable" computer, the Kaypro II. (There never was a Kaypro I, but since Apple was selling the Apple II, Andrew Kay, the inventor behind Kaypro, borrowed the number in a marketing ploy to make it sound more technically advanced.)

Compared with the bulky forty-eight-pound IBM 5150 desktop personal computer, the Kaypro was an amazingly *light* twenty-nine-pound portable that sold for $1,795. That was a great deal of money to an unemployed college graduate, but I thought no computer could ever get any smaller or lighter, so I felt this was an investment that would last me for many years to come. (I was so wrong. Forty-three iPad Minis combined weigh less than one Kaypro II.) I set up the machine, read the manuals, and was ready to change the world.

With my newly declared computer expertise, I printed up some business cards, and Jasmine Productions was born. In my mind's eye, Jasmine—which was a mash-up of my initials, J.A.S. (Jay Alan Samit), and the fact that it was "mine"—would be the low-budget alternative to George Lucas's Industrial Light & Magic, which had created all the amazing visual effects for *Star Wars* and *Star Trek II: The Wrath of Khan*. If you didn't have millions to spend on special effects, Jasmine could do it for a fraction of the cost. As one of the few people in Hollywood touting computer skills, I quickly found work creating computer graphic effects for television commercials and low-budget independent films.

As I've described, my first venture with IBM and Pioneer into consumer interactive laserdiscs had failed to take off. I wasn't ready to give up; I just needed to adjust my idea. The key to finding a big idea is first finding a problem in need of a solution. Every disruptive idea makes use of new technology to solve a big problem. I started analyzing the value chain of laserdisc sales. When I stripped away all the features of the laserdisc player, I realized that the real value was found in just one thing: it was nonlinear and interactive. Once I targeted this unique feature, I could determine who would benefit most from the laserdisc's real value. Consumers watching at home didn't care about interacting with their videos, but I knew there was someone, or some organization, who would benefit from this key feature.

The next step is to kill your big idea. If you can find a problem that will derail an idea, so will the marketplace. The quicker you can eliminate the business roadkill, the more capital you will have left to focus on the one idea that can't be killed. Pioneer had spent tens of millions of dollars proving that the home market for laserdiscs was dead. That still left dozens of other avenues to kill. I built music video jukeboxes, but the laserdisc players were too unreliable for video arcades. Philips was failing with a competing technology aimed at preschoolers, so

I killed that idea. I tried retail kiosks at shopping malls, gambling machines for Las Vegas—none of them proved to be the key to laserdisc sales. I learned later in my career that the faster you can kill the bad ideas, the quicker you can pivot to the successful one. "Speed to fail" should be every entrepreneur's motto. When you finally find the one idea that can't be killed, go with it.

> Kill your big idea. If you can find a problem that will derail an idea, so will the marketplace.

> "Speed to fail" should be every entrepreneur's motto. When you finally find the one idea that can't be killed, go with it.

I had stuck with the laserdisc and heeded the old codger's advice; I was the best in the world at what I was doing, precisely because I was the only one trying to do it. But the only way laserdiscs would be successful was if I could find an industry to disrupt with laserdisc technology. In other words, I needed a giant problem that only this technology could solve. Finally I discovered the one opportunity that was truly disruptive: corporate training. Companies spent billions on training manuals, videos, courseware, and seminars without any interactive way to customize learning to the speed and educational aptitude of each employee.

I knew that interactive learning made possible by laserdisc technology would be vastly superior to watching videotapes or reading manuals, but I knew nothing about the entire value chain and ecosystem surrounding corporate training.

Reading the newspaper (the printed daily newspaper was still going strong in 1982 and had yet to be disrupted by the digital age), I came across countless articles on the plight of the U.S. automobile industry in the wake of rising gasoline prices and the global energy crisis.

Detroit, which prided itself on making ever bigger and faster motor vehicles, had stumbled in its race to quickly come to market with smaller, more gasoline efficient cars. Ford introduced the Pinto, but its gas tank would explode when rear-ended. General Motors introduced the subcompact Chevrolet Vega (my first car), with an aluminum engine block that couldn't handle heat, causing it to melt, buckle, and leak. The Vega was so notorious for overheating, overfueling, and bursting into flames that the fear of more engine fires caused more than 500,000 Vegas to be recalled. Chrysler couldn't make the leap to fuel efficiency either, suffering massive recalls of the Plymouth Volaré and Dodge Aspen. Chrysler incurred such large operating losses that year that the federal government had to step in and keep the company afloat with $1.5 billion in loan guarantees. The slogan "Buy American" turned into "Bye-bye, American."

Japanese automakers met the demand for vehicles with better gas mileage by making quality cars at affordable prices. Toyota, Honda, and Nissan cars were so reliable that the companies could offer longer and longer bumper-to-bumper warranties without financial risk. The marketing departments of the Big Three in Detroit had no choice but to match those offers with extended warranties of their own. The warranties didn't mean that Detroit was building better cars; they just meant that when the car broke, the consumer wasn't stuck footing the bill.

This was a big problem for American car manufacturers. Prior to the advent of bumper-to-bumper warranties, when your car broke, you had to pay for the repair. It wasn't really the mechanics' fault that they didn't know how to fix Detroit's cars. Modern cars had become less and less mechanical. They were no longer a collection of parts that fit together like the inner workings of a clock; instead, they had complex electronic ignitions, microprocessor-controlled fuel systems, and interconnected electrical circuitry. Manufacturers sent thousands of pages of diagrams and documentation for each model of each car released every year. The average repair department had over forty thousand pages of instructions per model to sift through. Most of these manuals were written by engineers, for engineers—not car mechanics. If the auto mechanic didn't know what exactly was broken, he just kept replacing parts until the car worked. In fact, half of all parts replaced by U.S. auto dealers in the 1980s were good parts with nothing wrong with them. Trying to compete with the Japanese by offering extended warranties turned out to be a very costly problem for Detroit manufacturers.

One day, I read an article stating that Ford's extended warranty plan was going to cost the manufacturer $600 million in repairs that year. I had found my big problem. The unique value of laserdisc technology was that it was interactive. If quality training of mechanics could reduce the number of good parts that mechanics were unnecessarily replacing, Ford could save as much as $300 million a year. I had stumbled upon a new value chain perfect for disruption. Interactive video could transform corporate training from a cost center to a profit center by reducing unnecessary repairs. With all the confidence of a young entrepreneur, I knew my logic was impeccable, my plan foolproof, and that Ford would thank me for my brilliance. The only challenge was that I lived in Los Angeles and had never been to Detroit. I also should mention that I knew nothing about automotive repair, nor had I ever created any corporate training courses. And there was the little detail that I didn't even know how to get a meeting with Ford Motor Company, of Dearborn, Michigan.

Thinking about this opportunity, I realized that I didn't have to figure out how to solve a problem for all of Ford—I only had to figure out how to solve a problem for the one executive who would benefit most from my solution. I had to find the single executive who understood technology and had to deal with the challenges of modernizing the dealership systems. Reading an article on Ford's modernization, I came across the man I was looking for. It turned out his name was Ted Derwa. A Ford lifer, Ted had been at the company twenty years and knew how to get new projects launched.

By following my approach of solving the problem for the individual and not the entire organization, I tried to imagine who the key decision maker was at Ford and why he would take a meeting with a twentysomething tech geek from La-La Land. Realizing that he wouldn't, I tried to imagine whom he *would* like to meet. If you can imagine a solution, you can make it happen. Ford is as American as apple pie and football, so I hired as my head of sales the newly retired assistant coach of the Michigan State University football team, Ted Guthard, who had worked with the legendary head coach Franklin Dean "Muddy" Waters.

A hardworking, dedicated guy, Guthard knew nothing about computers, but he knew everything about football and the discipline it takes to achieve lofty goals. Our goal was to break into corporate training, and Ford was our end zone. Motor City automotive executives were all excited to meet Guthard and talk to him about his Spartan glory days. Within a few months we had our first meeting with Ted Derwa, followed shortly thereafter by a contract to produce an interactive laserdisc course on automotive electrical systems. Playing to my Hollywood hometown strengths, and to make the training program fun for the mechanics, I hired celebrity impersonators to appear in the video as consumers with car problems. We developed an interactive training laserdisc on which trainees could interview Lady Di, Elvis, and Michael Jackson (or at least people who looked like them) in order to diagnose a vehicle's electrical problem. It wasn't long before Ford had invested millions of dollars to produce over two hundred interactive laserdiscs for mechanic training. By figuring out whose problem the unique technology of the laserdisc could solve, we were able to disrupt the entire industry of corporate training. It wasn't especially sexy or glamorous work, but it sure was profitable.

WHAT'S A BIG IDEA?

"Most people don't tie up their dogs in the backyard anymore" sounds more like an obvious observation than a big idea. The fact that most Americans consider their dog part of the family isn't exactly a trade secret. But that one insight set one of my fellow board members on the path to becoming a multibillionaire. Clay Mathile, a midwestern salesman living in Dayton, Ohio, figured that if dogs were now sleeping in the house, people would pay more to feed these "family members" premium healthy food. So he set out to create a better, healthier dog food. His quality product was so expensive to produce that it had a wholesale cost greater than the retail price of the big-name competition's dry dog food. But Clay held firmly to the belief that the welfare of animals was as important as the welfare of people.

Mathile named his new premium brand Iams and set about building his company's reputation for producing the highest-end dog food on the market. Though he hadn't invented anything new (Iams was still just dog food), Mathile had disrupted the production and marketing links on the dog food value chain. He was producing a product of the highest quality and marketing it to a specific customer who equated spending more on quality ingredients with deeper love of the family pet. By making Iams's wholesale price more than the retail price of his giant competitors, Mathile was able to build his product's distribution while the young startup was ignored by the multinational corporations. During the decades he was growing his company, many people derided Mathile and dismissed Iams as a niche player. All that changed on September 1, 1999, when Procter & Gamble made the largest acquisition in the company's history by purchasing Iams for $2.3 billion.[1] Because he was the sole owner of the company, Clay's big idea had made him a very wealthy man.

We think that great disruptive ideas come from "eureka" moments—brilliant, insightful flashes of innovation that come to people fully formed. Think of Doc Brown, in *Back to the Future*, who discovers the flux capacitor while standing on his toilet hanging a clock. Even the word *eureka*—Greek for "I have found (it)"—comes from the story we are taught in school of how Archimedes discovered his displacement principle while getting into a bath. He was so excited with his discovery that he ran naked through the streets of ancient Syracuse yelling, "Eureka! Eureka!"

In reality, most discoveries come from the simple act of identifying life's problems. When University of Southern California engineering students take my class Building the High Tech Startup, most want to make millions launching an Internet company or writing the next killer iPhone app. Many of them feel that fame and fortune are a foregone conclusion. These students all tend to have just one minor obstacle on their road to success: they lack the big idea. The truth is, those eureka ideas are actually fairly easy to come across—but they don't come from chance moments of brilliance; they come from careful, methodical observation.

> *Most discoveries come from the simple act of identifying life's problems.*

If you want to disrupt the world, take a good, hard look at it. Ask yourself this question: *Is my world perfect?* Does everything function smoothly at your job or company? Are all your friends enjoying the stress-free lives they imagined for themselves when they were young? Are all the goods and services you use properly priced and easy to find? If the answer to any of these questions is no, then there is room for a disruptive idea. As Mahatma Gandhi so prophetically stated, "You must be the change you wish to see in the world."

The trick to creating disruption at scale is to identify the biggest opportunities where the existing value chain is most easily upended. Look for the piece of the business that will shift the most dollars away from their present course. Uber shifts the taxi market from thousands of small cab companies to one centralized software system that collects the money. Uber breaks one link of the chain—distribution—and it is the one that has the highest potential for profitability. Step two is then capturing as much of the newly unlocked value as you possibly can in the shortest time. It's that easy. Find a problem, disrupt it, and solve it. The bigger the problem, the more people your solution helps, and the more money you make. Disruptors are simply problem solvers.

Trying to identify such opportunities is what venture capitalists do for a living. Large, established Silicon Valley firms such as Andreessen Horowitz, Sequoia Capital, and any of the others on Sand Hill Road have teams of M.B.A.'s sifting through business plans and taking thousands of pitches just to pick the small handful of startups that they invest in each year. Those whose business plans are deemed as having the greatest potential are called in for a meeting with one of the firm's partners. Fewer than 1 percent of the startups that get a meeting are funded. Using this tried and true process, Andreessen Horowitz invested early in such phenomenal successes as Twitter, Skype, Facebook, and Airbnb, all the while generating billions of dollars in returns for their investors and partners. Top-tier VC firms consistently find great startups because they have what is known as *deal flow*. A steady stream of opportunities literally flows into their offices, and their job is to invest in what they see as the cream of the crop. Every day, dozens of startups are lining up to get a chance to pitch to someone on Sand Hill Road and, if lucky, then meet with all the partners at the firm. This path works for many, but it isn't the only road to success. The truth is, you don't need to be a venture capitalist or have a team of M.B.A.'s to have great deal flow. You just need to look around and be observant.

🐦 *You don't need to be a venture capitalist or have a team of M.B.A.'s to have great deal flow. You just need to look around and be observant.*

By carefully studying your environment and analyzing your daily frustrations, you'll find that opportunities for disruption start to jump out at you. Daily discipline is the key to this exercise. I tell my students to write down three things they notice could be improved every day. The world is far from perfect, and in the beginning this exercise is pretty easy. But as the days roll on, more attention to detail and careful introspection will be needed. Like Sherlock Holmes on the hunt for Moriarty, carefully observe how things function in your world and focus on where the maximum worth is created in each value chain. When you have a bad day, as we all do, challenge your assumptions about what went wrong and how systems we accept as "the way it is" can be altered. Were you stuck in traffic and late for an important meeting? Why didn't your car have the real-time information to crowdsource from other vehicles which roads were clogged and automatically inform you about which streets were open? This was the insight that led an Israeli startup to create Waze. After solving Tel Aviv traffic, they went global and in 2013 were acquired by Google for approximately $1 billion.[2] The worse your day is going, the better the opportunities to be discovered from your frustration. A disruptor finds opportunity and profit from his misfortunes.

🐦 *A disruptor finds opportunity and profit from his misfortunes.*

Women disruptors have an advantage when it comes to finding problems to solve. This is far from a sexist statement. According to research experts at Nielsen, women have generated virtually all the income growth experienced in the United States during the past twenty years, and they are responsible for 83 percent of all consumer purchases.[3] That's a huge market worth tapping into. What is not working for the American woman? Could that be a global issue?

I have my students identify the three best opportunities for disruption every day. By the end of a month, they have ninety new big ideas to pick from. The students who maintain this routine for a year generate massive idea flow. "All problems are opportunities in disguise," says bestselling author Mark Victor Hansen. "Every problem is a prospective opportunity." He should know: his series of books on problems, *Chicken Soup for the Soul*, have sold over five hundred million copies.

True disruptors understand that they can find problems to solve even while they sleep. The problems that literally wake you up in the morning can either ruin your entire day or make you millions of dollars. If you look closely, one of the first complaints most people have comes even before they get out of bed. The dreaded alarm clock always seems to wake us up when we are in our deepest state of sleep. How many times have you been startled from a deep sleep? Half awake, you then suffer through your morning and tend to spend the entire day in a groggy fog. In 2003, a college student complained to her friend at Brown University that her early-morning grogginess caused her to do poorly on her exams. "What if there was an alarm clock that could detect sleep patterns and awaken you in a light stage of sleep?" she wondered. Her friend considered the idea and ruminated on the science of sleep cycles. The Brown student went on to raise over $8 million to build such an alarm clock.

"There has been 20 years of research on sleep inertia, but no one had done anything with it," remarks Eric Shashoua. His product, Zeo, is a combination of a REM-reading headband and a smartphone app. Zeo is designed to wake up users at the time in their sleep cycle that will make them feel the most rested and refreshed. Whenever I think of Shashoua and his friend, I remind my students to keep a notebook and a pen next to their beds—they might find problems to solve even before they get up in the morning!

"We are really the first to come up with something that is not a gimmick, but a real product, based on real science," Shashoua adds.[4] The Zeo was born from a simple scientific insight. The science, the technology, and the market need had all existed before Zeo entered the market, but no one had bothered to build a business.

Problems are just businesses waiting for the right entrepreneur to unlock the value. How many other problems can be solved by applying existing science and technology?

> 🐦 *Problems are just businesses waiting for the right entrepreneur to unlock the value.*

My dear friend Lani Lapidus will kill me for sharing the origin of this next innovation: Odor-Eaters. Smelly feet are a timeless problem that has plagued people for as long as we've worn shoes. In college, my roommate's shoes smelled so bad that I made him hang them outside our dorm window at night. In Lani's case, her father, Herbert, couldn't deal with the smell of her mother's feet. The difference between my college problem and Herbert's problem was that he happened to be a chemist—and he was married to his roommate. He understood how activated carbon was being used in commercial filtration systems, and he thought he could apply that same concept to insoles. So Herbert experimented in his basement and invented latex insoles filled with activated carbon that actually neutralized foot odor. Odor-Eaters created a new category at retail and have gone on to sell tens of millions of units. Happy wife, happy life.

While Herbert was able to apply his training as a chemist to solving problems, not all of us have science backgrounds. We do, however, all bring skills and our unique creativity to how we solve problems in our lives. Whole websites have sprung up around "life hacks"—simple tricks to solve everyday issues. Some are as simple as putting your iPhone in a drinking glass to amplify the speaker, while others, such as making a cheap plastic shoe for the sauna (Crocs), made billions. So don't worry if you're not a computer programmer or a chemist—insight and drive are all the skills you need. Everything else can be hired.

> 🐦 *Insight and drive are all the skills you need. Everything else can be hired.*

BIG IDEAS CAN HAPPEN AT WORK, TOO

The same process for identifying problems in our daily lives applies to identifying opportunities for disruption on the job. And some of the most disruptive ideas don't require any special skill set, science, or technology to implement. Amy Berman was working with me at Sony when Sir Howard Stringer became our company's new North American chairman. One of the first tasks to be accomplished after Sir Howard joined the company was to send someone over to his Manhattan home and replace all his electronics with the latest Sony products. Televisions, DVD players, stereo equipment, and the Sony home theater controller each came with a new remote control and complex cutting-edge features. While these were great products to enjoy, they required a huge learning curve for any consumer to attempt to tackle on his own, and each remote functioned differently from the rest.

As much as Stringer loved his company's products, one can't expect the busy chairman of an $80 billion corporation to sit down and read all of the new product manuals, so Berman was sent over to help him learn how to use the Sony gear. While dealing with this obvious problem, she realized that Stringer wasn't alone in his frustration. Senior executives, celebrities, and professional athletes all have the money to purchase the latest and greatest electronics gadgets, but none of them have the time to learn how to use their new toys. Berman realized that this steep learning curve was actually a barrier to sales. Furthermore, she surmised, many of the rich and famous had multiple homes and would like identical electronics installed in each location. Not only would this luxury market be a source of increased revenues, but the prestige of having such famous customers would be a boon to Sony's brand image. Her solution was to create a new business unit within the company, Sony Cierge.

Cierge became a custom shopping service for elite clientele that not only delivered and installed the electronics but also trained the customer on how to use the devices. Members would pay $1,500 per year to have an exclusive private phone number with concierge-like shopping privileges. Call the number on your black Cierge card and installers would come over wearing white gloves to install your electronics and teach you how to use them. Within the year, Berman had been promoted to run the new division, and she quickly built a national clientele made up of thousands of the biggest names in the world, including such iconic celebrities as Howard Stern and Donald Trump. Berman had identified a hole in Sony's value chain, and rather than break it, she filled it in by adding a new business line for the company. Being an intrapreneur catapulted her career.

Every new experience or skill we learn has the potential to lead us to a big idea. Take, for example, middle school student Brittany Wenger. When she was in seventh grade, she learned about artificial intelligence as part of a future-of-technology project at school and was fascinated by its potential.

"I came across artificial intelligence and was just enthralled. I went home the next day and bought a programming book and decided that was what I was going to teach myself to do," Wenger said.

For fun, she began by creating a neural network that played soccer. This was a great learning experience and proved to her that she could build something that really worked. Then the teenager looked around her world at problems that could be fixed with a neural network. Women in her family had suffered from breast cancer, so why not work on a neural network that could potentially help detect cancer? Later, Wenger learned that breast cancer afflicts one out of eight women worldwide. If she could improve the existing methodology for early detection by just 10 percent, forty million women's lives could be improved.

"I taught the computer how to diagnose breast cancer," she told reporters after winning the 2012 Google Science Fair. "And this is really important because currently the least invasive form of biopsy is actually the least conclusive, so a lot of doctors can't use them."[5]

Coding in Java, and running her network in the cloud, Wenger ran 7.6 million trials and found that the network was 99.1 percent sensitive to malignancy. Her results were more accurate than any commercially available network being used by practicing physicians. Her neural network has the potential to radically improve women's lives, could save the health care industry billions of dollars, and could be applied to many other types of cancer.

CREATING A ZOMBIE IDEA

After finally honing all of their observations down to one big idea, most people are afraid to act on it. One of the most common misconceptions of having a big, disruptive idea is that if word gets out, someone with better connections and more money will steal your creation. After David Fincher's movie *The Social Network* came out in 2010, a paranoia set in with young entrepreneurs that they were going to get "Zucked." As in: if you tell anyone about your idea, the next Mark Zuckerberg is going to come steal your idea and become the billionaire whom you were destined to be. The result of this hysteria was that budding disruptors were afraid to tell anyone their brilliant ideas. Wanting to build creations in stealth mode, with no collaborators or funding whatsoever, is an unrealistic impossibility. Many first-time entrepreneurs approach me with nondisclosure agreements (NDAs) for fear that even one unprotected whisper of their concept could result in their fortune riding off like an unchained bike on a college campus. Nothing could be further from the truth.

"Nobody is going to steal your stupid idea," Founder Institute head and serial entrepreneur Adeo Ressi loves to tell first-time entrepreneurs.[6] The Founder Institute is the largest startup accelerator in the world. It has helped launch over 750 companies in five continents, and more than 40 percent of these incubated companies get funded.[7] Still, Ressi is so confident that ideas won't be stolen that he offers a $1,000 reward to anyone in the Founder Institute who *can* get their idea stolen.

When Steve Jobs went to technology leaders with his prototype for a personal computer, he was met with derision. Jobs recalled the experience in an interview with *Classic Gamer* magazine: "So we went to Atari and said, 'Hey, we've got this amazing thing, even built with some of your parts, and what do you think about funding us? Or we'll give it to you. We just want to do it. Pay our salary, we'll come work for you.' And they said, 'No.' So then we went to Hewlett-Packard, and they said, 'Hey, we don't need you. You haven't got through college yet.'"[8]

Instead of trying to promote your idea, as Jobs had done, Ressi's advice to young entrepreneurs is startlingly counterintuitive. According to Ressi, your goal is not to promote and protect your idea, but rather, "Your job is to kill your dumb ass idea."[9]

Ressi is absolutely right. A disruptive idea shouldn't be nourished like a seedling with the expectation that it will grow into a mighty oak. The trouble with most entrepreneurs is that they would rather be ruined by praise than saved by criticism. Your job is to try everything you can to kill your big idea and discover every way that it can fail. When you discover a crack in your plan, fix it, reshape it, and make it stronger. The Japanese have an art form called *kintsugi*. They fix broken pottery with gold lacquer resin, believing the repaired ceramics are more gorgeous and precious than they were before they were destroyed. The same applies to killing and reviving your big idea. Through that process you build a strong, defensible, beautiful business that the competition and market factors can't destroy. Much like forging steal, ideas are baked in a fiery cauldron to harden and solidify before being unleashed upon the world. You don't want a big idea; you want what I like to call a zombie idea: no matter what is thrown at it, a zombie idea can't be stopped or killed.

> The trouble with most entrepreneurs is that they would rather be ruined by praise than saved by criticism.

Keeping the idea to yourself isn't much help, either. If your idea is truly original, you will have to scream about it at the top of your lungs to get anyone to notice. You will take it to dozens of potential investors, friends, family members, and experts in the industry, who will all tell you it is the worst idea they've ever heard. Most will list a dozen reasons why it will fail. If your idea is truly disruptive to a market, get used to hearing the word *no*.

If your idea isn't original, then it is even harder to convince people to invest. They've heard it before, and they can rattle off the names of three companies that have failed in the space. For a so-called obvious idea, you will need to show why your approach is different and timely.

AN IDEA CAN BE A TEAM EFFORT

Surprisingly, the startup accelerator with the most successful track record at picking winning companies and creating billions of dollars in value for its investors doesn't even require that the startup teams they invest in have an idea. Since its founding in 2005, Y Combinator, based in Mountain View, California, has funded more than five hundred companies, including such mega-successes as Airbnb, Dropbox, Reddit, and Scribd. The average valuation for the first five hundred companies launched by Y Combinator is over $45 million.[10] What is their secret for finding great new companies?

Y Combinator knows that the right passionate team is far more important to a startup's success than the right idea. They invest in people, not ideas. To help attract teams, Y Combinator even publicly publishes a list, "Startup Ideas We'd Like to Fund," on its website. "When we read Y Combinator applications there are always ideas we're hoping to see," the accelerator's director, Paul Graham, writes in his list's introduction. "In the past we've never said publicly what they are . . . We don't like to sit on these ideas, though, because we really want people to work on them. So we're trying something new."[11]

Given that I'm a former music company executive, the idea at the top of their list to fund is near and dear to my heart:

> 1. A cure for the disease of which the RIAA is a symptom. Something is broken when Sony and Universal are suing children. Actually, at least two things are broken: the software that file-sharers use, and the record labels' business model. The current situation can't be the final answer. And what happened with music is now happening with movies. When the dust settles in 20 years, what will this world look like? What components of it could you start building now?[12]

"We invest in the entrepreneur first, not the idea," stresses Ron Conway, a super angel investor and backer of Y Combinator.[13] Conway, whom *Forbes* regularly lists as one of Silicon Valley's top dealmakers with the Midas touch, was an early-stage investor in Google, PayPal,

Square, and Twitter. Now a billionaire, Conway continues to seek out and fund the next generation of disruptors. "We are funding innovation. We are funding the next Facebook, Google, and Twitter."[14] Getting the next big idea funded is never as easy as it appears.

Putting the fictional movie *The Social Network* aside, when Harvard University student Mark Zuckerberg invited five trusted friends over to pitch them his new business idea in February 2004, only two people bothered to even show up. Even at Harvard, most people aren't seeking new ideas. The two friends who did show up had their lives changed forever. Facebook's IPO made Dustin Moskovitz $6.5 billion and Eduardo Saverin $3.4 billion. But sometimes, even with the most profitable business idea in history, it's hard to find anyone willing to invest.

Serial entrepreneur Bill Gross started IdeaLab, one of the first new business incubators in Southern California, in 1996. In 1998, they launched GoTo.com, which had a novel idea in the world of online advertising: monetizing search. AltaVista, Infoseek, Magellan, and Lycos—the main search engines of the day—made their revenue by charging websites for each search that was initiated using their technology. GoTo had a better idea. What if companies paid for positioning in search results, much the way that Yellow Pages directories had charged businesses to place ads in telephone books? If you searched "Barcelona Hotels," for example, the company that paid the most money would be at the top of the search results. Today we know that this one idea turned out to be the most profitable business model ever launched and has made Google one of the richest companies on earth.

But in 1997, the world looked at it differently. A year earlier, in 1996, OpenText had tried to launch a similar idea and folded under the negative press of trying to "commercialize" search at a time when the Web's commercial potential was not fully grasped by most of its users. GoTo .com pitched all the usual venture firms on Sand Hill Road, only to be rejected over and over again. One VC went so far as to tell the startup that this was "the dumbest idea he had ever heard." Eventually they raised their money, changed their name to Overture, and proved out the model. The company was successful enough to be acquired by its biggest customer, Yahoo!, for $1.6 billion.[15] However, Yahoo!, then the most successful Internet company, with a market cap of over $100 billion, was making so much money from display advertising that it deprioritized Overture's business model after the merger. Google, which had been powering the search results on Yahoo!, took notice of the new business model and jumped on the bandwagon. Without a competing revenue model to distract Larry Page and Sergey Brin, Google built out the business, which today grosses more than $50 billion a year. Sometimes you can't even give away your idea at any price. Before proving out paid search, Page and Brin tried to sell all of Google to Excite for a mere $1 million. Excite negotiated Google's price down to $750,000 but didn't close the deal, because they couldn't convince Excite's board that there was any value in owning Google.[16]

Disruptors looking for a big idea need only examine their worlds and their businesses: What problems do you confront every day? How do those problems provide the opportunity for value to be captured? More often than not, a big idea is just a simple solution to a small problem.

🐦 *More often than not, a big idea is just a simple solution to a small problem.*

Chapter Seven

Pivoting Your Energies

There can be no real freedom without
the freedom to fail.
—Erich Fromm

When I was global president of digital distribution at EMI, I did business with a guy who had the typical startup horror story. He had founded a high-tech company in Silicon Valley and created substantial value for his venture capital backers. But then competition grew and his market share fell below 5 percent. The same board that had applauded him when things were good kicked him to the curb the moment things headed south. They brought in a corporate CEO who didn't fit the company culture, and things continued to decline. After a series of failed attempts to right the ship, and faced with no other choices, the board reinstated the original founder. With no new products in development and the business in dire shape, he pivoted the company from making personal computers to revolutionizing consumer electronics and telecommunications. Oh, yeah, and this company was called Apple, and its cofounder, Steve Jobs, disrupted the world.

GE chairman Jack Welch was fond of saying, "Change before you have to," but for the first-time entrepreneur, knowing when to plow through it and when to change directions is the hardest decision to make. Emotionally, it can feel like abandoning your baby in a forest or, worse, selling it to a butcher to be cut into pieces. In a constantly changing world, learning when to pivot is a skill that is useful for any business. For every cliché about how "winners never quit and quitters never win," there is another that says, "If you always do what you've always done, you'll always get what you've always got."

Pivoting a business didn't come naturally to me when I built my first company. Jasmine Multimedia was like my first child. What I lacked in experience I overcompensated for in drive. Now I can acknowledge that chief among the lessons I learned from the process of building and growing that company is the lesson that pivoting is less an admission of failure and more a way to find new opportunities to be successful. This lesson applies to every business and every career.

With only the desire to survive guiding me, my first company pivoted from business-to-business custom productions to publishing, from CD-ROMs to the Internet. Each iteration of the business had to resolve new challenges to its assumptions about the value it was creating and the constant threats to its position in the market. This is never an easy task. The music industry pivoted too slowly from manufactured goods to digital distribution and didn't survive intact. As an executive vice president at Sony, I watched as the company couldn't pivot from being a stand-alone consumer electronics manufacturer to a creator of networked digital ecosystems. This failure to change course caused Sony to shrink rapidly from a market capitalization of $100 billion in 2000 to $15 billion in 2012.

True disruptors aren't afraid to pivot. When the creation of the World Wide Web disrupted the entire software industry in 1995, Microsoft chairman Bill Gates bravely pivoted the entire company, through his famous Internet Tidal Wave memo.

"The Internet is the most important single development to come along since the IBM PC was introduced in 1981," Gates wrote prophetically. "The PC analogy is apt for many reasons . . . a phenomena grew up around the IBM PC that made it a key element of everything that would happen for the next 15 years. Companies that tried to fight the PC standard often had good reasons for doing so but they failed because the phenomena overcame any weaknesses that resisters identified."[1]

With that thirty-eight-paragraph memorandum as a guide, Gates restructured all of Microsoft and pivoted the market leader in packaged software into a leader in a new digital economy. Microsoft may not be the dominant company that it was at the birth of the personal computer revolution, but Gates's timely pivot successfully positioned the company for the next dozen years.

For most businesses, pivoting is less about big changes in direction and more about adjusting to ever-changing market conditions. Businesses are sailboats cutting through choppy waters. In order to move forward through calm winds or storms, the captain must tack the ship back and forth in a constant series of minor adjustments. *Test, verify, and adjust* is the only way to stay on course. Data has no ego and makes an excellent copilot.

> Test, verify, and adjust *is the only way to stay on course. Data has no ego and makes an excellent copilot.*

"I tell entrepreneurs our business model is like going to the eye doctor. 'Better like this or like this? A or B? B or C?'" Twitter CEO Dick Costolo says. "'Oh, C's doing better than B? Let's do more C.'"[2] When small adjustments don't do the trick, look at what you have built and see if there is any traction or proof that you will be more successful pursuing a different direction.

When speaking with the most successful Silicon Valley venture capitalists on Sand Hill Road, they can all, to a person, share stories of companies that they had invested millions of dollars in that were so far off course that the board debated pulling the funding and closing the operation down. The punch line to the story is invariably that the company pivoted, and the result was not only the biggest success of the investors, but also the biggest success in the history of the venture firm.

The following are a few of my favorite pivot success stories friends have experienced in recent years.

Yelp was originally started by former PayPal coworkers Jeremy Stoppelman and Russel Simmons as an automated service for emailing recommendation requests to friends. "Can anyone recommend a pediatrician in Boston?" would be sent to one's social graph, and responses would be tabulated. The service, which launched in 2004 with more than a million dollars invested by PayPal cofounder Max Levchin, instantly bombed with the public.

Turns out that auto-email wasn't very appealing, but users enjoyed writing reviews about the local businesses mentioned in the email blasts. By studying their user data, the founders identified that it was the reviews that were the big draw to users. The service pivoted to follow its audience. Yelp, which was derided in the beginning as the "Friendster of Yellow Pages," now attracts fifty million unique visitors each month to its collection of over seventeen million consumer-generated reviews, and it is currently valued at over $2 billion.[3]

Burbn was a Foursquare-wannabe mobile app started by Kevin Systrom and Mike Krieger. The app gave users points when they checked into a location. But, unlike Foursquare, Burbn wanted to verify that the user wasn't gaming the system and was actually at the declared location, not checking in from some remote place. To prove that the mobile user was in the venue, Burbn had people take and post pictures that they could then share with other friends on Burbn. The young company's data clearly showed that people liked sharing the pictures more than the gamification of earning badges and points for checking in. The original premise of the company was changed by observing the data from this unanticipated consumer behavior. The founders ditched the whole check-in concept and pivoted to photo posting and social sharing. Within two years, more than a hundred million people would join. Now the app is so successful that more pictures have been posted to it than were taken on planet earth during the first hundred years of photography! Systrom and Krieger added some fun filters, changed the name to Instagram, and sold their eight-person company to Facebook for nearly $1 billion, without generating one cent in revenue.[4] A picture truly is worth more than a thousand words.

Tune In Hook Up was designed by three former PayPal employees to disrupt the online dating industry. Bolstered by the massive success of PayPal, the team was looking for another online business venture. Online dating, while immensely popular, had failed to incorporate any new features since the advent of broadband. Most dating sites featured only still images of prospective partners, and Chad Hurley, Steve Chen, and Jawed Karim thought showcasing dating videos would be a much more immersive offering. Their assumption was that users could get a better feel for a person's personality if they could see and hear them through video. The founders were convinced that this was their billion-dollar idea. No need to test the premise with potential online daters—all they had to do was architect the video site's infrastructure and the users would follow. While working on building the video-dating upload site, Karim noticed that he couldn't find the footage of Janet Jackson's Super Bowl "wardrobe malfunction" that all of America was talking about on-line. He realized that finding dating videos was just a subset of a more massive online video-discovery problem. Karim realized that a better discovery mechanism for online video would need to be created. Abandoning their original concept, the team focused on helping people search for any type of video they might possibly want. They changed the name of Tune In Hook Up to YouTube and were acquired by Google in 2006 for $1.65 billion, after being in business for just a year. Their site now has more than one hundred hours of video uploaded every minute of every day and boasts over a billion unique users per month.[5]

In 2005, Odeo was going to be *the* place for music fans to discover and share music podcasts. When Apple quickly conquered that space with iTunes, Odeo brainstormed new, unrelated ideas to try before finally running out of cash and going out of business. Pivoting before going broke is the cardinal rule for startup survival. Believing it would be easier to raise additional funds to keep the company going rather than start over again with a new company, the team discussed a wide range of unrelated concepts. Jack Dorsey liked the idea of a short-messaging app, and they debuted it at the SXSW music festival, in Austin (where they had already reserved booth space when Odeo was a music service). Today, more than 500 million registered users of the popular service generate over 340 million short 140-character messages a day. They changed their name to Twitter, raised over $1 billion in funding, and, as of this writing, are valued at over $30 billion.[6] Twitter's SXSW launch also changed the future of the conference, which today is known as *the* place to launch new digital companies.

RUSH TO FAIL AND TEST, TEST, TEST

Not all pivots end in success, and the vast majority of startups fail. But failing is part of the entrepreneurial process. Success doesn't teach as many lessons as failure does. Many great entrepreneurs who became brand names, including Henry Ford, Walt Disney, and Henry Heinz, went bankrupt before creating their billion-dollar empires. Sony cofounder Akio Morita's first product was an electric rice cooker that, unfortunately, burned the rice. After selling fewer than a hundred units, Morita pivoted to making transistor radios.[7]

> 🐦 *Success doesn't teach as many lessons as failure does.*

Even Traf-O-Data, the first company started by two of the world's richest men, failed. The concept of the business was to use a Traf-O-Data 808 computer to analyze a city's traffic data to reduce urban congestion. The idea seemed like a no-brainer. Unfortunately, their concept was decades ahead of the market, and local government planners didn't accept the idea of cities purchasing computer systems. So Bill Gates and Paul Allen had to pack it in and figure out something else to do.

"It's fine to celebrate success," Bill Gates famously said, "but it is more important to heed the lessons of failure." Undaunted by failure, Gates and Allen started a second company, then named Micro-Soft, which grossed $16,000 in 1975.[8]

Dealing with the failure of a business is never easy. In a sense it is an admission that the direction in which you were headed wasn't working. All too often, we stay the course a little longer or try the same thing over again because any other approach would be a tacit admission of failure. The problem with fearing change is wasting years on a course that will not lead to success—time that could be put to use pursuing new, more lucrative ideas. All financial and personal success comes from change. To the disruptor, change is a natural requirement.

Smart entrepreneurs learn that they must fail often and fast. Try an approach, quickly measure the results, and move on. Change is an iterative process. As inventor Thomas Edison wisely remarked, "I have not failed. I've just found 10,000 ways that won't work."

> 🐦 *Smart entrepreneurs learn that they must fail often and fast.*

For the startup entrepreneur, failing quickly is often the key to long-term success. Managing the burn rate of your capital while you test each new idea is as important to your long-term success as the initial idea itself. After coming up with your disruptive concept, determine the quickest way to validate your hypothesis while consuming the smallest amount of your capital. For today's mobile and Web-based businesses, data is everything.

I was mentoring a young startup in the ecommerce space that was looking to launch with a Hollywood superstar. Capital was easy to come by, because so many stars were cashing in on this new retailing trend. Britney Spears's perfume grossed over $1 billion in global sales, and Jessica Simpson's clothing line generated over $500 million in revenue.[9] What Kim Kardashian had done for ShoeDazzle, and Kate Bosworth for Jewelmint, this new venture wanted a female celebrity to do for intimate apparel. While going up against the category leader, Victoria's Secret—which grosses over $6 billion in sales each year—was a big challenge, there was plenty of room in the category for a competitor.[10] Pick the right star and fortune is almost certain; but partner with the wrong icon and your business is doomed from day one. So how do you know which celebrity will sell the most bras? As with any new concept, by testing what works and what doesn't.

Testing a concept before you roll out a new business is the iterative way to disrupt. The single biggest reason most startups fail isn't that the founders had a bad idea. They fail because they run out of capital before they discover how to bring their idea to market. For most new businesses, whether they are neighborhood restaurants or iPhone apps, the cost of customer acquisition is vastly underestimated.

In the case of the intimate-apparel company I was mentoring, Victoria's

Secret had already proved the market. We only needed to determine which celebrity had a big enough social media following in the bra-buying ecommerce space to launch a clothing line. We brainstormed lots of names and ran the short list by women we knew. How important was her age, race, cup size? Did it matter if she was married or single? Did it help if she had a sex-tape scandal in her past, or did we want a more aspirational woman? Trashy or chaste? Which was more important, her Twitter following or her Facebook following? We had heated discussions about why each of us thought our first choice was the woman to bet the company on. But with millions of dollars at stake, how could we know for sure? We needed empirical data.

Before entering into negotiations with agents and managers for our lingerie spokeswoman, we ran small, unauthorized online ad campaigns with the various female stars' photos. In one afternoon, without letting any of the celebrities know (and without the legal permission to do so), we could accurately and quietly determine each woman's market value and lingerie sales potential. All we had to do was put banners in front of a few thousand women in our target market to quickly see who drove the greatest response selling bras and who wasn't a perfect fit. By measuring the click-through rates on the ads, we knew which star worked best for our market. We had bankable data within a few days, and the total amount invested in the test was less than $1,000. What was most interesting about the test results was that the perfect choice was irrefutable. Data is the most rational and productive member of any startup team. Invite data to as many planning meetings as you can. Data may disappoint, but it never lies.

> 🐦 Data is the most rational and productive member of any startup team. Data may disappoint, but it never lies.

Online testing happens very quickly, while some business hypotheses take months and hundreds of thousands of dollars to test. It is fine to go into any venture as a management team with a strong point of view about what you think will work, but check your ego at the door once you have actual data. There is a surprise benefit to the iterative cycle of test-fail-retest: you uncover valuable insights hidden from anyone not testing. Some of the most successful billion-dollar businesses of the past decade grew out of this process. On the road of testing one assumption, a startup can discover a new direction that no one else would know about unless they had conducted the very same tests. YouTube, Twitter, and Instagram are just a few examples of companies that didn't give up when their initial concepts came up short. Instead, these entrepreneurs employed a process known as effectuation.

EFFECTUATION

Effectuation is a set of decision-making principles expert disruptors are observed to employ in situations of uncertainty. The process begins with simply defining what you know about your new business and its underlying market. How big is the market? How many competitors will you have? What is your target demographic? Are product offerings perennial or constantly changing? The list of questions should be exhaustive. Try to interview as many potential consumers as you can. The goal of the process is to become an expert on how the market for your idea currently functions. Next, add to that information what value you can bring to or capture from the market. The focus is to define your goals for the new business or idea. You know that sushi is popular in your city, but does your restaurant location have the same traffic pattern as its competition across town? How does your parking compare? What value can you add to offset any deficit resulting from your location? Why have other restaurants in the area failed (regardless of cuisine)?

When Hiroaki "Rocky" Aoki conceived his first Benihana restaurant in New York in 1964, he had analyzed what made most restaurants fail and specifically designed his concept to mitigate his risk. Most restaurants waste a great deal of food, because they offer too many selections, and not all dishes are ordered with a consistent frequency. So Aoki limited his menu to three choices. Rent is the single greatest fixed cost to a restaurant, and most establishments can't maximize the use of their space because parties of two or three take up tables with the seating potential of four or five. Aoki solved the occupancy issue by seating people only when an entire teppanyaki table could be filled—even if this meant that strangers would have to share a table.

He also knew that keeping people waiting at the bar until a full table could be seated had the additional benefit of increasing bar orders and thus the average revenue per customer. Through effectuation, Aoki became an expert in the restaurant industry instead of just an expert in Japanese dinner houses.

I can't stress enough the importance of the third step of effectuation: meeting with people in the target market. Just as Jesus had his apostles, you need to find a dozen consumers who are in your target demographic and bounce your ideas off them. These should not be friends or family, who will tend to think they are helping you by giving you false praise and encouragement. These should be actual consumers who feel their lives would benefit if your innovation was successful. The whole concept of crowdfunding grew out of this very idea: find enough customers who are so emotionally invested in your product that they would pay for it far in advance. Pebble, a smartwatch concept created by Eric Migicovsky, set out to raise $100,000 from future customers on Kickstarter in April 2012. By the time their crowdsourcing campaign ended in May, the company had raised more than $10 million from 69,000 consumers.[11] The crowd had spoken: there was a real market for Migicovsky's watch.

Working with potential customers to create a new product goes far beyond the tech sector. When I was with EMI, our classical music label had limited funds for recording symphonies and could release only a few new albums each year. So the label listed on its website upcoming orchestra performances that might be of interest to its audience. The top orchestras in the world perform some pieces of music only a couple of times and then those specific renditions are lost forever. Given that most classical music fans can't afford to traverse the globe to catch each unique concert, EMI worked out a system to record those performances using "presales." If enough consumers signed up to purchase the album, EMI went ahead with the expense of sending a team to record the project. Data is always right. If no one signs up to buy the product, listen to your customers.

Real consumers actually value their time as much as their money. If your ideas lack merit, they will let you know. If most of your focus group of users hates your idea, it's time to take another direction or abandon ship. All too often when I meet with young startups, they believe they can skip this step. They believe they know how people will think. I remind them that everyone else on the planet has one of seven billion points of view that are different from their opinion.

> 🐦 *Real consumers actually value their time as much as their money.*

Though he has already made billions, Sir Richard Branson actually flies commercially on Virgin Atlantic and talks to his fellow passengers. During one conversation with Upper Class fliers, Sir Richard realized that nearly all of them had hired a car service to take them to and from the airport. That one insight gave him an advantage over every other airline. Why not include a limo service to and from the airport as part of the Upper Class service? He realized he could raise his ticket prices to include the car service and that he'd attract more passengers by providing true door-to-door service, thereby eliminating the burden on travelers of having to coordinate and communicate changing flight schedules with their drivers. Passengers could check their luggage with their driver and have one less hassle on their trip. But it was only by talking to his customers that Branson learned they'd be willing to pay a premium for this service.[12]

Jeff Bezos has built Amazon into a $150 billion company by carefully analyzing his customer data. The data revealed that Amazon makes twice as much money from each of its Amazon Prime customers as it does from regular purchasers. Prime customers pay an annual fee for free two-day shipping. These consumers want to get the most out of their $79 investment, so they are inclined to do more of their shopping from the site. In 2013, the average Prime customer spent $1,340 per year, compared with $708 per year for non-Prime consumers.[13] Never stop talking to your customers and you'll never stop learning how to improve your business.

Once you begin getting commitments from stakeholders, your business has a base to build upon. A business's growth is then a factor of its virality and customer acquisition costs—both of which can be modeled very quickly, and marketing spend can be adapted accordingly.

But effectuation is an ongoing process that doesn't take place in a vacuum.

At the same time as you are building a community of stakeholders who want you to succeed, changes to the market, the consumer demographic, and the existing technological infrastructure are all impacting the original assumptions that led you to build your company or product. Unless you are diligent about always challenging what you know and what your market wants, a newer, more nimble upstart will come along as you once did and disrupt your business. Pivoting is not the end of the disruption process, but the beginning of the next leg of your journey.

> *Pivoting is not the end of the disruption process, but the beginning of the next leg of your journey.*

Most startup failures result from entrepreneurs who are better at making excuses than products. Customers and data instantly let you know how your business is doing and where it is heading. Yet too many people continue to pursue the same path in their life or their company without admitting that something isn't working. As the astounding successes of YouTube, Instagram, and Twitter illustrate, failing isn't the same as failure. The only true mistake is not realizing the value of the mistakes you are making.

> *Most startup failures result from entrepreneurs who are better at making excuses than products.*

"Make mistakes small and fast," advises Silicon Alley honcho Miles Rose, who assists New York–area startups with capital raises.[14] The faster you pivot, the more time, money, and energy you have to spend on a better idea.

Chapter Eight

Unlocking the Value Chain

Commitment unlocks the doors of imagination,
allows vision, and gives us the "right stuff" to
turn our dreams into reality.
—James Womack

Harvard Business School professor Michael Porter first popularized the concept of the value chain in his bestselling management book *Competitive Advantage: Creating and Sustaining Superior Performance.* Porter recognized that each enterprise builds value through a linear series of discrete steps that are always followed in the same order. Each link in the chain adds value to the final product or service sold to the consumer. Value is the commodity that a consumer actually purchases.[1] As I suggested earlier in this book, the key to self-transformation is understanding what makes you, as an individual, uniquely valuable. The same is true for businesses. Differentiating value is the only competitive advantage any single business enterprise can maintain over another. Are Beats headphones technologically better equipment, or do consumers pay for the value they perceive from the brand? Is Fiji water better-tasting or better for you than Dasani? Differentiation is the key to creating and capturing value for your business.

Unlike the uniform links in a bicycle chain, the five links in a company's value chain—research and development, design, production, marketing and sales, and distribution—are not equal. Auto dealerships, for example, make more money from servicing vehicles than from selling them, but the sales also help drive traffic into their service department. The varied properties of each link in the chain are what, in the end, make the entire ecosystem so vulnerable to disruption. Surprisingly, in many industries the most expensive part of the chain to operate may deliver the smallest financial return. For example, movie exhibitors compete to get the biggest blockbuster films into their theaters, even though they make the bulk of their profit from food and beverage concessions—but who would come to the theater if they didn't have a movie you wanted to see? Conversely, the least costly step may be the one that generates the greatest monetary value. Some links aren't worth breaking, while others hold the lion's share of the potential profit. It's easiest to make money from disruption by focusing on the most profitable links in the chain. So before one embarks on disrupting this system, it is important to understand a value chain's inherent instability.

> It's easiest to make money from disruption by focusing on the most profitable links in the chain.

A DIAMOND IS FOREVER

Diamonds offer a textbook illustration of the disproportionate links in the value chain. Think of the most glamorous star in the world dripping with bling or the joy of a bride-to-be basking in the glow of her engagement ring. Nothing says wealth and status like a diamond. But did you ever ask yourself why this one stone is so coveted?

Nearly $9 billion worth of diamonds are mined annually, employing tens of thousands of workers.[2] This is the most costly link in the diamond's value chain. Mining operations require massive investments in real estate, equipment, and manpower. Tons of worthless rocks must be dug out of the ground to make way for the literal diamond in the rough. By comparison, cutting the mined stones is an inexpensive step, but it adds the most value to the finished product. But it could be argued that the marketing campaign masterminded by N. W. Ayer & Son for De Beers nearly a century ago actually generated the most value in the diamond value chain: it created demand.

Prior to the De Beers campaign, which began in the 1930s, engagement rings were adorned with any number of gemstones or pearls. But

Ayer created an association between diamonds and love. He gave the diamond value chain one of the most recognized slogans of the twentieth century: "A Diamond Is Forever." The result of over seventy-five years of this advertising campaign is that engagement rings from Singapore to Saõ Paulo all sport diamonds. Ayer's campaign created demand for the product. Coupled with De Beers's near-monopolistic control over supply, this demand drives consumers to spend billions on an otherwise useless little rock.

Now imagine the disruption that would happen to the value chain if real diamonds could be made in the laboratory at a fraction of the cost of mining. Today around 2,200 pounds of synthetic diamonds are produced each year. But these stones are not intended for anyone's ring finger. Synthetic diamonds are produced for industrial uses. And while mining colorless diamonds runs about $40 to $60 per carat, gem-quality synthetics still cost fifty times more, at about $2,500 per carat.[3] Should scientists ever discover a way to fabricate synthetic diamonds that's cheaper than chemical vapor deposition, the entire multi-billion-dollar diamond business would be disrupted overnight. One innovation in the laboratory and there would be no further need for mines or miners. Two college students with a new technology could do to the diamond industry what Napster did to the music business.

Even more disruptive to De Beers's monopoly is the problem that inexpensive synthetic diamonds would remove the invisible hand of scarcity that holds the existing value chain in place. Sound impossible? It's happened before. When the Washington Monument was completed, in 1885, the monolith was the tallest structure in the world, at 555 feet 5 ⅛ inches. To crown this massive modern architectural achievement, the proud American designers chose to cap the obelisk with a hundred ounces of one of the rarest and most expensive metals of the day: aluminum! Aluminum, which cannot be found in its pure state in nature, was so rare in the nineteenth century that only one American, William Frishmuth of Philadelphia, knew how to make it. Frishmuth's skill was so valuable to the war effort that President Abraham Lincoln made him a secret agent in the U.S. War Department during the Civil War.

Today we know the process for extracting alumina from buxite and that aluminum is the third-most-abundant element on earth (after oxygen and silicon). Over 30 million tons of the inexpensive metal is produced each year. Once disrupted, a broken value chain is never repaired. The value shifts the market, and new, more efficient systems evolve. Aluminum proves that perhaps diamonds aren't forever.

BREAKING THE VALUE CHAIN

In the twenty-first century, the accelerating pace of advancement in technology continues to disrupt value chains that were once perceived to be as permanent and unmalleable as a diamond. With each disruption, wealth shifts from the entrenched to the innovator. To the disruptor, every threat to the status quo is an opportunity in disguise. Deconstruct the problem and solve for the new opportunity.

> 🐦 *Every threat to the status quo is an opportunity in disguise.*

Disrupting a simple value chain is how two guys in San Francisco went from not being able to pay their rent in 2007 to having a company worth $10 billion in 2014. To help cover their rent, Brian Chesky and Joe Gebbia created a simple website to rent out air mattresses in their apartment. Realizing that people visiting cities such as New York and San Francisco were forced to pay high hotel rates because there was no system to connect them with available rooms in people's homes, they raised $20,000 from Y Combinator and expanded their software. While famous venture capitalists such as Fred Wilson passed on funding them, Airbnb continued to grow. In 2014, after they'd achieved over 500,000 listings in 192 countries, TPG Capital invested $450 million in the company, at a valuation of approximately $10 billion.[4] Airbnb is not profitable, and its valuation is not based on current revenues but rather on the potential its business model has to completely disrupt the hospitality sector and capture much of the value that could be unlocked.

As illustrated in the diamond industry, each link in the value chain contributes a different amount to creating the overall value of the company or product. And depending on the industry, the least expensive link may yield the greatest return. Take the circus, for example. A circus is made up of a collection of entertaining acts. Some acts, such as trained lions and elephants, are very expensive to keep and transport, while others, such as clowns and contortionists, are both low-cost and low-maintenance. When the grand touring circuses like Ringling Brothers and Circus Vargas were struggling to make a profit, Canadian street performers Guy Laliberté and Gilles Ste-Croix dumped the more expensive acts and reimagined a circus experience with only value-generating links. Cirque du Soleil not only successfully disrupted the touring circus industry but it also quickly took over the Las Vegas Strip with its profitable formula for low-cost, high-margin entertainment.

My friend Bruce Eskowitz took the same approach to removing cost and maximizing the entertainment value in touring when he became president and CEO of Premier Exhibitions. Eskowitz, a twenty-year veteran of rock concert touring and sporting events, looked at the sky-rocketing costs of producing multicity tours. He analyzed the value chain and devised the most cost-effective tour ever imagined. He booked an act that was willing to tour the world without ever asking to be paid one dollar. The Body Worlds exhibition, originally created by Gunther von Hagens, took artistically dissected human cadavers to over fifty museums around the world. When I first asked Bruce about the appeal of the Body Worlds tour from a business perspective, he replied, "Do you know what the catering and hotel bill is for this tour?" He created the cheapest cast of any touring show in the world. And best of all, when they weren't touring, you could put the entire act on ice—literally.

Being able to quickly identify disproportionate links is the key to disrupting an existing value chain and capturing the greatest return for your investment. In the following chapters, we will explore techniques for decoding and disrupting each of the links in private- and public-sector value chains. Each of the traditional five links contributes different values and degrees of importance, depending on the industry. Innovation and marketing increase a company's revenue, while everything else is merely a cost center. But all parts of the chain contain value that can be released through disruption. The following chapters will each focus on one link of the value chain and illustrate how others have disrupted their industries by seizing opportunities available in one of those links. These chapters will share the stories of successful innovators who took advantage of opportunities to disrupt specific links in the value chain to make money and grow their businesses. I will also forecast how these links are transforming our world and predict some of the ways they are likely to be disrupted in the future.

Chapter Nine

Research and Development: Unlocking the Value of Waste

If we knew what we were doing, it wouldn't be called research, would it?
—Albert Einstein

Most scientists don't know what they are doing. Really. Millions and millions of research dollars are spent without any product or business rationale. This is not meant as a condemnation of the work of our best and brightest minds, but rather as another way of looking at the field of primary research. A scientist's job is to discover new knowledge through experimentation and observation. True scientific discovery is finding something that no one knew existed before. By definition, scientists are searching for the unknown. For the entrepreneur looking to disrupt the research and development link of the value chain, opportunity abounds, precisely because most scientists working in primary research and development are creating new discoveries with little thought about how, or why, to bring them to market. Engineers, scientists, and medical researchers create bodies of work without a business purpose in mind. Often it takes the fresh perspective of a disruptor to look at scientific breakthroughs with a market-driven set of eyes. This is where financial opportunity lies. Disruptors don't have to discover something new; they just have to discover a practical use for new discoveries.

> *Disruptors don't have to discover something new; they just have to discover a practical use for new discoveries.*

Real financial value is not created in the lab; it's created by determining which market, or use, will generate the greatest value for a newly discovered innovation. Sildenafil, the active ingredient in Viagra, was developed in the lab as a cardiovascular drug to lower blood pressure. When Pfizer's marketers learned that its side effect of creating harder, longer-lasting erections had test patients refusing to return samples of the medication, it gave rise to a more profitable $2 billion business.[1]

PROFIT FROM OTHERS' DISCOVERIES

Oftentimes, an entrepreneur can benefit from millions of dollars of research without investing a dime of his own money. Great wealth can be created by taking advantage of the research and development done by someone else. The R & D link has never been easier to disrupt than it is today. To the disruptor, this link of the value chain offers the distinct advantage that you can profit from a discovery that others might have spent years refining before ultimately abandoning it. Many inventions and scientific discoveries are cast off because they're ahead of their time or don't fit the strategic direction of the company developing them. In the case of universities and other research institutions, grant monies may have run out and forced a team to abandon a project after most of the expensive research has been completed. Finally, market factors that might have made something too costly or inefficient when it was being developed might have changed over time, making the development of the product more affordable. Billions of dollars' worth of discoveries are filed away and nearly forgotten, waiting for the disruptor to come along and breathe life into them. A great example of how a disruptor can rethink scientific research is the story of how one of the biggest failures of U.S. military research was turned into one of the most delightful products of my childhood.

🐦 *Great wealth can be created by taking advantage of the research and development done by someone else.*

During World War II, all United States private sector manufacturing was converted into aiding the war effort. Strategic resources like gasoline were rationed, and scrap metal was recycled into tanks and planes. One of the most essential ingredients for war production was rubber. Rubber tires kept our armies moving toward victory, and all those boots on the ground needed rubber soles. Gas masks, life rafts, and even fighter planes required rubber. Since most rubber tree production was in Southeast Asia, the war in the Pacific made supplies scarce. Civilians did their part in conservation and worked as communities to gather up old tires and raincoats. Recycling became a national obsession.

Behind the scenes on the home front, America's top scientists were busy spending millions of dollars in the laboratory trying to create a synthetic rubber made from domestic ingredients. In 1943, with the war raging on around the globe, General Electric engineer James Wright had a scientific breakthrough. Working in New Haven, Connecticut, Wright mixed silicone oil and boric acid to form a goop with several properties very similar to rubber. Wright's synthetic substance bounced when dropped, had a high melting point, and stretched farther than the natural latex tapped from trees. But it had a tragic flaw: as unique as this compound was, it couldn't be hardened or molded into a lasting shape. Wright tried everything he could to stabilize his strange liquid-solid, but he failed again and again. Still believing in his discovery, he open-sourced his goop and sent samples to leading American research scientists in the field. Because it was unable to retain its shape, no one found a practical use for Wright's goop during or after the war. The discovery looked like a massive waste of time and money.

But after the war, a Madison Avenue advertising man named Peter Hodgson was looking for a new product to bring to market. The goop may have been completely useless to scientists, but it was fun to bounce and stretch, and it could even copy color pictures from comic books.

"Everybody kept saying there was no earthly use for the stuff,"

Hodgson recalled to an interviewer years later. "But I watched them as they fooled with it. I couldn't help noticing how people with busy schedules wasted as much as 15 minutes at a shot just fondling and stretching it."[2]

Eventually Hodgson, who'd spent the last of his savings making samples, took the goop to New York's International Toy Fair in 1950 and called it Silly Putty. Hodgson sold 250,000 eggs of the putty in just three days. Since that time, over three hundred million eggs have been sold, sending Silly Putty to the moon—literally.[3] It took one of the greatest research organizations on earth, NASA, to find a practical use for Wright's goop. Silly Putty's unique adhesive characteristics made it the ideal substance for Apollo astronauts to secure their tools in zero gravity.

Hodgson's one disruption of the research and development link—putting Wright's research to new use—inspired a generation of inventors and tinkerers to create new chemical substances for the toy business. Norman Stingley sold his Zectron polymer to Wham-O, which went on to sell millions of Super Balls. Polyvinyl acetate and ethyl acetate were mixed by inventors to create Super Elastic Bubble Plastic, which was popular with kids despite its noxious fumes. Mattel marketed a liquid "Plasti-Goop" that, when heated to 360 degrees, allowed children to manufacture their own Creepy Crawlers. James and Arthur Ingoldsby created Magic Rocks crystal-growing kits. Joseph McVicker, working at Ohio-based Kutol Chemicals, created a safe, nontoxic wallpaper cleaner that was easy to mold and manipulate. When McVicker heard from a neighborhood schoolteacher that young children had difficulty sculpting clay, he gave her a box of his cleaning composition. It was so popular that orders started pouring in from all the Cincinnati-area schools. Since 1956, over two billion cans of Play-Doh have been sold, much to the delight of children everywhere.[4] Hodgson's Silly Putty disruption spawned a category of toys that continues today, with toys such as Brookstone's Sand, which sticks together but not to children's hands.

Research that was converted by disruptors into big profits isn't specific to chemicals and the creation of wacky new substances—even in the toy industry. Richard James was a naval engineer tasked with designing a suspended meter to monitor horsepower on battleships. While working on the device, he accidentally dropped a tension spring on the ground and was amazed how simple harmonic motion kept the spring moving. His wife, Betty, named the toy Slinky. James borrowed $500 and had four hundred units manufactured at a local machine shop. Though wrapped in yellow paper, the Slinky didn't sell without a demonstration. Philadelphia department store Gimbels allowed James to set up an incline and sold out of all four hundred units in ninety minutes. Over three hundred million Slinkys have been sold to date, and the toy continues to be a perennial bestseller.[5]

For the purposes of this book, the stories of success in the toy industry through disruption in the research and development link provide a nice example because the science feels approachable and understandable. The lesson, however, extends to research in medicine, alloys, electronics, materials, detergents, cosmetics, and so much more. The disruption is not in the category you create, but rather in the act of leveraging an investment made by others into a profitable business. Slinkys and Silly Putty were not disruptive technologies, but their "inventors" made money by disrupting the research and development done by other people. Hodgson and his peers were all looking for a product to sell, and they used others' financial investment rather than having to start from scratch. Disruption can come from learning to reuse, repurpose, and recycle the R & D of others to achieve new products in new categories never imagined by the original creators.

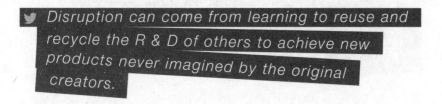

Disruption can come from learning to reuse and recycle the R & D of others to achieve new products never imagined by the original creators.

HOW THE INTERNET IS TRANSFORMING R & D

What Hodgson, James, and McVicker achieved can be replicated by today's disruptors with greater ease, thanks to the Internet and open-source research. Hundreds of government and university laboratories share their discoveries license-free in an effort to promote universal access to their work. At the University of Southern California's Stevens Center for Innovation, whose Board of Councilors I had the privilege of sitting on, an entire team is dedicated to transferring university-researched technologies to the private sector. Entrepreneurs who comb these resources have built businesses around open-source software, medical research, robotic engineering, and even beverages. In recent years, dozens of small companies have sprung up and started making millions in the open-source space. Adafruit uses open-source technology to enable over 350,000 of its customers to build cell phone jammers.[6] Bug Labs open-sourced Lego-like interlocking computers. In 2010, *Wired* magazine's editor in chief, Chris Anderson, launched an open-source company focused on creating military drones and quickly generated over $1 million in sales.[7] The cleverly named Evil Mad Scientist Labs creates open-source 3-D printers that "print" in caramelized sugar. The open-source movement is growing so quickly that an electronics retailer based in Boulder, Colorado, SparkFun, which embraced open-source technology early, now employs over 140 people and has grossed over $10 million in sales.[8]

Every entrepreneur has equal access to all of this research. Billions of dollars' worth of research knowledge lies dormant at American universities waiting for the right disruptor to come along and create a business. Some research institutions require licenses and royalties, while others allow their innovations to be freely open-sourced. This approach to sharing innovations is exploding globally.

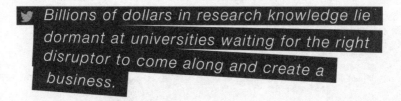

Billions of dollars in research knowledge lie dormant at universities waiting for the right disruptor to come along and create a business.

One of the most unusual open-source products on the planet is Blowfly Beer. Australian brewery Brewtopia open-sources every aspect of its beer production, from taste to packaging, and gives those who participate in the product's development shares in the public company. Liam Mulhall and his two mates wanted to start a microbrewery like the ones they saw in the United States. Unfortunately, the three partners knew nothing about making beer or how to market it. So they turned to the wisdom of the crowd. They asked all their family and friends, around 140 people, to sign up on their website. Each week, they polled their followers with questions on every aspect of the process: logo, shape of the bottle, T-shirt design, and so on. Furthermore, for participating in the creation of Blowfly, every site member would get a free six-pack and a share of stock when they launched. The open-source campaign worked. In the course of thirteen weeks, their membership list skyrocketed to thirteen thousand, and distribution at launch had reached twenty-eight pubs in Brisbane, three in Melbourne, and three in Sidney. The membership list also created mail-order demand, which makes up about 50 percent of their business.[9]

On the more philanthropic front, the Open Source Drug Discovery for Malaria Consortium is a collaboration between scientists, doctors, and researchers around the world working on open-source pharmaceutical development to fight a range of deadly tropical diseases. (For more on crowdsourcing, see chapter 15.)

Of all the research and development centers run by the U.S. government, the National Aeronautics and Space Administration (NASA) is the most user friendly. It actively encourages entrepreneurs to commercialize NASA discoveries. In just the past decade alone, technology spinoffs from NASA have created over fourteen thousand private sector jobs and generated over $5 billion in revenues.[10] Implantable medical devices, miniature smartphone cameras, and even kombucha tea products have been developed from NASA-funded research. Companies such as Rackspace, GreenField Solar, and Locus Energy have converted NASA discoveries into economic growth engines for their businesses.

Two of the most famous NASA-spinoff technologies are now found in millions of homes around the world. When government contractor Black & Decker had to create a self-contained drill capable of extracting lunar core samples for the Apollo program, no one imagined that the drill's computer-designed, low-power motor would become the genesis of the cordless mini vacuum we all know as the Dustbuster. NASA's Ames Research Center's work to improve the safety of aircraft cushions resulted in a polymer matrix foam with an open-cell structure that enables it to slowly spring back to its original shape. Today their creation is known as memory foam and is the technology behind the Tempur-Pedic mattress. The NASA Spinoff page on the agency's website tracks over sixteen hundred products that have been spun off to private entrepreneurs since 1976.[11]

With so many billions of dollars' worth of government and university patents sitting unused and gathering dust, three Ph.D. students realized there was a need for a crowdsourcing website dedicated to commercializing science. In 2012, Daniel Perez, Mehmet Fidanboylu, and Gabriel Mecklenburg started Marblar—a place where inventors around the world can showcase their patents and profitably collaborate with creative minds from all disciplines and experience levels. While they refer to their business as a "creative playground realizing the promise of science," NASA and other research centers have taken notice of the disruptive concept.

To speed up technology transfer and accelerate commercial development, NASA partnered with Marblar to provide entrepreneurs with the opportunity to profit from government research. This joint program empowers the crowdsourcing of products from forty of NASA's patents. NASA believes that if it opens up its discoveries to a global community, transformative commercial products will be created.

"Crowdsourcing has allowed NASA to tap into more than the usual suspects to get ideas and solutions that address an assortment of NASA needs," Jenn Gustetic, NASA's Prizes and Challenges Program executive, said in announcing the project. "Reaching out to innovators in a variety of fields through online crowdsourcing may provide a 21st century way for NASA to expand the reach of its technology portfolio for commercialization and use right here on Earth."[12]

In addition to NASA, Marblar makes available over $500 million worth of patents from top research institutions such as the University of Pennsylvania and the Electronics and Telecommunications Research Institute (ETRI). Anyone can access the technologies on Marblar and participate in their development—from initial concept through market research and technical feasibility. The more one participates in a project, the more "marbles" one earns. Marbles are the site's currency for determining final ownership and profit participation in the new business opportunities created. In May 2014, Samsung debuted a prototype for a wearable health monitor based on flexible personal sensors developed by Marblar. Dubbed the Simband, the Samsung smartwatch tracks heart rate, blood pressure, and electrocardiography in real time and may someday soon be able to predict a heart attack.[13]

CROWDSOURCE YOUR RESEARCH

Activating dormant science discoveries is just one way to disrupt the research link of the value chain. Another method is to crowdsource the research you need before anyone has even proved out the idea.

For those without a background in the sciences, Quirky helps anyone with a basic idea for a product crowdsource the entire value chain, from R & D through manufacturing to sales and marketing. By harnessing the skills of its half a million members, Quirky gives lone entrepreneurs a team dedicated to getting the best ideas to market quickly.

Jake Zien, a twenty-four-year-old designer, is the typical Quirky success story. Zien identified a simple problem that most of us face in this overly wired world: how to plug all of our gadgets into one compact power strip. Tired of fiddling under his desk trying to rearrange several chargers, Zien envisioned a flexible power strip with hinges that would bend to accommodate fat transformer plugs. With help from over seven hundred Quirky members, many of whom Zien had never met, the Pivot Power strip was created. To date, Pivot Power has sold over 750,000 units. After sharing the profits with Quirky and the community, Zien is on track to make over $1 million the first year from his idea.[14] One year, one idea, and the power of crowdsourcing and one disruptor makes one million dollars.

"It was Quirky that did the overwhelming majority of the work, and I see the product's success as a 'perfect storm' combination of factors, such as my timing in submitting the idea, rather than a complete testament to the quality of the submission," Zien says.[15]

Of the thousands of ideas submitted to the company's website each week, Quirky develops only three or four. The crowd decides which products get developed. The range of products incubated by Quirky truly matches its name. From a citrus spritzer that taps juice straight from a lemon and a squeezable egg separator for the kitchen to a customizable Swiss Army–style knife, Quirky products can now be found at Target, Bed Bath & Beyond, and Best Buy. Quirky is the brainchild of serial entrepreneur Ben Kaufman, the company's founder and CEO.

Instead of going to college, Ben convinced his parents to take out a second mortgage on their home to fund his first business, Mophie. Mophie, a maker of iPod and iPhone accessories, was so successful that *Inc.* magazine named Kaufman its number-one entrepreneur under thirty—when he was just twenty years old.[16] Today, Quirky's hundred-plus products are sold in over thirty-five thousand retail locations, and they generated over $50 million in sales in 2013.[17] Thanks to the speed and efficiencies of crowdsourcing research and development, Kaufman has taken development disruption mega-scale.

General Electric, one of America's oldest, most traditional companies, has recognized the potential for profit in partnering with an innovative startup like Quirky. In 2013, GE partnered with Quirky to allow the Quirky community access to GE's vast library of patents. One of the first products jointly developed by the two companies is the smartphone-enabled Egg Minder, which lets consumers know when eggs in their refrigerator are about to go bad. The Egg Minder, which debuted at a $79.99 suggested retail price, was marketed by GE as one of the first "Internet of Everything" products for the home.

Disrupting the research and development link doesn't have to mean inventing something new. Rather, the savvy disruptor will see how envisioning new purposes for products created by others opens up opportunity for profit. As the disruptors in this chapter have proved, the investments of others can always be leveraged by those able to see beyond the original scientific vision. All it takes to be successful is the ability to wade through the billions of dollars' worth of research with a fresh perspective. And now, thanks to the interconnected world of crowdsourcing, anyone can quickly and cost-effectively assemble a team to help bring their discoveries to market.

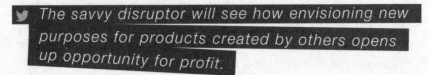

The savvy disruptor will see how envisioning new purposes for products created by others opens up opportunity for profit.

Chapter Ten

Design: Disruption Through Aesthetics

Design is where science and art break even.
—Robin Mathew

Think you can improve upon something already in existence? You are ready to disrupt the design link in the value chain. Michael Kors, Kate Spade, and Tory Burch didn't invent the handbag. Nike and Converse didn't invent the running shoe. Unlike innovators who try to disrupt through research and development and must find a new, previously unseen way to introduce something to the marketplace, design disruption focuses on the art of simply building something better. Most first-time entrepreneurs wrongly believe that they have to invent the next big thing in order to be successful. So many entrepreneurs have literally tried to "build a better mousetrap" that the U.S. Patent and Trademark Office has issued over 4,400 patents for mousetraps.[1] When our world was dominated by manufacturing businesses, innovation meant either inventing a new widget or engineering a more cost-effective way to manufacture an existing one. Yet in our interconnected mass-market world, even the smallest incremental improvement in design and manufacturing efficiency can yield billion-dollar results. When Nestlé Waters North America, maker of Arrowhead, Poland Springs, and Deer Park bottled water, reengineered its bottles to use 50 percent less resin, it not only saved millions of dollars on the twenty billion bottles it manufactures each year but also reduced its carbon footprint by 55 percent.[2] Oftentimes, the real disruption comes not from changes to the product itself but from innovations in packaging design. As with all disruption, design disruption comes from identifying problems where others failed to see a solution.

When I was a teenager, all motor oil came in big one-quart cylinders. These clumsy cans had tin tops and bottoms connected by cheap cardboard sides. For nearly half a century they were the only way to buy motor oil for your car. To open them, you savagely jammed an eight-inch spiked metal spout into the flimsy can and poured most of the contents into your engine. Inevitably, your hand slipped on the oily can and you painfully stabbed yourself while the oil dripped onto your engine block, your hands, and your shoes. If your car was down more than a quart, you had to yank out the sharp, slippery spike and hold a second quart steady in your oil-soaked hands to be stabbed again. Every car owner and every gas station used this same ridiculous method of getting oil from a container into a motor. With all motor oils being virtually identical in composition, Quaker State—the U.S. market leader—had a manufacturing advantage. Its factory had the largest, most advanced canning system in the world. Having invested millions in production, it could knock out more cans per hour than the next three competitors combined. While this reduced the cost per unit of its motor oil substantially, its huge investment in canning equipment locked the company into a set form of packaging. Quaker State had spent millions of dollars to buy its competitive advantage through superior means of production.

I guess someone over at Pennzoil saw the movie *The Graduate*. (For those who may have missed one of the best films of the twentieth century, it features a young college graduate named Benjamin Braddock, played by Dustin Hoffman, who is given advice by one of his parents' friends for making it in the business world: "I just want to say one word to you. Just one word . . . Are you listening? Plastics.") Unable to compete in the cardboard-and-tin-canning business, Pennzoil designed a plastic bottle in 1984. The bottle was cheaper to manufacture and easier to pour. You just untwisted the cap and poured the oil into the engine. The bottle was injection-molded from bright yellow plastic, which boldly stood out on store shelves. While Pennzoil's new, cheaper packaging improved the manufacturer's margins, it was met with resistance by service stations and automotive retailers because it didn't easily fit on the shelves with competing cans. Pennzoil gathered retailer and consumer feedback and continued to innovate and refine its packaging. It was determined to disrupt the market through innovative packaging design.

In 1986, Pennzoil opened its national sales meeting by unveiling a fifty-foot-tall inflatable blow-up of its new bottle, with the sales slogan "The Challenge of Change." Seriously: a generation ago, making a plastic bottle constituted innovation in American business. Since Pennzoil was fighting for limited shelf space, and retailers had thousands of SKUs to fit in their stores, Pennzoil designers had squared the bottle. The new bottle, which was similar to those used today, enabled retailers to put twice as many bottles in the same shelf space used to hold round cans. And because they were so compact, Pennzoil introduced a twenty-four-quart case that customers could easily throw in their trunks. Instead of stocking up on twelve cans, consumers began to buy twice the quantity. Sales of the squared plastic bottle soared. Based solely on its innovative design, Pennzoil disrupted the market and quickly became the number-one-selling motor oil in the United States—without reengineering its motor oil or changing its pricing. By 1998, the company that had introduced the square plastic bottle took over the lead, dominated the market, and merged with its onetime archrival Quaker State to form Pennzoil–Quaker State.[3]

While the plastic motor-oil bottle seems like an obvious improvement, it came about twenty years after shampoos had switched from glass bottles. In today's world, where every product comes with a lawyer-written warning label and fast-food restaurants are sued for serving hot coffee, it is hard to imagine that up until the mid-1960s, shampoo was sold in glass bottles. As a child, I lived in utter terror of dropping the shampoo bottle. Slippery, soapy bottles of glass being handled were constantly being dropped in hard-tiled showers and baths and shattering into a million clear shards that were indistinguishable from water droplets. Thousands of consumers cut themselves each year trying to pick up the pieces. Prell shampoo was the first to switch to plastic packaging, and it used television commercials to dramatize what happened when its bottle bounced off the shower floor.

Two important twenty-first-century lessons can be learned from these basic packaging examples. First, as Quaker State found out, no amount of capital can buy a long-term competitive advantage. According to Peter Senge, director of the Society for Organizational Learning at the MIT Sloan School of Management, "The only sustainable competitive advantage is an organization's ability to learn faster than the competition."[4] Having the largest investment in a given technology—in Quaker State's case, tin-and-cardboard can production—forced the corporation to amortize its investment over the long term. The company did not devote any additional resources to innovating in new areas of competitive advantage.

Second, it's often the case that the solution to one industry's problems already exists in another unrelated field. The surest path to finding a way to disrupt an existing value chain is to look beyond your industry and apply transformative insights from other businesses. Had one Quaker State executive used Prell shampoo, perhaps it would have dawned on him how packaging design could save the company.

DESIGN DISRUPTION THROUGH BRANDING

Disruption in design can be as simple as taking branding from a product in one market and applying it to another market. Instead of focusing on what is new about your improved product, turn the concept on its head. Leverage an existing brand to build on the established relationship consumers already have with the existing products that share the brand identity. Often referred to as brand extensions, this is an easy way to disrupt a category through design. When it's done well, you get products such as Reese's Peanut Butter and Chocolate Dessert Bar Mix or Arm & Hammer Advance White toothpaste. These new products seem familiar to the consumer because of the trust and reputation of the brand affiliation. The new products capitalize on brand goodwill and are quickly noticed on store shelves. When Deepak Chopra's son, Gotham, wanted to launch a new comic book line in a field crowded with dozens of publishers, he licensed a brand name already associated with creativity thanks to Sir Richard Branson, naming his company Virgin Comics. The young publisher gained quick distribution and sales because its consumer base related to the brand's rebel image. Branson has leveraged his brand name hundreds of times, embracing everything from Virgin Cola to Virgin Brides.

> Disruption in design can be as simple as taking branding from a product in one market and applying it to another market.

David Aaker, creator of the Aaker Model, has spent over twenty years studying and writing about the value established by brand equity. His research proves time and again that a new product that leverages an established brand's equity to enter the market benefits from reduced marketing costs. It also reassures potential customers who are familiar with the original brand and is immediately associated with quality. "A brand strategy can enable, sometimes crucially, the potential of an innovation to be realized," Aaker writes. "There are times when you literally need to brand it or lose it."[5]

When brand extensions are done poorly, however, you get such insanely bad ideas as Colgate's Kitchen Entrees (dinners that taste like toothpaste?), Frito Lay Lemonade, and my favorite, Bic Underwear. When Harley-Davidson tried launching a perfume line, I wondered, Who wants to smell like a motorcycle? The key is to license or partner with the right brand, one that will allow you to disrupt a category and grab market share. The fundamental principle behind successful brand extensions is tapping into consumers' feelings about the brand and matching your product to the attributes associated with the established brand. ESPN means sports to consumers in much the same way that Heinz is synonymous with ketchup, so it makes sense for ESPN to have a sports magazine and for Heinz to make pickle relish.

I learned the value of partnership and the power of leveraging brand recognition to launch a new product early in my career. In 1993, my startup software company, Jasmine Multimedia Publishing, had fewer than a dozen employees and none of the connections I needed to enter the big leagues. I had raised a few hundred thousand dollars to publish CD-ROMs, and our products were winning awards and being used by tens of thousands of business professionals, but I dreamed of creating consumer titles that could sell in the millions. My big break came when I figured out how to hire a billionaire and a dozen rock stars without spending one thin dime.

I had founded Jasmine to create a new form of video entertainment that combined the interactivity made possible by the personal computer with the immersive imagery of full-motion video. We were publishing interactive video that branched from one scene to another, which allowed for a new storytelling experience. In the early days of video on computers, this was groundbreaking work, but I knew we could do more. I wanted people to be able to actually get inside each frame and play with the video image itself. At the time, PC video games were mostly simplistic 2-D graphics with a limited selection of sound effects. I was imagining creating real immersive and interactive video games that popular audiences could play on their computers.

Jasmine had been working with Microsoft on the development of Video for Windows (which Microsoft released as a dual-logoed product, with our name *proudly* displayed in barely visible two-point type). We discovered that we could cut up the moving picture of a video into a checkerboard grid and then move the individual pieces around. As the small squares moved around the board, each piece continued to play at a full thirty frames per second. When we cut up the video into a five-by-five grid, putting a twenty-five-piece video back together became a pretty challenging game. The shorter the video clip, the quicker you had to solve the puzzle. The more edits in the video, the harder it was to beat the clock. In 1993, at the height of MTV and the music video, it didn't take us long to realize that a puzzle game made of music videos would be a colossal hit. If we had the greatest bands and the best music videos, we would have the biggest chart-topping game in our company's history. Just two small obstacles stood in my way: I didn't know a soul in the record industry, and I had no money to pay the bands for their participation.

This idea for a music video game was a decade before *Guitar Hero*. Back in the 1990s, the video game industry and the world of rock and roll had nothing in common. Video games sounded like electronic beeps, blips, and boinks, and record companies didn't have licensing departments that knew how to cut a deal for their acts to appear in a video game. And even if we found one band or label that would give us a music video from which we could make our first game, it might take years before we could possibly sign real rock stars or negotiate with music publishers. And even if we did resolve all of these business issues, fewer than a million American households had a personal computer with enough speed and RAM to play our game.

I realized that I needed to find a way for my big idea to solve someone else's problems. The computer industry needed to sell more Americans computers. Microsoft needed to get more consumers onto its operating system. Since our technology worked only on a Windows PC, our game would make Microsoft's new video technology cool. I realized that this was how I was going to get Bill Gates to help me. I had developed something that benefited him, his company, and the entire industry. So I sent an email to Gates, asking if he would write a letter of introduction for me to music mogul David Geffen. At that point in my career, I had never met Bill Gates, but I had nothing to lose, and Microsoft had a lot to gain. I should say that there were a number of heroes inside Microsoft who championed our cause, including a very persuasive multimedia general manager named Melinda French. Unbeknownst to me at the time, Melinda was dating Bill and would marry him the following year. I got lucky; luck plays a big role in success. But as the old saying goes, "The harder I work, the luckier I get." Gates graciously sent David Geffen a letter of introduction and mailed me a copy.

🐦 *"The harder I work, the luckier I get."*

As you can imagine, when the richest man in the world sends a letter suggesting you meet someone, you take the meeting—even if you are a billionaire in your own right. Soon enough, I had an appointment on

Geffen's calendar. Geffen had started his first music label, Asylum Records, in 1970. He signed Jackson Browne, the Eagles, Joni Mitchell, and Linda Ronstadt and owned the California sound being created in the 1970s. A decade later, he started Geffen Records, which would release albums from John Lennon, Guns N' Roses, Sir Elton John, and Cher. Geffen was the first person in history (Sir Richard Branson would later be the second) to sell a music label for over $1 billion. David was at the pinnacle of his music career when he agreed to take a meeting with me. But at that time, he had never used a computer or played a single video game.

I am not the nervous type. Outwardly, I treat bartenders and billionaires, postmen and popes, the same. As my mother would say, "They all put their shoes on one foot at a time." But inside, I was a wreck. This was one of those life-changing meetings. If I blew it, I couldn't go back to Bill Gates and ask him for another letter. This was my make-it-or-break-it moment. I had a working demo of the game. I wore my best tie and sport jacket. (To be honest, I think it was my only sport jacket.) The morning of our meeting, my business partner, Lenny Lebowitz, and I drove over to Geffen's offices on Sunset. The meeting was in full swing when I noticed Lenny staring at my shoes. I kept demonstrating the game but saw Lenny making an odd face. When I finally looked down, I discovered that I was wearing two different shoes. Somehow in my nervousness when I got dressed that morning, I had managed to walk out of the house with one lace-up shoe and one loafer!

I had brought along a poster from one of our distributors showing that Jasmine Multimedia Publishing had produced seven of the top-ten-selling CD-ROMs in the country. In our own minds, we were to the nascent computer software industry what Geffen Records had been to the music industry: a gutsy little startup upstaging the big guys. I offered Geffen, for no money or financial risk on his part, a 50 percent ownership of what we believed would be our bestselling title of all time. I would pay all the costs and assume all the risk, while he would get half of all the profits. This got his attention. All I wanted in exchange was ten music videos to put into our CD-ROM game. My offer, however, came with one caveat: the music videos couldn't be just from Geffen Records acts. For our game to be huge, I needed the ten biggest acts from across the entire music industry. It took guts to tell the most successful man in the history of music that his label's roster of talent wasn't big enough for our game, but I had one shot, and I decided to go big or go home. Whatever Geffen did or did not know about computer software, he knew what made a hit. If he was going to own half of this game, he too wanted the biggest acts in the world to be part of it. As they said in *The Godfather*, I "made him an offer he couldn't refuse." Just as I had done with Bill Gates, I made the success of my product important to David Geffen and the music industry. We could prove that video games could become a new source of revenue for artists, and David Geffen wanted to be the first to open up to this new revenue stream.

Geffen and I made a deal. In reality, I had given away nothing. Without those music videos, I had no product. It was a no-brainer to give Geffen 50 percent of our potential profit—100 percent of nothing is nothing, but 50 percent of something can be worth millions. I hold strongly to the belief that I'd rather own half of the Pacific Ocean than all of Lake Erie.

> 🐦 100% of nothing is nothing, but 50% of something can be worth millions. I'd rather own half of the Pacific Ocean than all of Lake Erie.

To get the artists and their management to sign off on the game, I traveled around doing demonstrations for the bands and their managers. Steven Tyler and Joe Perry loved the game so much, they agreed to be in the television commercial for free. This might have just been smart marketing on their part to get more exposure for their new music video, "Cryin'," but to me it was incredibly generous.

Chasing down the other potential acts for the game was a challenge in itself. Whenever I got word that an act—or their management— was in Los Angeles, I drove over and demonstrated the game. As buzz built around the project, managers were eager to get their bands into the game, but word got out that the CD-ROM compression technology could accommodate only ten videos. With only a few slots remaining, one manager was so committed to getting her act onto the game that she personally drove over to our Van Nuys offices to deliver the video-tape. Sharon Osbourne personally handed me a master tape for "No More Tears," assuring her husband, Ozzy, a spot in the game.

At the time, Soundgarden, which had just released *Superunknown,* was the hottest band around, and I was told it would be a huge score if we could get them and fellow Seattle band Nirvana. Including grunge would ensure that gamers would love the product. The folks at Geffen told me Soundgarden was shooting a new music video at the A&M lot in Hollywood and I could set up the game for them to see on their break. I was really never into the whole grunge/alt-rock made popular by Nirvana's *Nevermind* and Pearl Jam's *Ten.* In fact, prior to driving across town, I had never heard of Soundgarden. But when the coolest guys at the coolest label tell you Soundgarden is the band to get, you listen.

I raced over to the stage with a large desktop computer and a bulky seventeen-inch CRT monitor, a mouse, an external amp, a Bose sub-woofer, and speakers. The security guard had me park at the other end of the lot, far from the soundstage, so I would have to make tons of trips back and forth to set up the computer gear. Luckily, this nice young guy who was hanging around the soundstage offered to carry all my gear so that I could concentrate on setting up the equipment. I wanted to make sure the game looked and sounded fantastic. The guy seemed to know a bit about computers and was so helpful that I let him play the game as we waited for the band to go on break. He got hooked playing, quickly rising through the levels, and I stared anxiously at my watch. The band was going to be here any second, and he had been play-ing for twenty minutes. Politely, I thanked him for all his help but told him he had to leave so that I could be ready when the band came. He told me how much he enjoyed our game, but he understood and left, smiling. Not five minutes later, he returned with a bunch of other guys and introduced himself to me. "I'm Chris Cornell," he said, "and we are Soundgarden."

We named the sliding puzzle game *Vid Grid,* and Geffen more than lived up to his end of the deal. When we shipped the game to retailers a few months later, it included music videos from Metallica, Aerosmith, Guns N' Roses, Soundgarden, Jimi Hendrix, Peter Gabriel, Van Halen, Ozzy Osbourne, the Red Hot Chili Peppers, and Nirvana. (After Kurt Cobain's suicide, we decided to move "Smells like Teen Spirit" to a hidden bonus level so as not to exploit his death.) *Vid Grid* debuted at Comdex to rave reviews and generated press beyond our wildest dreams. We won numerous awards and launched the relationship between the music and video game industries that continues to this day. As computer and game console sound systems improved, more video games came to have real soundtracks. The little company that I had started with only a box of business cards had earned a spot in the major leagues. After more than a dozen years in business, I was finally an overnight success.

Every company can't go after every market niche, but there are plenty of trusted brands that can easily be licensed by entrepreneurs introducing new products or product categories. Through partnerships and licensing, disruptors can save the millions of dollars it takes to establish a new brand and allow entrepreneurs to focus their limited resources on building a better product.

DESIGN DISRUPTION THROUGH CUSTOMER EXPERIENCE

In the digital age, disruption through design doesn't have to be as complex as leveraging a brand's equity in a thoughtful partnership; it can be as easy as simply rethinking the user interface of a website. A great example of this is how the first generation of digital travel agencies—the disruptors that put the brick-and-mortar travel agents out of business—were bested by a design team focused on a great consumer experience and a clean user interface.

One of the first value chains shattered by the Internet was travel. The advent of Expedia, Priceline, Orbitz, and Travelocity wiped out the independent travel agency business. Before the Internet, consumers had to call or go into a travel agent's office to find out about travel packages, flights, or even hotel rates. With the Internet, millions of consumers could use self-service sites to book flights, make hotel reservations, and even rent cars. The shift to online booking happened nearly overnight. By 2010, bookings with the online travel agencies (OTAs) exceeded $300 billion and showed no signs of slowing down.[6] How could the multi-billion-dollar online travel agency ecosystem—an industry that was itself recently built by disruptors—be disrupted? The answer: through design.

Anyone who's ever booked online knows that most of the travel sites are difficult to use and aren't especially consumer-centric. The original OTAs based all of their booking systems on the same interfaces used by the professional travel agents, rather than reimagining the process from a consumer's point of view. Finding the right flight was sheer torture. But one man's problem is another's opportunity.

Two serial disruptors, Reddit cofounder Steve Huffman and Book-Tour cofounder Adam Goldstein, founded Hipmunk in 2010 to solve travel agony. The user experience was clean and visual. Travelers could visually see each possible flight as a color-coded bar, and the information could be customized with one click. Hipmunk allows travelers to sort flights by price, schedule, and "agony." In Hipmunk-speak, agony is the combination of price, flight duration, number of stops, and flight times. For business travelers like me (who make up the majority of all tickets purchased online), agony is more important than price alone. Hipmunk built an agony algorithm to help travelers find the easiest routes. Because I regularly fly in excess of 100,000 miles per year, the moment I used Hipmunk was love at first sight. I wasn't alone in valuing design function. After less than a year in business, *Time* magazine named Hipmunk one of "The 50 Best Websites of 2011."[7]

Beyond the Rack, the innovative Web retailer that specializes in flash sales for its members, looked at its data and saw a need to vastly improve its mobile design. Since 2009, the online private shopping club had focused its business on desktop and simply mirrored the experience on mobile phones and tablets. BTR's data showed that mobile customers had the lowest conversion rate. The company committed to making 2012 its "Year of Mobile" and doubled its sales simply by redesigning its app.[8]

Disrupting the design link in the value chain can come from designing a better product or a clever interface, or through brand extension. Design is crucial to how products are perceived by consumers; it determines how users feel about a product. Poor design presents a world of opportunity for disruptors looking to make their mark without having to invent or introduce a new product to the world.

> Poor design is an opportunity for disruptors looking to make their mark without having to invent or introduce a new product to the world.

Chapter Eleven

Production: Reuse, Repurpose, Re-create

*Innovation is taking two things that already exist
and putting them together in a new way.*
—Tom Freston, former president and CEO of MTV

Two hundred and fifty years after the birth of the industrial revolution, hasn't every innovation in manufacturing already been implemented? How can a small startup possibly disrupt the production link of the value chain? How can a modern factory compete with the low-cost industrial complexes found in China? How can one possibly disrupt production?

While we feel as though we live in the postindustrial age, most of the items we purchase, wear, and consume are manufactured in factories overseas. Factories haven't stopped making things; it's just that in America we have stopped making factories. Even if the raw materials for our goods come from America (cotton, iron, wood), production has migrated to countries with cheaper labor. Many of the largest factories in America's industrial centers sit idle and rusting. Reversing this trend in outsourced production requires another form of disruption.

There is a difference between economic transformation in a global economy and disruption. In a free market economy, there will always be a cheaper labor market to outsource manufacturing to, but the endless shifting of factories around the globe isn't a viable long-term solution. As developing economies increase the standard of living for their skilled workers, costs go up and jobs shift to less mature economies. Disruptors need not tackle the systemic problem of labor supply and demand. Value that can be captured from production can be disintermediated from a labor force. Just as the creation of synthetic diamonds would replace the need for a massive mining workforce, postindustrial production is shifting the location and definition of the modern factory. Disruption in the production of physical goods is bringing jobs back to America and other developed economies by reinventing how manufacturing is being interpreted. The assembly line approach to production pioneered by Henry Ford over a century ago for the 1913 Model T assumed that an efficient industrial production line required access to workers. Large cities like Detroit grew because large factories required access to large populations of workers. The era of mass production enabled cost efficiencies to bring thousands of new innovations to the masses. But mass-manufacturing an identical product to a world made up of billions of individual consumers is not the only way to imagine production. To disrupt production, and capture value, one must look to on-demand manufacturing. This idea isn't new; it is just being newly empowered by changes in technology.

> To disrupt production, and capture value, one must look to on-demand manufacturing.

One of my favorite examples of disruption through production happened over five hundred years ago. In the Middle Ages, very few people knew how to read or write, because books were incredibly expensive. All manuscripts were handwritten by scribes, and it took months to make copies. With such a scarcity of talent, only those books deemed essential were ever reproduced. Centuries' worth of human knowledge was trapped in the few private libraries of church and royal leaders. But while the book business was virtually nonexistent, wine making was a hearty industry.

In the late Middle Ages, Germany's Rhineland region was prospering. Thanks to the efficiency of the mechanical screw press, fifteenth-century vintners could make more wine with less labor than ever before. The screw press, which had been used to make olive oil for nearly a millennium, was adapted by Germans and modified for viticulture. Smaller growers, with fewer workers, could make more wine, more cheaply. The result: everyone was making Rieslings, and there were a lot of drunken Germans. By the year 1500, German vineyards covered four times more land than they do today, to serve a population of twelve million, as compared with today's population of eighty-two million.[1] The bacchanalia didn't last long. Overproduction led to oversupply. Oversupply reduced the value of the wines, and most winemakers went out of business. Thousands of used screw presses were available, and a young Rhineland disruptor named Johannes Gutenberg figured out how to solve the problems of one industry with the detritus of another. Why not use the wine press to automate printing with movable type? Had the wine market not imploded, had he not been able to purchase the used industrial equipment so cheaply, Gutenberg's Bible would not have come to be.

Gutenberg's printing press made books affordable to the masses and disrupted the ruling class's control over the dissemination of knowledge. Within fifty years of its creation, printing presses in Europe had churned out more than twenty million volumes on a wide range of subjects, spreading the newfound knowledge of the Renaissance.[2] This one simple invention so transformed the structure of the Western world that by 1620 the English writer Francis Bacon, who penned the famous aphorism "Knowledge is power," wrote:

> Printing, gunpowder and the compass: These three have changed the whole face and state of things throughout the world; the first in literature, the second in warfare, the third in navigation; whence have followed innumerable changes, in so much that no empire, no sect, no star seems to have exerted greater power and influence in human affairs than these mechanical discoveries.[3]

DISRUPTION THROUGH PRODUCTION AND THE CREATION OF NEW BUSINESS MODELS

Gutenberg not only invented a printing press—he created the entire publishing business model. Instead of every new book being a custom work for hire, works could be commissioned once and sold multiple times. When I began Jasmine Productions as a work-for-hire interactive video producer, I was no different from the scribes of old. I made money only when I was creating a custom training video for a corporate customer. When Nissan or Merle Norman Cosmetics hired us to make a video, we made money. If no one hired us, my production company sat idle. One day it dawned on me (albeit five hundred years after Gutenberg) to turn my little company into a publisher and unlock previously unnoticed production value.

With the federal government's breakup of AT&T's monopoly in 1982, each of the Baby Bells had to find new vendors for all of its various corporate needs. Pacific Bell, one of the companies created out of the breakup of AT&T, needed to hire and train an entirely new staff without access to any of AT&T's resources. To fill this void, Jasmine Productions created a custom interactive laserdisc course to teach defensive driving skills to Pacific Bell's thousands of field staff. Pac Bell employees drove over a hundred million miles a year for the company, and reducing accidents would save the company millions of dollars in workers' compensation claims, vehicle repairs, and increased productivity. The telecommunications company had used linear videotapes in the past, but by testing each driver individually during the course— interactivity enabled only by a laserdisc—the company could be assured that everyone was learning the lesson's material. If a driver answered a question incorrectly, he was immediately given remedial instruction. Self-paced learning meant that while some drivers took twice as long to get through the course, everyone left knowing 100 percent of the information. The results of having all their drivers take the refresher driving course were truly astounding. Pacific Bell cut its accident rate in half, and because the company was self-insured, it saved a small fortune.

As excited and proud as I was of this achievement, it didn't mean a penny more in revenue for Jasmine Productions. Once again, we had created new value for our customer without capturing any of that financial reward for our bottom line. The biggest flaw of this B2B work-for-hire business model was that each production was created as a one-off to fit the needs of the specific corporation that hired us. We made a profit on that single production, and that was it. Our driving course, which was produced for around $150,000, was providing tremendous value for Pacific Bell, but Jasmine wasn't profiting from any of the value we had created.

The solution was simple, and a variant of what had led me to originally contact Ford in the early days of my company. I could turn Pacific Bell's corporate training department into a profit center by licensing back the course from Pac Bell and selling copies to other companies with fleets of drivers. Unlike with Ford, which had taken a leap of faith in hiring us, this course had proved itself over millions of miles and thousands of drivers. If I could license it with the Pacific Bell name attached, the course had brand recognition as well. I didn't have to sell anyone on the merits of the course because of the trusted values imbued by the name on the packaging. I didn't face the startup challenge of explaining why our product was good; I only had to show customers how their organization had the same needs as the telephone company that had already benefited by using our product. Surely Federal Express, UPS, DHL, state highway patrols, police departments, and school and municipal bus companies could all similarly benefit from this branded content. So Jasmine Productions pivoted and became Jasmine Multimedia Publishing. Our professional courses led us to publish more consumer "edutainment" titles, and within the year our products were sold at CompUSA, Circuit City, Fry's, Tower, and hundreds of other retailers across the country. We had recognized that in order for innovation to be successful, it has to be about not just value creation, but value capture. We had disrupted corporate training with better technology, but we'd disrupted the production value chain by creating branded corporate courseware. Thanks to the publishing business model, for the first time in my life I was making money even when I wasn't working.

> 🐦 *For innovation to be successful, it has to be about not just value creation, but value capture.*

DISRUPTION THROUGH PRODUCTION AND THE RISE OF 3-D PRINTING

Gutenberg has another lesson to teach the world about production. What happens when everyone can become not just a publisher of ideas but also a manufacturer of finished products? The biggest revolution in production since the dawn of the industrial age is happening around the world with a new take on the classic Gutenberg printing press. Today's printing press, the 3-D printer, can manufacture anything one can imagine.

The 3-D printer is shattering the existing value chain for physical goods the way the Internet destroyed the value chains for intellectual digital goods such as music, movies, and books. Camera parts and pharmaceuticals can be downloaded and printed as quickly and easily as a song. Any physical item can be produced anywhere, at any time. Mass production is being disrupted on a massive scale. Never has so much manufacturing capacity been available to so many people. The McKinsey Global Institute estimates that 3-D printing will impact over 320 million manufacturing jobs globally.[4] The opportunities for disruption abound in countless fields.

In much the same way that the personal computer industry grew out of a group of geeky hobbyists, 3-D printing is emerging from the open-source RepRap project, which was founded in 2005 by British mechanical engineer Adrian Bowyer and is quickly becoming a billion-dollar on-demand manufacturing industry.[5] Initially costing tens of thousands of dollars to build, today's RepRap-designed 3-D printers can be constructed from $500 worth of parts. (Inventor Afate Gnikou, Africa's version of MacGyver, has even built a working 3-D printer from electronic waste and parts he found in Nigerian scrapyards.[6]) By being able to manufacture on-site one-off designs, 3-D printing is poised to disrupt everything from prototyping automotive parts inventory and space station repairs to custom toys and clothing. Printers are already being created that print in plastic, metal, chocolate, and even living human tissue. In 2014, startup Local Motors 3-D-printed, in forty-four hours, a working automobile dubbed the Strati, which consisted of fewer than fifty parts. The electric vehicle can reach fifty miles per hour and cover up to sixty-two miles per charge.[7] Disruptors are launching businesses to create everything from lifesaving artificial human organs to deadly weaponry.

3-D printers grabbed global headlines when "the Liberator," the first 3-D-printed all-plastic gun, was demonstrated in a YouTube video in 2013.[8] More than 100,000 copies of the gun's model were downloaded before the federal government forced the gun's inventor to take down the plans. "Significant advances in three-dimensional (3D) printing capabilities, availability of free digital 3D printer files for firearms components, and difficulty regulating file sharing may present public

JAY SAMIT

safety risks from unqualified gun seekers who obtain or manufacture 3D printed guns," warned a federal report, adding, "Limiting access may be impossible."[9]

The disruption to the production link caused by the 3-D printer will destroy many traditional manufacturing value chains while giving birth to an entirely new series of specialized industries. Moving from home-hobbyist experiment to a mass-market, Internet-enabled appliance, MakerBot introduced the Replicator2 in 2012, with a retail price of only $2,200. Companies such as Bukobot, Gigabot, Printbot, TangiBot, and Ultra-Bot quickly copied MakerBot's success.[10] Many of these startups went after specific subgenres of 3-D printing and raised their capital from crowdfunding sites such as Kickstarter. Jumping on this exploding market, Staples became the first major U.S. retailer to carry 3-D printers when it started selling 3D Systems' Cube for $1,300 in 2013.[11]

As with all disruptive technologies, a whole new ecosystem of opportunity will develop around the new equipment. Think of all the new industries that the personal computer gave rise to thirty years ago. 3-D printing will launch a wave of disruptive innovation around shared 3-D models, collaborative design software, and printing materials. Websites are popping up offering to replicate objects out of resin, plastic, ceramic, and silver. Lifestock is a startup that 3-D-prints slaughter-free synthetically produced meat at one-fortieth the cost of current culture methods.[12] Even the president of the United States acknowledges the disruptive power of these new printers. "A once-shuttered warehouse is now a state-of-the-art lab where new workers are mastering the 3-D printing that has the potential to revolutionize the way we make almost everything," President Barack Obama declared in his 2013 State of the Union address, adding that with congressional help we can "guarantee that the next revolution in manufacturing is made in America."[13]

One of my fellow USC professors, Behrokh Khoshnevis, is using 3-D printing to disrupt the construction industry. Khoshnevis, who teaches industrial and systems engineering, has built the world's first large-scale 3-D printer that is capable of building a 2,500-square-foot house in a single day. His technology, known as Contour Crafting, replaces construction workers with a computer-enabled robotic gantry and a concrete-squirting nozzle. By removing most of the labor costs associated with home building, the professor envisions a world where inexpensive 3-D-printed homes can be used to improve the unsanitary living conditions of the nearly one billion people living in slums.[14] 3-D-printed buildings also solve the challenges of construction in harsh or remote environments. NASA's Desert Research and Technology Studies is studying ways of adapting Contour Crafting for extraterrestrial applications such as using large-scale 3-D printers to construct buildings on the moon or Mars. The opportunities for 3-D printing are both expanding and contracting our world.

3-D printing allows consumers to have greater customization of the products they order. Entrepreneurs are cashing in on this desire with on-demand manufacturing of shoes, jewelry, and even furniture. For the first time in history, anyone can now *own* the means of production. Virtual factories can give the solo designer all the "tooling" of a major factory without any of the overhead expense. Everyone has the power to compete on a global scale without having to raise millions of dollars for equipment and tooling.

> Everyone has the power to compete on a global scale without having to raise millions of dollars for equipment and tooling.

Companies such as Sculpteo, Shapeways, and Ponoko leverage a network of other entrepreneurs that own specific pieces of manufacturing equipment to enable distributed production. Ponoko's free downloadable software connects designers with a "Licensed Personal Factory" to offer online laser-cutting services in the United States, Europe, and New Zealand. The company links creators with material suppliers and digital fabricators in a seamless way, where it used to require a team of specialists and huge inventory costs. With the expensive barriers to entry removed, more entrepreneurs are able to bring their products to market without having to raise the massive amounts of capital required for a traditional factory's infrastructure.

The personal factory system democratizes the marketplace so that size is no longer an advantage. Designers can use social media to market their creations and manufacture items only after they are purchased. A personal factory is by definition profitable from its very first sale.

Taking this disruptive concept further, Ponoko markets the designs of the independent creators so that others can manufacture and retail the new products. A great designer might not also be a great marketer. Just as technology transfer of research opened the door for creative disruptors to benefit from existing patents, Ponoko is opening the door for marketers to bring finished goods to new verticals. Anyone can peruse the thousands of items created by the Ponoko community and bring them to their local market. Everything from modernist foam lampshades to coffee tables is available as a "digital product" for sale on its site.

Most manufactured goods today face the costs and constraints associated with managing their supply chain and inventory. Stockpiling materials, parts, and packaging tie up valuable capital that could be better deployed generating more sales or developing new products. Given how rapidly the 3-D-printing market is evolving, it is important to understand how these changes can and will affect the launch of every production.

Just as Netflix embraced the mailing of millions of DVDs while waiting for consumers to catch up with the concept of watching Internet "flix" (streaming content), a smart disruptor may have to develop a hybrid strategy for employing traditional manufacturing and on-demand production in concert. As the cost of custom printing continues to quickly decrease, the transition to on-demand will become more cost-effective for a wider range of products. Being ahead of this curve is the best way to disrupt this link of the value chain.

One note of caution: such rapid disruptions in production are quickly outpacing the way governments and established businesses think about intellectual property, patents, trademarks, and copyrights. Some countries recognize design patents, while others don't. In a borderless networked world, it will become increasingly hard to protect ownership of investments in intellectual property. Pirated goods can be produced in any place that has an Internet connection and a 3-D printer. Just as Napster challenged many of our assumptions about file sharing, 3-D printing will have an impact on our laws governing copyright, homeland security, trademark, and trade secrets for decades to come. As with all economic disruption, many companies that rely on the existing production ecosystem are destined to go the way of the music labels if they continue to cling to old legal constructs and fail to adapt to the new world of digital production. Those who recognize the inevitability of such changes stand to benefit the most.

> *Those who recognize the inevitability of changes stand to benefit the most.*

Chapter Twelve

Marketing and Sales: Finding the Problem to Fit Your Solution

Everyone lives by selling something.
—Robert Louis Stevenson

When I was in high school, I sold shirts at the swap meet on the weekends. I had worked out a deal with a local shirtmaker to sell its factory seconds on consignment. Some days I sold a bunch, other days I would stand there bored in the sun. Trying to come up with a better way to drum up sales, each week I would make a new sign on poster board. I looked at other traditional retailers and tried to copy what I saw in real stores. ON SALE. HALF OFF. JUST IN TIME FOR SUMMER. Nothing really made a difference, until one day, out of boredom and as a joke, I made a sign that read, SHIRTS $1.50 EACH OR 3 FOR $5. Business boomed. I quickly sold out of my shirts as most people went for the value of three for $5. Not a single person that weekend stopped and asked me if they could just buy three for $4.50, since the regular price was $1.50 per shirt. And that was how I learned what's at the heart of all sales and marketing: creating demand even in the absence of logic.

> 🐦 *What's at the heart of all sales and marketing: creating demand even in the absence of logic.*

But you don't need gimmicks or tricks to disrupt the entire process of sales and marketing. For example, people hate waiting in lines to check out at retail, so Apple Stores reimagined the consumer experience, designing their stores without cash registers or checkout lines. Priceline became a $60 billion company by empowering consumers to "name your own price."[1] Jay Walker and Michael Loeb looked at the steep drop-off rates magazines faced annually when consumers were asked to renew their subscriptions. Seeing that magazines had become not so much a disposable product as a content service for consumers, they invented the continuous magazine subscription, which charged users monthly like a cable company. Walker and Loeb formed Synapse and quickly grew to thirty million subscribers.[2]

Andrew Mason disrupted retail sale pricing by creating ThePoint.com, a website that allowed consumers to sign up to purchase items at a group discount. If enough people signed up to buy pizzas from the same pizzeria on the same night, everyone got a discount. The concept proved so successful with Chicago consumers that the company expanded nationally, under the name Groupon. Hewlett-Packard, faced with ever-growing offshore competition for cheaper printers, completely disrupted its model of making money on hardware and decided to sell printers as a loss leader in order to make its profit on toner. HP's toner is now more expensive than Chanel No. 5 perfume.[3] Switching from a razors model to a razorblade model thrust the company's growth into overdrive.

Disrupting the sales link of the value chain is really about deciding what business your company or your product is in. Recognizing the value that can be both created and captured through creative pricing models can disrupt any business sector. In the 1950s, the Haloid Company developed the technology to make photocopiers. The $4,000 copier machines appeared doomed from the start, since they couldn't compete with the cheap carbon paper used by most office typists. Haloid's disruptive move was to own the machines and sell five-cent copies. Haloid became Xerox—a name that is still synonymous with copying fifty years later.[4] The challenge is not in coming up with a new and creative marketing campaign, but rather in developing completely new sales strategies, channels, and business models. Differentiation of the sales model can be as powerful as differentiation of the product itself.

SALES DISRUPTION ON AIR

One of my favorite examples of disruption in the sales link comes from Clearwater, Florida. Radio stations sell advertising. That business model has been etched in stone since Hawthorne Court Apartments ran the first-ever commercial on New York station WEAF in 1922. But how can a radio station make money when its advertisers can't afford to advertise?

In 1977, WWQT 1470 AM station manager Lowell "Bud" Paxson, in Clearwater, Florida, was faced with a problem when his station had an advertiser with plenty of manufactured inventory but no money left to pay for its radio spots. Figuring he had nothing to lose, Paxson told his afternoon talk show host to get on the airwaves and sell the $20 avocado-green electric can openers live on the air for the special price of only $9.95. There was no pick-pack-and-ship department at WWQT, so listeners were instructed to come down to the radio station with cash or certified checks to pick up their appliances. Within the first hour, the station sold out of all 112 can openers, and a new industry was born. Instead of just selling ads, Paxson discovered he could make more money by changing the station's sales model. A radio station could become a direct marketer and retailer. Paxson disrupted the sales channel. He and his financial partner, Roy Speer, realized they could sell much more product if only they had visuals for consumers at home to see the products. Television, which also had until then focused solely on the advertising sales model, was the logical next step. The two men founded a local cable TV channel and launched the Home Shopping Club (later renamed Home Shopping Network).

"I want to be the United States Post Office of eyeballs," Paxson proudly told *The New York Times* in an interview.[5] Today, HSN employs approximately 6,700 employees, generates over $3 billion in sales annually, and reaches 95 million households.[6] Paxson didn't invent television, but he reinvented its business model and created an entirely new industry. Retailing on television has earned Paxson a personal fortune estimated at over $400 million.[7] Not a bad financial return for a local Florida AM radio spot advertising an electric can opener.

DISRUPTING THE SALES LINK THROUGH PRICING

Disrupting the sales link involves rethinking how an item is priced as much as how it is sold. As I learned when I sold my T-shirts at the swap meet, changing how an item is priced can yield great returns.

How much elasticity is there in the pricing of any item? By now most consumers have accepted the fact that we pay variable pricing for items such as airplane tickets and hotel rooms. Airlines have sophisticated algorithms that can dynamically change a specific flight's cost based on demand, seasonality, availability of aircraft, past purchasing history, and a host of other factors. In fact, some websites will even cookie your computer and raise the cost of a ticket when you return an hour later to buy the flight you were previously considering. In 2008, Amazon endured the wrath of its most loyal customers when it was discovered that Amazon Prime customers were charged more for certain products than people who rarely shopped on the site.[8] Amazon's data revealed that its best customers weren't price-comparison shopping and took advantage of that fact, until the retailer got caught.

Many startup disruptors are taking this same concept of dynamic pricing to brick-and-mortar retailers, thanks to a range of new disruptive technologies. Radio-frequency identification (RFID) tags are inexpensive stickers that can communicate an object's location or its proximity to customers or other devices. In much the way that bar codes made it easier for retailers to know what products were selling, RFID can communicate with a smartphone to alert a customer of a promotion, track special merchandise, or use big data to create variable pricing. If you are standing in the printer aisle of your electronics retailer, technology exists to track how long you are in the proximity of the products and to query Hewlett-Packard in real time to see if they want to offer you a $10 coupon to close the sale.[9] In the very near future, two shoppers whose carts are full of the same items at a supermarket might pay dramatically different prices based on the purchasing history of each individual shopper.

But what if a retailer did away with the entire concept of setting a retail price? In one of the most disruptive sales models, penny auction sites are letting consumers name their own price for dozens of luxury items. While this business model appears to be a variant of Priceline's name-your-price concept, it is actually a clever pay-to-bid model. Unlike eBay, where only successful bidders pay for the items they purchase, penny auction sites charge users for each bid they place. Whether or not consumers are successful in winning the item, a user is charged a small fee every time he or she tries to bid for a product.

Bids on these sites are sold in bulk, from a few cents to as much as a dollar per bid. By factoring in the revenue from losing bidders, penny auction sites can advertise name-brand electronics and other items for up to 95 percent off manufacturer's suggested retail prices. A $500 iPad sold for only a dollar may generate 3,600 bids and garner $2,000 in revenue. While sites like Beezid continue to advertise iPads that have been won for as little as 83 cents, several state attorney generals have filed complaints, and the Federal Trade Commission has even issued an alert. The line between clever and fraudulent gets muddied as new business models are explored. Class action lawsuits will decide whether these sites are scams or just a fun form of gambling, but, either way, the millions of dollars generated by penny auction sites prove how the sales link can be disrupted with a little creativity.

DISRUPTING THE SALES LINK THROUGH CONTENT

On the marketing side, the biggest form of disruption is in the area of branded entertainment. The line between what is programming content and what is a commercial has become increasingly blurry. While consumers are fast-forwarding through the commercials, brands are getting more and more aggressive with product placement and integrated marketing. Ever notice how perfectly lit that SUV is on your favorite police show? Or how every character on your favorite prime time drama seems to be using the latest mobile phone or portable electronic device? Branded content is now a key revenue driver for film, television, and online video content. Brand Finance chief executive David Haigh estimated that Red Bull's video of Felix Baumgartner's record-breaking twenty-four-mile free fall from space, which was watched live around the world, generated at least $5 billion worth of brand value.[10]

Creating branded content for your new product or service is very simple. The more you know about your potential customer, the easier it is to identify opportunities to utilize branded content. My go-to right-hand man at three of my most successful ventures has been a genius creative marketing officer named Larry Lieberman. When I tapped him to be CMO for ooVoo, I knew we needed a breakthrough way to stand out from the competition.

Engineers at ooVoo had built an amazing multiparty video-chat platform, but usage of the service had stagnated. The startup faced formidable competition from Apple's FaceTime, Google's Hangouts, and the granddaddy of them all, Microsoft's Skype. All four services were free to use, so disrupting sales wasn't an option. Larry and I quickly focused on capturing value through marketing, and to do so we analyzed who our users were and how the service made them feel.

It turned out that ooVoo's audience was dramatically different from our competition's. Our users were young, urban teens looking to have fun and connect with friends. As we zeroed in on how different our audience was, our plan emerged. We decided to raise ooVoo's status from a communication platform to a lifestyle brand. Larry reached out to the urban music community and placed ooVoo at the center of the culture. A young R & B singer named Trey Songz loved the service and agreed, for a small fee, to include ooVoo in his "Simply Amazing" video. The key to making branded content work is for the product placement to feel organic. The video was a love ballad, with Trey and his lover staying in touch with each other via ooVoo. The magic worked. The song and video quickly rose to number one on the UK R & B charts and number three on the U.S. Bubbling Under Hot 100 Singles chart. It also garnered Trey award nominations for best R & B male performer and song of the year.[11] While YouTube plays of our video skyrocketed past ten million views, use of ooVoo soared from a few million users to a hundred million users. Young urban teens were ooVooing for over a billion minutes a month. The total cost of the promotion was less than most brands spend to shoot a television commercial. When Trey went on the road to promote his *Billboard* number-one album, ooVoo supported the tour.

Within a year, ooVoo became the seventh-most-used social app in the world and a top-one-hundred app in over a hundred countries. To attract advertisers to ooVoo's platform, it was important to use non-traditional marketing methods to build the brand. A company can't claim to be disrupting a field such as advertising and then use established media to grow. By connecting with entertainment content and artists, ooVoo was able to monetize its service with film studios, television networks, and music labels.

THE VALUE OF CUSTOMER SERVICE

Another piece of the sales-and-marketing link that is often overlooked is customer service. Customer service should be thought of as marketing, because it influences how customers feel about your company. Great customer service creates brand loyalty and product differentiation. The challenge in the digital age is that etailers never actually get to see their customers walking in the door, but the benefit is that etailers have access to data that tells them when and if those customers come back. The key value captured by great customer service is a reduction in customer acquisition costs. If a business has to market and advertise to get each and every sale, its costs are substantial. On the other hand, if each customer tells five friends, then the business grows virally.

> Customer service should be thought of as marketing, because it influences how customers feel about your company.

"If there's one reason we have done better than most of our peers in the Internet space over the last six years, it is because we have focused like a laser on customer experience, and that really does matter, I think, in any business," Amazon CEO Jeff Bezos says. "It certainly matters online, where word of mouth is so very, very powerful."[12]

Zappos CEO Tony Hsieh passionately agrees: "At Zappos.com, we decided a long time ago that we didn't want our brand to be just about shoes, or clothing, or even online retailing. We decided that we wanted to build our brand to be about the very best customer service and the very best customer experience. Our customers call and email us to say that's how it feels when a Zappos box arrives," Hsieh says. "And that's how we view this company."[13]

Sir Richard Branson built Virgin into one of the most loved brands in the world by focusing on business from the customer's point of view. Sir Richard is legendary for both understanding the consumer and making quick decisions. Knowing that Virgin America can't control the weather and that occasionally flights are delayed, Virgin's social media teams frequently respond to the tweets of frustrated travelers with gifts at the gate or surprise travel vouchers.

"Further proof that Virgin America is incredible, it just sent me a $200 credit because my flight was delayed," one happy customer tweeted. Virgin also rewards those who follow the airline on Twitter with flash sales. Virgin America's Fly Forward, Give Back promotion was one of the top five events in the company's history for selling tickets.[14]

The last challenge of extracting value from customer service is the old adage that your brand is only as good as your people. The heart and soul of good customer service is building a great company culture. Far too many businesses play lip service to company culture, not realizing that it is an investment that pays dividends in better customer service, lower employee turnover, reduced absenteeism, and lower payroll costs. Tony Hsieh has written an entire book on Zappos company culture, entitled *Delivering Happiness*. Employees enjoy a wide range of perks, including free health care, a nap room, free lunches, and no-charge vending machines. Each year, the employees publish a 480-page book filled with essays by the staff about the company culture and what it means to them.

Zappos managers are even trained to spend up to 20 percent of their time outside of the office goofing off with their team. One secret that Tony shared with me that isn't in his book is how he intentionally closed off the back doors of the headquarters that were closest to the parking lot to force all the employees to walk through the front door and bump into their coworkers more frequently. If people could easily get to their desk without interacting with others, the opportunities for friendships and camaraderie would be diminished. Tony talks a lot about encouraging "serendipity" that leads to friendships at work. What Tony knows, and countless employment studies have proved, is that people are less likely to seek jobs elsewhere if they have friends at work. And happy employees are employees who better serve their customers. Sam Walton, who founded Walmart and built it into the world's largest employer and third-most-valuable company, also focused on customer service. The retailing genius wisely wrote, "The goal as a company is to have customer service that is not just the best, but legendary."[15]

As a teenager working in my parents' deli, I had my first face-to-face experience with customer service over a jar of pickles. My father had a large glass barrel filled with pickles on the counter of the store. One day a woman became agitated because of the live goldfish she thought she saw swimming in the pickle barrel. There was nothing I could say to convince her that there were no fish mixed in with the pickles, just pimiento peppers. She demanded to speak to the manager. My father came out and calmly apologized to the woman for the goldfish and said that if the fish bothered her, she should take her business elsewhere. "The customer is always right," my father said. "Even when they're wrong."

> 🐦 *"The customer is always right. Even when they're wrong."*

That experience stayed with me when I launched my software company and I wanted to make sure that everyone who created Jasmine software had an appreciation for our consumers. I required everyone in the company to take turns answering our technical support number. My theory was that by having all of our team in the position of speaking directly with our customers, we would build better software. Engineers learned firsthand what consumers understood and what frustrated them about our products. Graphic designers could gather ideas for improvements in our user interface. Our sales team gained insights into why consumers purchased our products and which future products they would most like to buy. As a leader who prefers a flat organization, I too learned from these calls. One afternoon when I was doing my shift answering our customer support line, I got a call from Timothy. Timothy was having difficulties with one of our CD-ROMs, and I asked him to reboot his computer. While we waited, I made the usual small talk and asked what he did for a living. He said he was a father. I told him I was, too, that I had two sons, and asked the ages of his kids. Timothy said he didn't have any children. He was a *Jesuit* father, a priest. In the most unlikely of all possible calls, Father Timothy explained that he worked in IT at the Vatican. When I picture the Vatican, I think of St. Peter's Square, the basilica, and the Sistine Chapel. It never occurred to me that running a 1.2-billion-member religion from Rome probably also involved computers and a sophisticated information technology department. I explained that I was the president of the company and that I had always wanted to make an educational CD-ROM on the Vatican Library and its art collection. He shared some fun trivia, including the fact that the library contained a thirteenth-century letter from Genghis Khan's grandson to Pope Innocent IV and that the archives even contained an invoice from Michelangelo in 1550 requesting back payments from the Church. We talked about the Church's role in the evolution of Western art and music. We had a wonderful conversation, and when his computer rebooted and everything worked, he thanked me for my help. I forgot about the conversation until a few weeks later, when we were contacted by the Vatican about doing a CD-ROM on the history of the Church, its art, and its music.

That CD-ROM, *Inside the Vatican,* was the most in-depth and spectacular product Jasmine Multimedia ever produced. Working with Thirteen/WNET, BBS Productions, and Multimedia Entertainment, we were given access to incredible filmed re-creations of the greatest moments in Church history, with Sir Peter Ustinov hosting and narrating. Oxford University collaborated with us in creating a two-million-word hypertext history of Catholicism. We were granted access to thousands of photos of the art collection and even recorded the Holy See's choir singing a range of hymns from various historical periods. When the CD-ROM was released, it was a global hit with consumers, as well as a critical success with reviewers. "CD-ROME: Pope Blesses PBS Disc" was *Variety*'s headline. "The Pope and the Vatican have given their blessing to a CD-ROM project."[16] All of these blessings from one customer service call.

There are dozens of software apps dedicated to unlocking value from customer service and customer relationship management (CRM). Website analytics can slice and dice big data in a thousand ways to better maximize ecommerce sites' yields or advertising's rates of engagement. Better methods for targeting and retargeting are evolving by the minute, and access to consumer profiles and mobile GPS signals can now measure the who, what, when, where, and why of every purchase decision. With so much technology changing how we interact with customers, the key is to not lose track of how our products make consumers feel. Effective sales and marketing results in a happy customer. And a happy customer is the only one who comes back to purchase from you again and again, which reduces the costs of new-customer acquisition.

To disrupt and capture value from the sales-and-marketing link, it is imperative that you think about how your customers and employees feel about every interaction they have with your brand, from the way they purchase the products to how they hear about them, through advertising and word of mouth.

> A happy customer is the only one who comes back to purchase from you again and again.

Chapter Thirteen

Distribution: Unlocking Unattained Value and the Challenge of Unlimited Shelf Space

Distribution has really changed. You can make a record with a laptop in the morning and have it up on YouTube in the afternoon and be a star overnight.
—Bonnie Raitt

For those of you reading this book electronically, the technology to do so existed long before electronic manufacturers could get their heads around the concept of digital distribution. The greatest example in my career of missing the opportunity for disruption through distribution was the creation of the first ebook reader, by Sony in 2004. Back then, Sony was the ruling consumer electronics brand around the globe. Sony televisions, DVD players, PlayStations, Walkman portable audio players, and other electronics commanded a premium at retail. Sony's dominance over consumer electronics was so massive that one-third of all dollars spent at Best Buy were spent on Sony products. Sony's engineers were constantly creating new and exciting hardware devices that delighted consumers year after year. In 2003, engineers in Tokyo created an entirely new category of device: a reader for electronic books, or ebooks. Using breakthrough electronic paper technology, which required a fraction of the electrical power of similarly sized laptop screens, the Sony Librie could perform virtually all the same book-reading functions as today's Kindles and tablets. Sony Electronics, with over fourteen thousand retail locations selling its hardware in North America, was eager to be the first to retail with this breakthrough device. Unfortunately, Sony didn't understand the value chain it was disrupting and the role of content in the world of digital distribution.

At the time, I had just been promoted from head of global strategy at Sony Music to executive vice president of Sony Corporation. I was tasked with building an ecommerce platform to deliver music and movies to consumers digitally. The moment I saw the Librie, I knew it wouldn't sell. No one buys an ebook reader without being able to buy ebooks. It was ridiculous to expect consumers to figure out on their own where to buy electronic books and which titles from which publishers were available on the new device. In the portable music world, Apple had proved that a device's retailer also needed to provide the consumer with content for the device: iTunes drove hardware sales. I knew that in order to sell the Sony Librie, we'd have to sell the ebooks to be read on the device. If I was building a store to sell digital music and digital movies, shouldn't I also be offering digital books? As obvious as this seems in hindsight, Sony corporate headquarters saw the world very differently.

Disruption of the distribution link in the value chain is about redefining the customer. Ford, General Motors, and other car manufacturers sell and distribute their vehicles through a network of independently owned automobile dealers. Elon Musk's Tesla disrupted this approach by cutting out the middleman and selling directly to the consumer. Record labels sold complete albums at stores before Apple's iTunes unbundled the album to sell ninety-nine-cent tracks. As the line between online advertising and transactional ecommerce continues to blur, more and more companies are looking to disrupt long-held methods and assumptions about distribution in order to unlock and capture more value from the products they sell.

As I've said, one of the reasons it is so easy for startups to disrupt major corporations is that big companies are set up to preserve the status quo. The bigger the conglomerate, the less influence and control at its center. Just like the giant *Stegosaurus* with the walnut-size brain, these corporations are being doomed to extinction by the speed of today's market forces. In large multinational companies, each division is given autonomy in its own vertical market, and the various silos rarely play well together. Sony Electronics knew how to build great hardware but didn't want to be in the software or content business. Its strategy served it well for nearly five decades, going back to its introduction of the first transistor radio, in the 1950s. Even though my division reported directly to the chairman of the company, we did not have the authority to tell another division how to design or market its products.

> One of the reasons it is so easy for startups to disrupt major corporations is that big companies are set up to preserve the status quo.

For over a year, my Los Angeles–based team and I made trip after trip to Tokyo to make our case for why we needed to develop a digital ebook store to support the launch of the Librie. We understood that no one buys a device to own it; consumers buy devices to play content. My team and I believed that failing to create the complete ecosystem, of which the hardware product was just a part, would result in the failure of the product itself. Our pleas fell on deaf ears, and Tokyo management said no to partnering with book publishers. Sony Electronics saw the Librie as just another hardware appliance to be sold to consumers in much the same manner as Walkmans or televisions—Sony made hardware, and it was up to book publishers to sell consumers book titles. And so the first Librie was released and bombed. With no book titles at the ready, few retailers even stocked the device.

We continued our shuttle diplomacy, and after nearly two years we were given the go-ahead to work with publishers to develop a distribution ecosystem. But by then Amazon—which had never developed or manufactured hardware—had taken over our market. Amazon, which is the world's largest retailer of books, understood that the real value to capture in digital distribution is the relationship with the consumer. In the digital era, distribution is no longer about supply chain efficiencies, but rather about the ability to connect directly with the end consumer. As more products go digital, this final link of the value chain becomes the most critical to capturing value. Using the same electronic paper technology that Sony had used, Amazon released the first Kindle in 2007, and it sold out in five hours.[1] By capitalizing on its direct relationship with book-reading consumers, Amazon controlled the distribution. Manufacturing hardware was not the etailer's primary business, but rather a necessary component for reinforcing its distribution hegemony. Unlike Kodak, Amazon had the foresight to cannibalize its original sales models in order to own the emerging distribution channel. As Peter Diamandis, founder of X Prize and chairman of Singularity University, explains, "True disruption means threatening your existing product line and your past investments. Breakthrough products disrupt current lines of businesses."[2]

By 2011, sales of ebooks eclipsed the sales of all paperback books on Amazon.[3] Today, as many of you are reading this on an electronic device not manufactured by Sony, it is clear that the company misunderstood the importance of the distribution link in the value chain of the book market.

DISRUPTION THROUGH DISTRIBUTION AND THE TRANSFORMATION OF RETAIL

Prior to the Internet boom, research, development, design, and production accounted for most of the successful value chain disruptions. Distribution, it turns out, holds the most value in the digital age. The U.S. Postal Service, which has been slowly dying since the physical distribution of first-class mail was replaced by email, should have been the bellwether for a wide range of industries, including advertising, television, print media, and retail shopping.

The introduction of ecommerce in the 1990s forever changed the global face of retail. Once consumers overcame their initial fear of entering their credit card numbers on the Web, the Internet became an endless store with unlimited shelf space. A well-stocked inventory, once the hallmark of a quality shop in the brick-and-mortar world, was no longer a competitive advantage. Now that so many purchases are made online, the only difference between a store with ten thousand square feet and a big-box retailer with sixty thousand square feet is that the latter pays substantially more rent. The shopping mall, America's postwar contribution to suburbia, is quickly becoming a vast wasteland as many chains struggle to adapt. Borders and Circuit City, once viewed as retail innovators by Wall Street, became dinosaurs doomed to extinction.

"Traditional brick-and-mortar retailers are being threatened with 'economic destruction' by their advantaged online competition," Andreessen Horowitz partner Jeff Jordan writes on his blog, adding, "Unfortunately for mall owners, the content on deadmalls.com is about to expand substantially. There just are too many malls in America, and this will only get worse."[4] Changes in distribution are affecting commercial real estate values, local economies, and the makeup of the American middle class.

For most products, ecommerce has removed any added value to be garnered from shopping at a local brick-and-mortar retailer. Almost overnight, chains like the Gap and Victoria's Secret discovered that their highest-grossing location was their website. Even that classic mantra of the three most important factors in retail, "location, location, location," can't compete with the ease of shopping from one's home at any time of day or night. Since its first mention, on November 28, 2005, Cyber Monday has become the second-biggest-selling day of the year (after Black Friday).[5] Changes in distribution, the penultimate link of the traditional value chain, are poised to create the largest disruption the world's economy has ever witnessed. In 2009, *Newsweek* writer Daniel Lyons wrote a manifesto railing against ecommerce, entitled "A Decade of Destruction." Ironically, the article appeared in a print publication that was itself being disrupted. Lyons characterized the disruptive power the Internet has on distribution, writing, "The past decade is the era in which the Internet ruined everything. Just look at the industries that have been damaged by the rise of the Web: Newspapers. Magazines. Books. TV. Movies. Music. Retailers of almost any kind, from cars to real estate. Telecommunications. Airlines and hotels. Wherever friction could be polished out of the system, those industries suffered."[6]

Since "A Decade of Destruction" was published, in 2009, retail carnage has only accelerated. In 2012 we saw the greatest number of store closings in U.S. history. Sears Holdings, once the champion of retailing, shuttered nearly two hundred Kmart locations and over one hundred Sears stores.[7] With same-store sales down more than 26 percent, J. C. Penney closed over three hundred stores.[8] GameStop and Radio Shack, both traditional fixtures at nearly every major mall in America, each shuttered nearly five hundred stores.[9] Add to that the hundreds of closings for Office Depot, Barnes & Noble, and Office Max and the pattern is unmistakable. Disruption of traditional distribution is shifting the fundamental nature of most businesses.

"As a company, we are culturally pioneers, and we like to disrupt even our own business. Other companies have different cultures and sometimes don't like to do that," Amazon's Jeff Bezos declares. "The music industry should be a great cautionary tale: Don't let that happen to you. Get ahead of it."[10]

FINDING THE RIGHT BUSINESS MODEL

If your startup idea involves digital content, selecting the correct business model is as important to the success of your business as building the right technology platform. Disrupting digital distribution is no longer just about competing or replacing physical products, but rather understanding the economic realities of each potential financial structure.

> The correct business model is as important to the success of your business as building the right technology platform.

Having served as the head of digital distribution for three of the world's largest content companies, I've had the opportunity to experiment with virtually every possible revenue model: subscription, rental, ownership, streaming, downloads, on-demand, advertising-supported, sponsored, reward-based, windowed, geo-fenced, or variants of all of the above. The short answer is that none have matched the profits enjoyed by companies that sell physical CDs and DVDs to consumers. Physical dollars are always replaced by digital dimes. Yet several companies have figured out successful models that allow them to capture the greatest value through distribution while disrupting the content producer's ability to maintain its profit margins.

By disrupting the value chain through distribution, Amazon, eBay, and iTunes generated combined sales of $82 billion in 2012.[11] All three companies continue to expand and innovate. In May 2013, the Apple App Store's fifty billionth app was downloaded and at the same time the store launched subscription services for music and television.[12] All three have taken different paths to disruption through distribution while offering the consumer the maximum available selection of product. Each was able to cleave off a different slice of the value it had unlocked. Each provides a different road map and lesson for the disruptor focused on distribution.

"There are two kinds of companies: those that work to try to charge more and those that work to charge less," Jeff Bezos declares. "We will be in the second."[13]

From the very foundation of the company, Bezos correctly identified Amazon's competitive advantage as being able to have the most complete selection of inventory. While traditional brick-and-mortar stores could stock anywhere from ten thousand to forty thousand book titles, Amazon was able to offer consumers a virtually unlimited selection by investing heavily in state-of-the-art automated distribution centers and by partnering with other suppliers that would drop-ship directly to the customer. Major disruption can require major patience (especially from investors). It took Amazon nearly $1 billion of capital and six years to make its first profit, but by then the mighty retailer was grossing over $1 billion in sales and had trained the consumer to be a cyber shopper. With that as a base, Amazon was able to expand into the digital goods ecosystem with its Kindle and content services.

So Amazon, which grew to prominence by disrupting physical distribution, quickly came to see eBay as its major retail competition. The once divergent business models now compete at selling consumers the greatest selection of new and used items.

eBay founder Pierre Omidyar's insight about accurately matching buyers and sellers who can agree on the exact value of any product at any given moment revolutionized both pricing and distribution. eBay is the most efficient global marketplace ever created. All of the usual supply chain constraints of distribution and pricing were removed simply through connecting a willing buyer with an equally willing seller.

"I built a system simple enough to sustain itself," Omidyar succinctly points out.[14] Just as the Internet has enabled airlines and hotels to have variable pricing on tickets and room rates based on real-time fluctuations in supply and demand, eBay has created a world where all products benefit from variable pricing. eBay focused on connecting the buyer and the seller, thereby eliminating any direct company cost associated with distribution. Billions of dollars of products are sold without eBay owning a single warehouse or delivery truck. In fact, the U.S. Postal Service, which taxpayers subsidize, actually serves as an outbound logistics arm of eBay. During much of the year, nearly one-third of all packages shipped by the USPS are eBay products![15]

With the auction model as a base, eBay has evolved to include flat-pricing "Buy It Now" capabilities and competes directly with Amazon on thousands of new products. Together the two etailers so dominate shopping that the big-box retailers are suffering from the new ailment known as showrooming, where consumers touch and feel the product they would like to own and then comparison-shop right on their smartphones in the store's aisle. Knowing how showrooming will affect your product is imperative to having successful distribution.

One of the most disruptive approaches to digital distribution I stumbled upon quite by accident. Here I was, supposedly one of the foremost authorities on digital distribution, and I would have totally missed a new business model if it weren't for my personal passion: magic. I've loved magic since I was a small child. I saved up for college by doing magic shows at restaurants and birthday parties, and even today I am a performing member of the Academy of Magical Arts' Magic Castle, in Hollywood. One day, a friend sent me a viral video of a young magician named Brad Christian doing an original trick on YouTube. In the video was a link to Christian's website, Ellusionist.com, where he sold the secret. Some tricks involve only know-how and could be sold via downloads of instructions, while other tricks require props to be mailed. In either case, Brad had leveraged YouTube's infrastructure to distribute his content and marketing at no cost. Ellusionist, which he founded in 2001, also encourages other young magicians to sell their tricks through his site.[16] And *presto*—one of the most successful new brands of magic paraphernalia is created, and a globally fragmented hobby has a community hub. This same model is being used to distribute a wide range of hobbyist content and products that otherwise couldn't garner traditional distribution or awareness on iTunes or a similar large-scale generalist site.

Apple's iTunes took yet a third approach to disruption through distribution by adopting an "agency" business model. In an agency model, the retailer takes a predetermined commission on every sale. In my EMI days, when we originally negotiated the first iTunes deal with Steve Jobs, Jobs was adamant that all songs retail for ninety-nine cents, regardless of a song's variable costs. So while many consumers benefited from that flat pricing, behind the scenes there were many songs that EMI sold to Apple for substantially more than a dollar. Initially, classical pieces of music that could be up to seventy minutes in length and used to command the price of an entire album could have a wholesale price of $6 and yet still retail on iTunes for just ninety-nine cents. With a virtual monopoly on which digital products can sell on their proprietary electronics ecosystem, Apple is being accused of anticompetitive behavior and has been sued by the Justice Department.

"I don't think you understand," Apple's senior vice president of Internet software and services, Eddy Cue, told the court. "We can't treat newspapers or magazines any differently than we treat FarmVille."[17]

Apple's aggressive stance against the Justice Department is core to its long-term strategy. If Apple can maintain its margins on all content, games, magazines, movies, and so on, iTunes can command the majority of retail profits. Whether Apple's electronic store is a monopoly or not is for the courts to decide. Either way, the company has extracted the greatest possible value out of its combined bricks-and-mortar and ecommerce strategy. Apple Stores don't suffer from showrooming—they benefit. Because Apple is both the retailer and manufacturer for all its products, it doesn't matter whether consumers buy iPads online or in the store; the company's margin is the same. How successful is Apple's unique distribution strategy? As of April 2013, it has amassed over $145 billion in cash—enough to buy every man, woman, and child in the United States a 32GB iPad Air.[18]

"No technology company has ever reported results like this," Apple CEO Tim Cook boasted about the company's 2013 first-quarter results of $54.5 billion in revenue and record quarterly profit of $13.1 billion.[19] And now Apple has its eye on disrupting the television market.

DISTRIBUTION DISRUPTION ON THE SMALL SCREENS
The television industry sits on the precipice of disruption, thanks to all the companies working to disrupt the distribution of video. DVRs and digital distribution of video content have already cracked the value chain,

but who will capture the benefits has yet to be determined. At the birth of television, the business model was simple. Three networks competed to buy programming that would attract an audience, and that audience attention was sold to advertisers. Financial syndication rules prevented networks from just airing shows they owned and produced, while ratings agencies calculated how many eyeballs each ad garnered. Fast-forward to the twenty-first century and the fifty-year-old-wall of a business model is displaying massive cracks and fissures. The average American cable subscriber gets over 189 TV channels, yet watches only 17 of them.[20] Further eroding those numbers is the fact that only 38 percent of viewers watch television live, which is causing advertisers to question when and if their ads are being seen.[21] According to Interpublic Group's Magna Global, the $62.7 billion television advertising business declined by 3 percent in 2013, while the overall $154 billion U.S. advertising market grew by 2.7 percent.[22] Even more disconcerting, television is losing the most valuable demographic to advertisers: eighteen-to-twenty-four-year-olds. According to a 2014 Nielsen study, Americans in that age bracket watched only twenty-two hours of television per week—a ninety-five-minute decline from the prior year, or 7 percent year over year. Nielsen noted that this is the fourth such year of declines for this demo.[23]

For all the promise of the Internet and mobile, most media advertising dollars are still flowing to the living room. Historically, more media has been consumed via the television than from any other device. Gaining control of this screen and its command of advertising dollars has been the goal of major technology, consumer electronics, and telecommunications companies for the past decade. Billions have been bet on disrupting this market, yet few understand how quickly consumer behavior is changing.

"History shows that pay-TV subscribers flee in droves to alternative providers when there is even a rare service disruption," states National Association of Broadcasting president Gordon Smith, "demonstrating a quantifiable value for 'must-have' broadcast programming."[24] Disruptors around the world are seizing on this multi-billion-dollar shift in advertising by creating a new generation of programming and advertising options. Multiscreen monetization is the cornerstone of companies ranging from software provider Seachange International to consumer apps such as tvtag and Beamly. Large media companies are working hard to maintain their positions, with Hulu and HBO Go leading the way in increasing consumer engagement.

When Apple first announced iTV in 2006, the company joined a host of major corporations determined to conquer the twenty-first-century living room. It took aim at Sony, Samsung, Time Warner, and Comcast and has recently warily eyeballed new entrants Hulu and Netflix. But while Apple and others continue in their attempts to stake out turf in front of the sofa, each will soon realize that they are in fact tilting at windmills. With the release of the revamped Apple TV and Samsung Connected Living TV, conquering the living room still remains an elusive quest. If Google, with Google TV and YouTube, is the Don Quixote of this journey to reach the unreachable, then Microsoft—longing to once again dominate a market the way it did during the era of the personal computer—is surely the sidekick Sancho Panza. Microsoft, once the leader in bringing video to the computer screen, has struggled to connect with a generation that expects video where, when, and how they want it.

Years before Jobs entered the consumer electronics space, Microsoft sought to have its operating system dominate the television set of the "future." Microsoft first entered the living room with the UltimateTV, way back in 2000—a year before Apple's first iPod was announced. UltimateTV was designed to smash television networks' value chain by offering consumers a DVR with commercial skipping and the ability to record thirty-five hours of programming. Microsoft's reach was then thwarted when EchoStar acquired DirecTV and UltimateTV lost its programming distribution. As a result of the EchoStar development, cable and satellite providers wrote big checks to Hollywood content owners and pushed back hard to maintain the value chain's status quo. If television networks can't guarantee that ads are seen, their business evaporates. But Microsoft remained undaunted.

As yet another way to gain distribution and plant a flag in the living room, Microsoft then entered the gaming-system market with Xbox. Its strategy was simple: the best gaming system, Xbox, would be hooked up to the best television, within the home. This approach proved to be very effective with the introduction of Xbox Live, in 2002, enabling consumers to download games, pay for subscriptions, and purchase music and movies. With forty-six million users as of 2013, owning the living room seemed within reach for Microsoft.[25]

But something unexpected happened while the tech titans valiantly fought for control of the couch. Like the ferocious windmill giants of La Mancha, the twenty-first-century "living room" became nothing more than an illusion.

"Everything is artifice or illusion," Quixote exclaims in Cervantes's novel, and no exception is made for the twenty-first-century living room. Families are no longer gathered around one single TV set, sharing in a passive experience. Video is now consumed all the time, everywhere, on a myriad of portable devices. Tablets in bed, smartphones on the go, and DVRs delivering programming to sets throughout the household are more the norm than Homer, Marge, Bart, Lisa, and Maggie gathered together on the couch. With 64 percent of millennials consuming content on multiple screens at the same time, the question of *where* one consumes media has been replaced by *how* one consumes media.[26] The so-called second screen is now becoming the primary screen on which most Americans get their news and stay connected to their world.

Proof of this disrupted landscape can also be found in who is cord-cutting, who is time-shifting, and who is demanding unbundled programming. Social media has further impacted the shifting dynamics of content consumption, allowing friends to share the viewing experience with one another and with their broader communities. Television programming is the number-one topic on Twitter, and dozens of start-ups in the social space are linking second-screen experiences.[27] Multi-party video chat companies such as ooVoo and Hangouts are enabling friends all around the globe to watch videos together and chat. Consumers are becoming rebroadcasters, and distribution of content is slipping past artificially constructed walls and borders. People no longer need to sit on the same couch to enjoy shared experiences. The disruption in the distribution of television programming is also affecting how shows are produced, marketed, and designed. Smart TVs and second-screen apps are evolving every day to more efficiently match advertisers to viewers, and viewers to the programming they desire.

A new generation of entrepreneurs is creating opportunities for connections around the content without ever being tied to the cost of creating that content. Just as eBay mastered physical distribution without owning the products or the trucks that delivered those products, today's startups are leveraging the programming experience without owning the content. Moreover, the social aspects pioneered by music services such as Spotify and Deezer will soon expand to video and further enable advertisers to engage directly with viewers sharing video content. The majority of marketers, though, continue to cling to the living room to reach consumers, despite innovation across every possible screen in the home.

> 🐦 Today's entrepreneur is creating opportunities for connections around the content without ever being tied to the cost of creating that content.

While broadcasters and cable networks cite increased demand at advertising up-fronts as proof that nothing has changed in the living room, one should recall that 1999 was the music industry's biggest year, before it saw its business model implode.[28] "Facts are the enemy of truth," Quixote famously says, adding, "Every man is the son of his own works."

If today's content creators are bemoaning the fact that disruptions in distribution are reducing dollars of revenue into digital dimes, the emergence of smartphones is turning digital dimes into mobile pennies. Six billion mobile users still have the potential to add up to a lot of pennies.

> 🐦 Smartphones are turning digital dimes into mobile pennies. Six billion mobile users still have the potential to add up to a lot of pennies.

As the prices of smartphones continue to drop and the proliferation of 4G mobile broadband continues to grow, the global market for digitally distributed content will continue to explode. Over 85 percent of the world now has a mobile phone, and the opportunities for video-distribution disruption abound.[29] When a simple mobile game such as Candy Crush Saga can gross a half a billion dollars in a year, there is clearly money to be made through the distribution of mobile content.[30] With so much content available, however, the real challenge is no longer access to that content but discovery of it. Curation, collaborative filtering, and personalization are all paths for entrepreneurs to cash in on digital distribution without having to invest costly dollars on content creation. As Internet writer Clay Shirky points out, "It's not content overload. It's filter failure."[31]

Curation and discovery are hard work. Flipboard, N3twork, Maker Studios, and dozens of other startups are taking different paths to crack the challenge of curating video in a world where over a hundred hours of video are uploaded to YouTube per minute.[32] With over $66 billion a year in television ad spending at stake, collaborative filtering, social network recommendations, and a host of algorithms are being developed by disruptors seeking to satisfy viewers' thirst for multiscreen content while providing advertisers with a way to monetize all of this consumer engagement. Starcom MediaVest, one of the largest ad-buying firms, shifted over $500 million of its clients' video advertising from television to digital in 2014.[33] If the pattern follows the disruption exacted on the music industry, the new entrants will become more valuable than those they displace, because viewers will actually consume more content (and more advertising). But as vexing as content discovery and curation may be, entrepreneurs must remember that long before you get consumers to consume your big idea, you need investors to discover you and your company.

Chapter Fourteen

Capital Revisited: Other People's Money

Always borrow money from a pessimist.
He won't expect it back.
—Oscar Wilde

The single most common complaint for entrepreneurs is lack of funding. "I could change the world if I could only raise $1 million." "Our startup would have been worth hundreds of millions of dollars if the IPO window hadn't closed." "If only I had pivoted earlier, I would have had the funding to take advantage of this amazing opportunity."

Every new business or disruptive idea will, sooner or later, require additional funding. Even the most successful of ventures require growth capital to keep pace with consumer demand. Raising money from angels, VCs, and private equity is a full-time job for most startup CEOs. There are countless strategies for raising everything from seed capital to multi-million-dollar rounds and going public. Over the past few decades, I have raised over $800 million for startups. The process of raising money to launch a new company—and the pros and cons of each source of capital—could be the subject of an entire book. But it is possible to disrupt the funding process to uncover my favorite kind of money. This money isn't borrowed, so it doesn't put you in debt. It isn't invested, so it doesn't take away your hard-earned equity. This money is freely and gladly spent to aid you in building your business or to implement your new idea. I am speaking of OPM: other people's money.

OPM is not about taking money and refusing to pay it back; it is about learning how to position your idea so that it is more valuable to suppliers of the OPM than the cash they are spending. It is money that is given with no requirement of paying it back, nor ownership of your business involved. It is about solving for someone else's problem in order to cost-effectively solve for your own. It is about creating opportunities for those with more capital than ideas. It is your chance to monetize your own creativity. It is the fuel that propels the disruption rocket, and your startup gets a free ride.

> OPM is about positioning your idea so that it is more valuable to suppliers of the OPM than their own cash.

SOURCES OF CAPITAL

First, here is a quick primer on raising traditional sources of capital. Most tech entrepreneurs flock to Sand Hill Road, in Silicon Valley, to raise money from venture capitalists. Sequoia, Benchmark, Accel, and dozens of other top firms all take money from limited partners and invest it into a wide range of startups. Since most of the young companies fail, the VCs need to make tremendous returns on their few hits. Facebook, Google, Yahoo!, and eBay have returned billions to venture firms and, in turn, to their investors. But the true cost of venture capital's batting average may surprise you. A comprehensive 2012 report by the Kauffman Foundation entitled "We Have Met the Enemy . . . and He Is Us" shows that, contrary to popular belief, most venture capital funds don't make returns for their investors better than the average return from the public stock market.[1] The era of VCs making huge returns peaked in 1997, and for the years since, 62 percent of the venture funds that the billion-dollar Kauffman Foundation invested in failed to beat the stock market once fees and carry were paid.[2]

Be cautious when raising money for your startup through VC funding: venture firms are under enormous pressure to improve their performance, so you will have to make sure that the hyper-growth potential of your disruptive business matches the expectations of your investors. Venture money comes at the expense of giving away a portion of your company. Each time you return to the well for your series

B, C, or D round of funding, your ownership gets diluted. While I continue to work with VCs and value not just their money but their business guidance and expertise, OPM is still a safer model whenever possible. The quickest way to show a return on the capital you have invested is to not invest any money in the first place.

I am not suggesting that it doesn't take money to build a new startup or disrupt an industry, but if you can figure out how to spend someone else's money to achieve your goals, you are earning profit from day one. You are doing off-balance-sheet financing. The true costs of launching your product aren't borne by your company. If you become disciplined at spending OPM, the results can be astounding. I should know: I've built my career doing it.

Throughout my formative years in business, years in which I was running my own company, I spent every dollar as if it were my own. This frugality both benefited our company's bottom line and trained me to be a very resourceful executive. Though there were times when my credit cards were maxed out, my car was repossessed, and my kids ate a lot of macaroni and cheese, I pride myself on the fact that I never once missed payroll to my employees (even when I was unable to pay myself). When I arrived at Universal Studios, I was accustomed to finding OPM and used it to build Animalhouse.com without spending any of my division's budget.

So by the time I was recruited by Sir Howard Stringer to launch Sony Connect, Sony's alternative to iTunes, finding OPM for my projects had been ingrained into my very DNA. Apple was spending over $100 million a year advertising iTunes, and I was going to market up against them without any approved launch budget. I knew I was outgunned. Senior management in Tokyo still didn't believe in digital content, and my idea wasn't funded by the board. Corporate boards usually don't volunteer to spend their money on your marketing priorities, especially unproven ones. As the disruptor from within the organization, I had to go outside the company to get my project properly funded. The secret to OPM is to find someone else's problem and make your product their solution.

Following my principle of solving for others to solve for you, I looked for partners who would benefit so much from a well-publicized launch of Sony Connect digital music service that they would gladly pay us to do it. But unlike a startup asking for assistance, Sony was one of the world's largest corporations and spent over $2 billion annually on advertising. There was no good reason for anyone to want to help Sony. So as I had done when I was first trying to launch my laserdisc business, I started scanning the news to find out which major corporations were in trouble. If I could use Sony Connect to solve their problems, perhaps I could leverage the other company's marketing-and-advertising budget to solve mine. It didn't take long to find companies that were in the news and wished they weren't.

🐦 *Solve for others to solve for you.*

Two corporations in completely unrelated fields were having problems and making the headlines in 2004: United Airlines and McDonald's.

Years of union contract disputes, coupled with the downturn in airline travel following the September 11 terrorist attacks, had forced UAL Corporation to file for Chapter 11 bankruptcy protection in December 2002. To survive, United Airlines furloughed thousands of workers and closed several travel routes, and it was in desperate need of some good press. The airlines had weathered the storm and wanted to tell the traveling public that they were back and better than ever. Every day their planes were flying with too many empty seats and not enough travelers. What they lacked was a creative idea to lure their frequent fliers back without increasing their marketing budget.

At the same time, McDonald's was facing a super-size problem. In 2004, director Morgan Spurlock premiered his film *Super Size Me* at Sundance and unleashed a public relations disaster for the company. The documentary chronicled thirty-two-year-old Spurlock eating at McDonald's three times a day for a month. He gained 24.5 pounds and watched his cholesterol shoot up to 230. The film ended with an image of Ronald McDonald's tombstone and the rhetorical question "Who do you want to see go first, you or them?" The debate over fast food was impacting McDonald's sales and its bottom line. The fast food giant needed positive PR. But how do you make McDonald's cool again? What would bring back those sought-after young adult customers?

And, most important, what did United Airlines' and McDonald's problems have to do with my launching a digital music store for Sony?

The answer was to find a solution for United Airlines and McDonald's that also worked for Sony's new digital music service. All three companies were brand leaders in their respective fields. And all three appealed to a very broad consumer demographic. All I needed to do was examine McDonald's and United's problems through my Sony-tinted glasses.

What if travelers' frequent flier miles could be used as a currency in the Sony Connect store? What if every Big Mac sold came with a code for a free music download? What if we could announce these programs with a giant PR stunt that the press would have to write about? And, following my OPM credo, what if I could pull this off without spending any of my nonexistent marketing budget?

The answer that tied the needs of these three unrelated brands together was the first-ever concert at thirty thousand feet. On May 4, 2004, singer Sheryl Crow performed the "Concert in the Sky" on a United flight from Chicago to Los Angeles. We filled the plane with press and filmed the concert with nine cameras. (The movie of the concert, which was brilliantly produced by Ty Braswell, would then play on every United Airlines flight for the next month—exposing the event to millions of travelers.) The plane was painted with the Sony Connect logo on its engines, and when we landed at LAX, the entire planeload of passengers and crew had their picture taken on the tarmac in front of the airplane. United got positive front-page news all across the globe, and our new Sony Connect music service was front and center in every story.

At the same time, McDonald's launched a fantastically creative television spot that showed how the world became one giant music video every time you held a Big Mac in your hands. The commercial ran in heavy rotation in nine countries. The Big Mac Meal Tracks promotion explained that on the side of every Big Mac box was a code for free music tracks that could be downloaded from Sony Connect. To make sure everyone noticed, the commercial even featured a very cool cameo by Justin Timberlake. (This was the first time Timberlake had ever been in a television commercial, which generated even more press and buzz.) Timberlake, McDonald's, and I held a press conference in

Los Angeles to launch the worldwide music giveaway. Over one hundred journalists attended the event. The results of these two OPM promotions were instantaneous.

Traffic to Sony Connect rose by 3,000 percent, and 79 percent of these new users returned to purchase more music within the first week. More important for McDonald's, which had spent tens of millions of dollars on the promotion, same-store sales increased 9 percent, and its business got back on track. Later that year, McDonald's and Sony won the prestigious Promotion Marketing Association's Gold Reggie Award for best promotional event of the year. (The name Reggie refers to making the cash register ring.) This was a true win-win-win situation that didn't cost Sony (or my division) a dime. OPM also earned me an award from the Sony board—the company's highest recognition!

One footnote to the McDonald's promotion: it almost didn't happen. After months of negotiations to put the deal in place, in which we haggled down to the penny with McDonald's over what each digital song would cost, I was blindsided by a last-minute requirement. Although the Sony board had approved my promotion (how could they refuse—it wasn't costing us anything), McDonald's business affairs lawyer explained that the restaurant chain always took out an insurance policy on redemption promotions in case a greater-than-expected percentage of the song codes issued were actually redeemed by customers. The potential financial exposure to McDonald's if every coupon was actually redeemed was over $100 million. I did my best estimate of the percentage of customers who would go to the trouble of downloading a free song, but no one knew for sure what the actual results would be. McDonald's had been burned in this situation before. Its marketing department had misjudged redemption rates on a promotion it ran for the 1984 Olympics, and it cost the company over $50 million.[3] With tens of millions of digital song codes going out, a mistake on this promotion could prove even more costly. To avoid such mistakes, Lloyd's of London would insure the Big Mac Meal Tracks promotion. The policy was $6 million, and Sony was expected to pick up half the bill. So much for the joy of using OPM! My program was days away from launching, and it suddenly looked like it would cost me $3 million.

The problem was that I didn't have $3 million in my budget. I had already presented my program to the board, and all of my sister divisions were participating. (We had included bonus prizes of electronics, PlayStations, DVDs, and other electronics for consumers who redeemed their codes.) If I pulled the plug, I would go from hero to zero overnight. If I went to the chairman for the money, I would look like I didn't know what I was doing. Now, not only was my big idea in jeopardy, but so was my career at Sony and the launch of my new service.

As I've said, disrupting from within a large corporation is no different from disrupting at a startup. It requires facing every challenge as an opportunity and finding the solution that solves for the most pressing issue first. My solution was simple: since Sony was a multi-billion-dollar corporation, we would self-insure the promotion, and McDonald's could write us a $3 million check. Now I had engineered a successful promotion using OPM *and* we were $3 million in the black before the first bite of a burger was taken or the first song was downloaded from our site.

As nerve-racking as the McDonald's experience was for me, it reinforced one of the most important lessons of being a disruptor: never give up. We are all our most resourceful when backed into a corner. My first instinct might have been to throw my hands up in the air and surrender, but I didn't. I forced myself to look at the problem from every possible angle. Every constituent's point of view was debated until a logical solution emerged. You'll never know how close you were to victory if you give up.

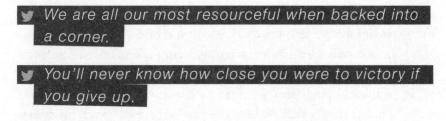

> We are all our most resourceful when backed into a corner.

> You'll never know how close you were to victory if you give up.

THERE'S NO SUCH THING AS RUNNING OUT OF MONEY

Too many entrepreneurs give up because they've run out of cash or can't find investors. There's always another point of view, another company that will benefit. Look at your challenges from others' perspectives and the source of OPM will become obvious.

Blake Mycoskie, founder of Toms Shoes, built his company around the principle of doing well by doing good. His "One for One" business model was to give away a pair of shoes to a child in need for every pair his company sold. While Toms had gained some Internet buzz, it wasn't until he put OPM to work that his business skyrocketed. In 2009, AT&T featured Mycoskie and Toms in a national television commercial. The premise was to showcase how he was able to run his international company thanks to AT&T's "more bars in more places." AT&T got an authentic, emotional spot as viewers witnessed Mycoskie giving poor children their first pairs of shoes, and Toms got millions in marketing for free. The spike in sales from the commercial exposure enabled the company to sell more than one million pairs of shoes—and to give away that many as well. This innovative model of featuring a local business and catapulting it to national fame has since been repeated dozens of times by companies such as American Express and Pinkberry.

For the entrepreneur looking to utilize such OPM opportunities, the process is very straightforward. First, identify and define your target market. What is the specific audience that your product appeals to, and what are the emotional attributes attached to your value proposition? Once you are armed with that information, your next step is to make a list of the other, noncompetitive products marketed to the same audience.

If you are launching a new weight loss supplement, for example, think of health clubs, exercise equipment manufacturers, sports apparel companies, and so on. Study the slogans and ad campaigns of the biggest players in each of those categories until you find a fit. Finally, search the Internet to find that company's ad agency and contact the creative team for the account. With few or no connections, I have used this formula with soft drink companies, automakers, clothing companies, and even makers of feminine hygiene products. It is rare that an ad agency would pitch such an idea to a client without already having a partner, and that's exactly why these pairings are so successful. Your bringing the idea to them only makes the agency's team look smart.

Another variant of OPM is cause marketing. As Toms Shoes proved, consumers like it when their normal activities can actually make a positive impact on the world around them. Avon's Walk for Breast Cancer and the Ronald McDonald House Charities are great examples of pairing a brand and a cause to benefit both. General Mills' Box Tops for Education, which raises cash for school supplies, has been so successful that dozens of other brands have joined in to leverage the attention and goodwill created by the cereal company.

For the smallest of companies, I also recommend cause marketing as an internal team-building exercise to increase job satisfaction and reduce employee churn. Cause marketing is a wonderfully selfish selfless activity. You donate your time and energies with the sincere desire to help others, when in fact you and your company come away from each activity more enriched, more inspired, and more empowered to face the humdrum problems at the office. When I was building my first company, we had more time than money, and more talent than paying work. So each year we gathered the whole company together to work on a pro bono project that could best utilize our talents. Graphic artists could create their vision unfettered by the demands of a color-blind client. Programmers didn't have to sacrifice functions or features to make artificial deadlines. Salespeople could reach out to potential clients to collaborate instead of negotiate. We created educational software for children with special needs, made science and Holocaust museums more interactive, and created video games that helped hospitalized children recover quicker. Whenever I run into former employees I haven't worked with for many years, it is the charity projects we remember most fondly.

During my corporate years, there were many times when I was the source of OPM for others. Just as I had given 50 percent ownership of my video game *Vid Grid* to David Geffen to get support from the music industry for my new technology, when I was president of digital at EMI, Bob Bernardi and Raju Puthukarai walked into my office in the Capitol Records building to offer me 50 percent of their new digital music company. Little did they know that I was the one executive in the music industry who was ready to listen. In the years before iTunes or legal digital downloads, MusicMaker was a company with a new idea for monetizing music. Let consumers pick which songs they wanted online and the songs would be burned onto a CD and mailed to them. And just as I had done in my Jasmine years, MusicMaker had built the technology but lacked the music content. Without hit music, the company had little prospect for survival.

We took the equity stake, and I joined their board. EMI granted MusicMaker license to thousands of songs in its catalog. Acts from the Beach Boys to Eric Clapton, from the Band to the Ramones would now be available legally online. Within a few months of signing our deal, the company went public on July 7, 1999. With only $20,000 in sales that year, MusicMaker's market capitalization reached over $600 million on opening day, and EMI made tens of millions of dollars.[4] EMI proved that money could be made from digital music, and other deals and IPOs soon followed. The OPM model was a turning point at EMI and gave my team the freedom to pursue new revenue streams such as digital downloads, Internet radio, and digital subscription services.

OPM and cause marketing are two ways to expand the marketing reach of your company without reducing your runway. Changing your industry and disrupting your value chain will take capital, but OPM is the only nondilutive source available to all entrepreneurs. Cause marketing is also becoming a core value of twenty-first-century companies wishing to recruit and retain the best and brightest who desire a career with purpose. Pursuing other people's money is a great way to make industry contacts with people who think collaboratively and creatively and who might care about more than just hitting their numbers.

> *OPM and cause marketing are two ways to expand the marketing reach of your company without reducing your runway.*

Chapter Fifteen

Disruption in the Era of the Crowd

A man who wants to lead the orchestra
must turn his back to the crowd.
—Max Lucado

The Internet has given billions of people access to centuries' worth of knowledge. While many squander this power on videos of cats playing the piano, others are committed to sharing their expertise—free of cost—with those in need of their skills and experience. Technology now allows for the aggregation of knowledge from endless points and unlimited points of view. While YouTube and others built business models around monetizing crowdsourced content, two of the most successful of these new crowdsourced enterprises, Wikipedia and Craigslist, chose by design not to capture the value they created. Both founders turned down billions of dollars in personal wealth to pursue their personal visions for a better world. Both approached the market from vastly different points of view, but together they challenged our assumptions on the power of the crowd to enlighten and inform. They pioneered the sharing economy.

For those looking to build a nonprofit, champion a cause, or change a public policy, crowdsourcing is the answer. With few or no resources, anyone with Internet access can connect with like-minded individuals to gather, share, and redistribute knowledge. Crowdsourcing is changing the ways in which products are funded, data is collected, and excess human capital is deployed. Crowdsourcing is the ultimate disruptor of distribution, because, in a most Zenlike fashion, the content is controlled by everyone and no one at the same time.

The greatest example of the power of crowdsourcing is Wikipedia. Wikipedia has become the virtual repository of the entirety of human knowledge in less than a decade. Perhaps more significant to the dissemination of learning than Gutenberg's press, Jimmy Wales and Larry Sanger made a conscious decision at the outset not to commercialize their creation.

"Imagine a world in which every single person on the planet is given free access to the sum of all human knowledge," Wales says. "That's what we're doing."[1]

Prior to Wikipedia, most collections of human knowledge were copyrighted and owned by authors, publishers, and corporations. Wikipedia disrupted the business of encyclopedias, reference books, and almanacs by having the crowd contribute for the betterment of all. In disrupting the distribution of knowledge, Wikipedia also pioneered the new business concept of crowdsourcing and user-generated content. Seventy thousand unpaid editors routinely patrol Wikipedia to ensure the accuracy and quality of the content. They spend countless hours volunteering because they embrace the site's mission and feel it gives their lives meaning. With nearly 5 million articles and counting, Wikipedia is more comprehensive and up to date than any encyclopedia that preceded it. More important, Wikipedia knows no boundaries, and its articles are available in some 285 languages. The site has become a self-sustaining, living community, universally embraced by its 350 million unique monthly visitors.[2] (I should confess that the capitalist in me tried early on to get Jimmy Wales to accept advertising on Wikipedia. The revenue generated would have been astronomical, but it would have irrevocably changed the core values of the site. Wales knew advertising would destroy the site's image of impartiality and would risk tainting the content to please sponsors. He was absolutely right, and not convincing the Wikimedia Foundation to monetize through advertising is one of my business failures I am proudest of.)

While Wikipedia was envisioned from the outset as a not-for-profit enterprise, Craig Newmark had much more modest aspirations when he launched Craigslist in 1995. When the World Wide Web was still in its infancy, all Craig wanted to do was help his friends find local events. So Newmark published an email list of San Francisco happenings. The list grew and became an easy-to-use website where anyone could list virtually anything. Craigslist now handles more than fifty million queries per day.[3]

"Our sites are run by the people who use them," Newmark said. "We just pretty much provide the infrastructure."[4] As usage quickly spread to over seven hundred cities in seventy countries, Craigslist singlehandedly eviscerated the extremely profitable classified ad revenue of daily newspapers.[5]

"Newspapers are getting wiped out because the Internet robbed them of their mini-monopolies. For decades they had virtually no competition, and so could charge ridiculous amounts of money for things like tiny classified ads," Daniel Lyons writes in "A Decade of Destruction." "This, we are told by people who are wringing their hands over the demise of newspapers, was somehow a good thing. Good or no, it's gone, thanks to Craigslist, which came along and provided the same service at no charge."[6]

Newmark could have made billions of dollars in the digital classified advertising space, but he chose not to pursue these revenue streams. In fact, his egalitarian approach to distribution disruption actually destroyed market value. Much like Napster would do to the music industry, Craigslist didn't shift monetary value, but rather disrupted the market to the point that no one could charge for a service that Newmark had made universally free. Blogger and startup entrepreneur Mark Bao sums it up best:

"In actuality, Craigslist is not so much taking business away from a certain market, but rather destroying their market entirely, as they make a sliver of the money that used to be in the classifieds market, while owning it. It's like if a competing coffee shop stole all of Starbucks' customers as they sold good coffee for $0.01 per cup. Sometimes creative destruction equates to market destruction."[7]

THE VALUE OF FREE

Wikipedia, Craigslist, and Napster pioneered a new business model: reduce competition by making services and products free. Large corporations do this to gain market share—for example, Google introduced Gmail to reduce Microsoft's Office revenues—but always with the motive of capturing the revenue from another sector of their business. In the case of Google, they were better able to target their advertising by reading every email users sent and could therefore justify the expense of Gmail. But crowdsourcing isn't always about capturing the value it unlocks. The power of crowdsourcing is that it prevents any business or organization from controlling access by democratizing the process.

> The power of crowdsourcing is that it prevents any business or organization from controlling access by democratizing the process.

Any business based solely on its access to proprietary data can easily be disrupted by crowdsourcing. Airbnb, Uber, and the new sharing economy are extensions of this phenomenon that could be disrupted by communities of users willing to offer competing services free of charge. Who would pay a service for a ride if an equitable system was created for sharing rides? Why would each house on the block purchase a lawn mower if a shared mower could be scheduled among neighbors? A recent study found that the average American owner of an electric drill uses it for a total of only thirteen minutes of drilling.[8] Why then do we collectively own eighty million drills? The possibilities of migrating from an economy based on owning to one based on sharing are limitless. Whole industries will be disrupted as consumers shift from "consuming" to "sourcing." Crowdsourcing is not the end of consumerism; it is a step in a cycle of disruption. Eventually this cycle comes full circle when consumers are willing to pay for a better version of an existing free service.

With advances in mobile technology and consumer behavior, inevitably even the disruptor will eventually get disrupted. As one of the oldest sites on the Web, Craigslist is continually being challenged by the next generation of Internet entrepreneurs who are able to charge for a better version of something Craigslist offers for free. With New-mark failing to adapt the simple user interface to meet growing de-mand, dozens of startups have captured value by breaking the Craigslist value chain into smaller, more efficient and manageable pieces.

The broadness of Craigslist's offerings has spawned more than fifty single-purpose alternatives. Airbnb, Care.com, 99designs, and oDesk are refined verticals of Craigslist classified categories. Airbnb cofounders Brian Chesky and Joe Gebbia had used Craigslist to find short-term rentals near trade conferences when hotel rooms were scarce. Identify-ing a business opportunity to fill the void between couch surfing and hotels, they quickly built out their air-bread-and-breakfast site into a $10 billion business. (How they first funded the idea has become legend-ary. During the presidential election of 2008, the entrepreneurs created and sold "Obama O's" and "Cap'n McCain's" cereal. In two months, they sold eight hundred boxes of cereal, raising $30,000 to launch Airbnb.) Their service quickly grew to over 250,000 listings in 30,000 cities in 192 countries.[9] While politicians argue over the long-term le-gality of the service in the same way the music industry tried to fight Napster, the proverbial genie is out of the bottle—consumer behavior has been fundamentally altered. The power of crowdsourcing always remains with the crowd, not with the technological implementation.

> The power of crowdsourcing always remains with the crowd, not with the technological implementation.

THE SOCIAL ECONOMY

By building a vertical market out of a single Craigslist category, a dis-ruptor can add more functionality to better serve the consumer. Clas-sified ads can become interactive and transactional, and they will grow beyond the few geographic locations served by Craigslist. The same opportunity exists today to unbundle functionality from leading social networks such as Facebook, Twitter, and LinkedIn. As with Craigslist, generic social networks satisfy a broad base of consumers. Disruption will occur when a valuable subsegment can be identified and better served by additional functionality. Those looking to disrupt through crowdsourcing need to focus on three key elements.

First, analyze what data a startup is now able to gather. Airbnb gathers and leverages the data on all available rooms and couches available for rent. As the public inputs both the supply and demand data, the company only has to create a platform for connecting the two. The result is an efficient dual-sided marketplace where no such business existed before. In the new shared economy, dozens of entrepreneurs are utilizing this same model for everything from power tools and lawn mowers to ride sharing and wardrobe rental.

The second requirement for successful crowd disruption is efficiency. Gathering the data on all available rooms makes sense only if the rentals it makes available are cheaper than those offered through the existing model. In markets where hotel rooms are most expensive (New York, London, Tokyo), Airbnb provides the greatest value to users. By leveraging the crowd to handle most aspects of the crowd model, a business greatly reduces its overhead, and those efficiencies can be passed on to the consumer.

Finally, the net result has to be of consistent quality and transparency. When eBay pioneered crowdsourced retailing, a system of trust had to be created so that buyers and sellers could trust that each party would hold up its own end of the bargain. No one would send a thousand dollars to a stranger with the faith that they would then receive the item they were purchasing. A publicly visible rating system solved most potential issues. If a seller listed a product with a price that was hard to believe, the prospective buyer could see how many successful transactions the seller had completed and read the reviews from other customers. Feedback is the engine that improves the overall quality of crowdsourced businesses and is the one aspect of the crowd economy that big businesses are struggling to embrace. The more open the system is to consumer interaction, the more robust the market will become. Smartphones now empower consumers to provide nearly instantaneous feedback on any product or service. Social media, the ultimate crowd business, is benefiting the most from this move to mobile.

As the world migrates to mobile for social media experiences, Facebook's dominance is being usurped by apps such as Instagram (which Facebook later purchased for nearly $1 billion),[10] WhatsApp (which Facebook purchased for $19 billion),[11] WeChat, Ello, and ooVoo. Each of these services looks at leveraging the crowd to improve systems of communication. By combining social functionality with communication, ooVoo pioneered a new form of social networking centered on multiparty video calling.

When I joined ooVoo as president in 2012, I knew that mobile communication technology would create a demand for a new form of social experience: the connectivity of social media combined with the intimacy of telecommunications. I also knew we would have to figure out how to access the crowd and then watch the experience grow virally. Much like texting a decade earlier, multiparty video communication would begin in urban centers, where technology is plentiful and usage patterns fluid. So we focused all our marketing on the youngest segment of Internet users and quickly grew our service to 100 million registered users. Young users were more social, more mobile, and less likely to make a voice call. Unfettered by the telephone habits of their parents, teens quickly realized that text was the most efficient form of communication, yet they still yearned for a more personal form of communication with their closest friends. Combining the ability to have face-to-face interactions with groups of friends, ooVoo fills a need: it connects with those living a mobile-centric life by allowing users to communicate through free instant voice messaging and voice and video chat. Within six months, comScore had identified ooVoo as the top app with American teens.

Voice-only telephony, which experienced growth every year between 1876 (when it was invented by Alexander Graham Bell) and 2012, makes no sense to this new generation. In fact, the easiest way to annoy millennials is to leave them a voice mail. Giant mobile providers like Verizon, Sprint, T-Mobile, and AT&T are going to have their business model completely disrupted by this generation, which communicates in a fundamentally different manner. Either telecommunication companies will learn to quickly evolve their business models or they are going to be reduced to dumb "pipe" utility firms paid to move data around. The crowd, once again, is more powerful and important than the technological infrastructure that connects them. A 2012 study by Ratemizer showed that while iPhone users increased their data usage by 68 percent, voice minute usage dropped by 13 percent over the same ten-month span.[12] Ratemizer, an app that compares carriers' rate plans to find the cheapest one available, is itself a crowdsourced gatherer of consumer data. As the majority of the United States migrates to smartphones, the financial impact to U.S. mobile carriers' voice-centric revenue model will be substantial.

Twitter, with its 270 million users, has evolved from short text messaging to a wide range of multimedia. But it is also being disrupted by services like Snapchat, Quibb, and Yammer, which focus on richer experiences for subsegments. Yammer, which combined features of LinkedIn and Facebook to create private social networks inside companies, was acquired by Microsoft for $1.2 billion in 2012—just four years after launching at the TechCrunch50 conference.[13]

I am not predicting the demise of Twitter, Facebook, or Craigslist, but history shows that as any service grows to hundreds of millions of users, the opportunity for disruption becomes inevitable. Large organizations' requirement to focus on the lowest common denominator opens the door for entrepreneurs to come in and grab the piece of those organizations' audience that is underserved. Combining crowdsourcing with crowdfunding opens up entirely new industries for disruption. Television shows are being created from crowdsourced videos by companies like Joseph Gordon-Levitt's hitRECord, while feature films are being crowdfunded on Indiegogo and Kickstarter (for example, *Veronica Mars* and *Wish I Was Here*). DonorsChoose.org and Kiva combine both crowdsourcing and crowdfunding to reduce the waste and friction associated with philanthropic giving.

There is no question that the power of the crowd will inspire change in all areas of our economy. All of the pieces of this emerging financial ecosystem came together for me when I was approached by a millennial who was set on disrupting an $11 trillion U.S. industry. His vision for change was elegant and simple.

In the spring of 2012, I spoke before the Los Angeles chapter of the Founder Institute and met first-time entrepreneur Jeff Hoffer and his partner. They had identified a huge market ripe for disruption: commercial real estate. As they pitched it, millions of American investors would like to diversify their investments by buying into apartments, homes, or pieces of shopping centers and office buildings. But these investors don't want the hassle of dealing with tenants, toilets, and trash. Nearly half a trillion dollars in U.S. commercial real estate is transacted annually, and yet no one had brought it into the twenty-first century. Every equity raise and transaction is treated as a unique one-off event, with each piece of the capital stack being uniquely negotiated by property owners, real estate promoters, financial institutions, and investors. The Internet had already enabled efficient marketplaces for stocks and bonds (E-Trade), used goods (eBay), new merchandise (Amazon), and dozens of other categories, yet real estate has been bought, sold, and financed in the same manner for hundreds of years.

As I would learn in the coming months, disrupting this market involved more than just understanding real property. Their concept, Realty Mogul, benefits both sides of real estate transactions by reducing transactional friction and creating market transparency. Realty Mogul is a website where people can either invest in property or raise the money they need to buy real estate. Those seeking to raise equity funding can use the Realty Mogul platform as an outsourced capital markets arm, and those wishing to invest gain access to deal flow previously available to only a select few insiders. Investors have the potential to generate better returns from less of a commission load of traditional real estate investment trusts (REITs) while benefiting from the tax advantages of the depreciation that flow through to them. Unlike Amazon, which had to displace Barnes & Noble, Realty Mogul's main competition when it launched was nothing other than an inefficient existing market. When you are searching for an industry to disrupt, the best opportunities are those where inefficiency is your only competition. Realty Mogul's pitch was a zombie idea that I couldn't find a way to kill, so I agreed to join their board, and within a year I was working as executive chairman.

Best of all, Realty Mogul was built on the premise that transparency and efficiency will drive market acceptance. Within our first year of launching the platform, Realty Mogul helped crowdfund over $100 million in commercial real estate and earned millions of dollars for its users. This is still a very small slice of the commercial real estate market, but the seeds for disruption have been planted. With innovation comes competition and further refinement of the model. Fundrise, Patch of Land, RealtyShares, Fquare, Globerex, and others have each combined crowdfunding and crowdsourcing targeted at various aspects of the real estate market. With dozens of other crowdfunding real estate companies perfecting the business model and specializing in different vertical or regional markets around the globe, the question is no longer whether the method of investing in property will change, but which firms will grow to dominate this new sector.

The Internet's efficient ability to connect millions of people who have never met but who share a common need, interest, or desire will ultimately disrupt all businesses based on being the "middleman." Just as many of the functions of banks are being replaced by peer-to-peer lending sites (for example, Prosper, Lending Club), likewise advertising agencies, insurance companies, retailers, publishers, transportation companies, hoteliers, and movie studios are all ripe for disruption or further disruption. For the aspiring disruptor, the possibilities to capture value by using the crowd to revolutionize these multi-billion-dollar fields are nearly limitless. Barriers and borders are vanishing daily as the majority of the world is now connected via wireless Internet. The scale of industries to be disrupted and the opportunities embodied therein have never been greater.

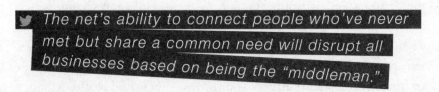

The net's ability to connect people who've never met but share a common need will disrupt all businesses based on being the "middleman."

JAY SAMIT

Chapter Sixteen

Disrupt the World

In today's knowledge-based economy,
what you earn depends on what you learn.
—President Bill Clinton

Sitting in the White House waiting for my first meeting with the president of the United States was one of the most unnerving experiences of my life. At the time, I was a small-time entrepreneur barely making a living. How had I been called to the White House? As nervous adrenaline raced through my veins, every fear and doubt crossed my mind in a series of unanswerable questions. *Did they call the wrong guy? Do I really know what I'm talking about? Did I put the right shoes on? Can I, a thirty-five-year-old technology geek with no government experience or advanced academic degrees, transform the entire educational system of the greatest country on earth?*

A month earlier, working at my software company in Los Angeles, I couldn't have imagined in my wildest dreams that President Bill Clinton would call and ask for my help. In fact, when my assistant ran into my office to tell me that the president was on the phone, I asked her, "President of what?"

For the first few moments of the call, I thought it might be a friend doing a really great impression of Clinton's Arkansas drawl. But as the president explained that he and Vice President Al Gore liked the idea of using the information superhighway (as the Internet was called in 1996) to "build a bridge to the twenty-first century," I knew that my personal dream could become a reality. I had proposed wiring the Internet into every classroom in America so that no child would be denied access to the latest information and the best resources available. My big idea had been inspired by the accomplishments of another disruptor at the dawn of the last century.

In the early 1900s, billionaire industrialist Andrew Carnegie recognized that access to information was the most important tool for improving society. Long before the concept of a public library was the norm, he agreed to build and stock them for any city that would donate the land and budget for their continued operation.

"A library outranks any other one thing a community can do to benefit its people," Carnegie wrote. "It is a never failing spring in the desert." In his lifetime, Carnegie gave away billions of dollars, creating 2,509 public libraries and founding the Carnegie Institute of Technology (now known as Carnegie Mellon University).[1] When I was in college, I had gotten a job writing for Ralph Nader at his Center for the Study of Responsive Law, in a building that had once been the Carnegie Institution of Washington, at 16th and P Streets in Washington, D.C. When I worked there, I learned about Carnegie's vision, and it stuck with me. I became convinced that the Internet could once and for all put an end to "separate but equal" and replace it with "connected and equal."

While the idea germinated in my mind, and as my career grew over the next fifteen years, I began speaking about this vision at conferences and with like-minded tech leaders. As personal computers became cheaper and more powerful, the concept of disrupting education through the Internet became more and more obvious to parents, students, educators, and government officials. In 1995, fewer than one-fifth of American households had Internet access,[2] but the medium had complete cultural awareness. When President Clinton and the White House staff decided to convene a meeting on the subject, I had made enough of a name for myself in the industry that I made the list. I was humbled by the accomplishments of the other people in the room at the Old Executive Office Building, next to the White House. These were the people who actually ran the country and made things happen. As trite as it might sound, sitting there among the leadership of our nation, I didn't want to let my country down.

I was surprised when the president challenged us to make it happen by the year 2000. I took the challenge personally. With the president's bully pulpit empowering us, I didn't know the steps we would have to take to make so momentous a change happen, but I knew it was possible, because that is the power of disruptive ideas. A big idea attracts big thinkers and big doers. It is a magnet for bringing out the best in people and making the impossible possible. The only problem was how to pay for it. No tax dollars were available for wiring our nation's schools, and paying to retrofit thousands of classrooms could cost billions.

After being invited to the White House and meeting others who shared the same vision, we created a nonprofit organization to build this road to the twenty-first century. As director of the National Education Technology initiative, and with the support of thousands of volunteers, unions, and corporations, I set out to achieve something meaningful through crowdsourcing. We broke down the herculean problem of how to provide all our nation's public schools with Internet access, dividing it into manageable tasks, and set out to change the future of our educational system.

AOL founder Steve Case and Microsoft gave us seed funding to get started, but this project would need more help. We thought about a charity dinner with a silent auction, but the people involved were spread out all over the country. That was when I came up with a simple idea: why not throw the first-ever *online* charity auction? We found a one-man company called Auction Web, which had just been started by a twenty-eight-year-old engineer in San Jose. Dozens of corporations, including Sony, Epson, and ViewSonic, donated software and hardware products. Even Miss California pitched in by auctioning off a date. President Clinton announced the auction on May 1, 1996, and Vice President Gore closed the auction with a videotaped speech at the Electronic Entertainment Expo (E3) on May 16. The response was tremendous, and the event would have been a flawless success except for one minor problem: logistics.

Auction Web's software worked great. Pierre, the company's founder and sole engineer, made it really easy for people to bid on and pay for the donated items. The logistical issue was that we'd had all of the donated items shipped to my company, and now it was up to my staff and me to figure out how to match all of the merchandise to the winning bidders. We'd created a pick-pack-and-ship disaster. I had also failed to anticipate how much work it would be to match the hundreds of bids, checks, packages, and addresses. It ended up taking us nearly six weeks to manually print out all of the manifests and match them to the corresponding packages. Since this was the first online auction, many donors got impatient and thought they had been duped out of their money. Everyone eventually received what he or she had paid for, but some of us got more than we bargained for. From challenges spring profitable solutions.

Volunteering to help others was everyone's sole purpose for working on this project. But giving, it turns out, is a very selfish act. The more you give, the more the karma bus brings back. Auction Web solved the logistics issue for future auctions by developing a rating system that built trust between buyers and sellers so that they could ship items directly between themselves. If you haven't figured it out yet, that company's founder was Pierre Omidyar: one year later, he renamed his company eBay and changed the world of commerce forever.[3]

Our online auction raised hundreds of thousands of dollars. Combined with the other donations, this gave us enough to get rolling. Within a few months, as classrooms started to get their computers, the president and the vice president came out to Concord, California, to help us pull Cat 5 cable and hook up a school to the Internet. In California alone, thousands of volunteers were able to lay six million feet of cable and wire 20 percent of the state's schools in just one day. The cost to California taxpayers was zero.

"We must bring the information-and-technology revolution to every classroom in America," President Clinton said that day.[4] Seeing so many people come together with a common desire to provide equal access to knowledge was a heady experience. I got to work with and meet wonderful people at that school. Sun Microsystems' John Gage, cocreator of NetDay, gathered everyone with the president and the vice president to celebrate and have the official White House photographer take pictures. A month later, I received a very nice note and a signed photo of Vice President Gore standing between me and another one of Sun's employees who volunteered that day. Though the photo hung proudly on my office wall for years, it wasn't until the other guy in the picture got a new job in 2001 that I discovered his name was Eric Schmidt, the new chairman and CEO of Google.

In 1996 alone, the movement had motivated an estimated 250,000 volunteers to pull cable and wire the Internet into more than fifty thousand schools for free. To complete the effort, later that year Congress got the FCC to pass rules to create discounted access to the Internet for all classrooms.[5] By the time the twenty-first century arrived, our dream had become a reality. We had wired every public school in the United States without one dollar from the government. Citizens were literally pulling together to provide greater opportunities for the next generation.

The Russian author Leo Tolstoy said, "Everyone thinks of changing the world, but no one thinks of changing themselves." In the first part of this book, we examined ways disruptors adopt a mind-set of creativity and innovation to achieve professional success and personal satisfaction. *Disrupt You!* goes on to demonstrate how to apply those principles to disrupting different links in the value chain of the business world. But not all disruptors are motivated by profits. The biggest big ideas go beyond the reach of any balance sheet and encompass the most existential of goals: freedom, equality, health, and justice. When Dr. Jonas Salk developed the polio vaccine, he was not motivated by the billions he could earn by patenting his discovery, but rather by the millions of children he could save from a lifetime of living with paralyzing disabilities. In fact, when he was asked who owned the vaccine's patent, Salk famously retorted, "There is no patent. Could you patent the sun?" We live in a world challenged by pollution, global warming, energy poverty, limited access to clean water, and a host of other problems that demand big ideas and committed disruptors.

> 🐦 *"Everyone thinks of changing the world, but no one thinks of changing themselves."*

Gandhi, Mother Teresa, Nelson Mandela, and countless others looked at major issues of injustice and dedicated their lives to solving some of our world's biggest problems. They were disruptors who thought differently and transformed the world to make a lasting difference. As the revolutions of the Arab Spring recently proved, the power of the Internet and the interconnections billions of us share every day have made disrupting governments, educational systems, and banking as easy as disrupting Fortune 500 companies.

This final chapter of *Disrupt You!* takes a look at how the same principles needed to successfully transform one's career or business can be applied to even larger social institutions. By championing big ideas that unlock never-before-realized value for the average citizen, the disruptors highlighted here are literally changing our world.

DISRUPTIVE IDEAS IN EDUCATION

Dozens of entrepreneurs are tackling the important task of educating the world. When retired hedge fund manager Salman Khan started his free online school in 2008, Khan Academy was little more than thousands of videos of him teaching math. But the videos made an impact. With financial support from the Bill and Melinda Gates Foundation as well as Eli and Edythe Broad, Khan Academy's 100,000 practice problems in math, biology, physics, and chemistry are now used by more than 350,000 registered teachers and reach over ten million students per month. Fundamentally democratizing access to knowledge, Khan's videos have been played more than 500 million times.[6]

What Khan has done outside the mainstream other major institutions of higher learning are doing from within the university structure. MIT, Tufts, the University of Michigan, and others have joined together to create the Open Education Consortium (the OEC). The consortium is an international community of hundreds of institutions of higher education committed to opening knowledge to the world. With over fifty million video plays on YouTube, the OEC enables anyone, anywhere, to access quality education for free.

An entire global movement has grown up around disrupting education. Massive open online courses (MOOCs) are a movement to provide great online lectures for free or for a greatly reduced price. The goal is to enable students to get university degrees more affordably. One MOOC champion, Coursera, has over eight million registered users. Another, Udacity, partnered with AT&T and Georgia Tech to develop an online master's degree in computing. Even the school that invented the M.B.A., Harvard Business School, has announced plans to offer an online pre-M.B.A. for as little as $1,500.[7]

With U.S. student loan debt exceeding $1 trillion, Starbucks CEO Howard Schultz saw a great cause-marketing opportunity that would not only reduce employee turnover but also ingratiate the brand to its core customers. In 2014, Schultz announced a plan to help Starbucks' 135,000 workers earn online degrees from Arizona State University. Starbucks would pay the college tuition for all employees who wanted to pursue a degree.[8]

While digital startups such as Coursera, Skillshare, Dabble, edX, and Udacity are bridging the gap between real-world skills and formal education for adults seeking cost-effective alternatives to traditional universities, other educators are focused on disrupting the K–12 experience. Taking a market-based approach to solving the problem of America's shortage of scientists and engineers, MIT decided to partner with Khan Academy to create video courseware designed to inspire elementary and middle school students to pursue careers in STEM (science, technology, engineering, and mathematics). Fewer than 5 percent of American university students get engineering degrees, compared with 19 percent of the students in Asia.[9] So MIT School of Engineering dean Ian Waitz is creating demand by showing students how fun and creative working with technology can be. Named MIT+K12, the video series draws on the talents of MIT's ten thousand students and features topics ranging from flying robots to basic chemistry.[10]

Even more disruptive than sharing lessons is having elementary students build the courseware on their own. Globaloria, which was founded in 2006 by educator Idit Harel, combines technology and game theory to transform elementary school students into child designers. Students create learning games and are responsible for teaching others. Over ten thousand students have participated in this experimental learning paradigm, and more than five hundred teachers are now trained for incorporating it into the classroom. "We have seen great results: 95 percent course completion and 95 percent school renewals," says Harel. "Kids naturally gravitate to video games. So we designed STEM education courses by introducing them to how the games are made."[11]

More engineers and scientists will lead to more innovation and more solutions to world problems. With global adult literacy rates hovering somewhere around 85 percent, that still leaves more than seven hundred million adults around the world without any basic education, according to UNESCO.[12] These educational disruptors are leading the way in democratizing the access and spread of knowledge. Just imagine all the problems an educated world could solve.

HUMAN CAPITAL DISRUPTION

As Will Rogers famously said, "It's not what you pay a man, but what he costs you that counts." The only thing in life as certain as death and taxes is the fact that every business or social endeavor requires two things to grow: people and money. The best big idea is going to be only as good as its implementation. Anyone who has ever tried to scale their business knows how hard it is to find great employees and how much time it takes to raise capital. Together, these tasks become a second full-time job for a business's founder. Recruiters and bankers traditionally help companies find the resources they needed, but at a hefty price. C-suite headhunters can charge in excess of $100,000 per recruit, and some in Silicon Valley require an additional equity kicker. With human capital and actual capital playing such a momentous role in every enterprise, it was only a matter of time before these elements were radically disrupted.

> The best big idea is going to be only as good as its implementation.

In every organization, there are support systems to the value chain that enable it to function. The two most important, and thereby the most ripe for disruption, are capital and human capital. Even with the creation of sites like Craigslist and Monster.com, the basic process for finding and recruiting talent changed very little during the first wave of digital disruption, in the late 1990s. Realizing the importance of human capital to any enterprise, Reid Hoffman set out to disrupt the entire global employment ecosystem with the creation of LinkedIn, in 2003. Hoffman was convinced that there could be a better marketplace that matched jobs and job seekers. Could the nature of networking with friends—and friends of friends—be systemized and globalized? Would the world understand the value created by utilizing the crowd to power the network effect?

The network effect is the geometrically increased value a network gets from each additional node added to it. When Alexander Graham Bell invented the telephone, he could just call Thomas Watson in the next room. The network itself was of limited value. When millions of people have telephones, the network is indispensable as a means for communication. Robert Metcalfe applied the same network effect when he co-invented Ethernet and saw the ever-increasing power of adding more Ethernet cards to the net. Metcalfe's Law states that the value of a telecommunications network is directly proportional to the square of the number of connected users in the system. If Metcalfe's Law worked for telephones, fax machines, and Ethernet cards, could it work for human capital?

As a senior adviser to LinkedIn during its formative years, I was amazed by Hoffman's astoundingly detailed vision for how creating a professional social network would change the market for both job seekers and employers. But the idea of disrupting the employment industry, which had been virtually unchanged by the Internet, was anything but a guaranteed success.

"At the end of our first year we had 4,500 members in the network," Hoffman recalls. "Tech early adopters tried it, but it just wasn't growing fast enough to survive."[13]

Survive it did. By its tenth year in business, the $19 billion company employed over 3,700 people and had 225 million users.[14] As with all crowdsourced networks, the value created is more than just the efficiency it brings to the market. LinkedIn does more than help people find or make great hires; it enables a deeper understanding of the market of human capital. Where are the jobs being created, and where are they being lost? Which job titles are vanishing, and which skill sets are in short supply? The predictive ability of the volumes of data that LinkedIn generates becomes a revenue stream unto itself. The data LinkedIn collects gives the company more insight into global employment trends than has ever existed, and the marketplace

Hoffman created for finding talent generates nearly $1 billion annually in revenues.[15]

Hoffman's success with PayPal and LinkedIn makes him one of the most experienced people in understanding what makes a disruptive business grow. Maximizing his know-how, he is also one of Silicon Valley's most successful serial investor/entrepreneurs, with investments in over a dozen disruptive startups. In addition to LinkedIn, Hoffman was a first-round investor in Facebook and even arranged the introductory meeting between Mark Zuckerberg and Peter Thiel, which resulted in the first $500,000 angel investment in the startup. Building a startup, Hoffman is famous for saying, is like "throwing yourself off a cliff and assembling an airplane on the way down."[16]

With U.S. companies spending over $120 billion a year on talent acquisition, recruitment will continue to be a target of disruption.[17] Hiring great talent is just the first challenge of human capital disruption in the twenty-first century. With companies constantly transforming their missions and their products, aligning talent with ever-changing priorities is a daunting task faced by HR departments and managers at even the most successful companies. While Silicon Valley companies such as Google are notorious for luring workers with a panoply of perks, other entrepreneurs are applying big data and analytics to increase employee satisfaction, performance, and retention. For example, Visier systematizes workforce analytics so that senior management can increase competitiveness by identifying and incentivizing top performers within their organizations sooner.

CAPITAL DISRUPTION

Mark Twain once wrote, "A banker is a fellow who lends you his umbrella when the sun is shining and wants it back the minute it begins to rain." I'm sure he would agree that if any industry once seemed immune and impervious to disruption, it is banking. Modern banking goes back at least as far as ancient Greece, and the oldest continuously operating bank, Italy's Monte dei Paschi di Siena, has been lending money in much the same manner since 1472—twenty years before Columbus set sail for America. Intellects from the far left and the far right both detest banks and their control of society. "Let me issue and control a nation's money," banker Mayer Amschel Rothschild said in the eighteenth century, "and I care not who writes the laws."

But as entrenched and established as banking is, nothing is impervious to disruption. The shocker is how little capital it took to reengineer the international banking industry. One man disrupted the entire structure of the multi-trillion-dollar financial services sector with just $27. Yes . . . twenty-seven dollars.

Today, with the world's top banks each controlling over $2 trillion in assets, the likelihood of disrupting this system seems minuscule.[18] But for all the good that is accomplished by a stable international banking system, there are many downsides. The financial crisis of 2007 and 2008 wiped out $34 trillion of wealth globally by March 2009, according to the Roosevelt Institute.[19] Yet even that financial calamity couldn't unseat the value chain of modern banking as government officials around the world propped up those flawed financial institutions that were "too big to fail."

The real banking disruption comes from the other end of the financial system: the billions of people struggling at the bottom fringes of society who are known as the "unbanked." The disruptor threatening our banking system wasn't camped out in Manhattan trying to occupy Wall Street with clever chants and cheers. He is an economist working in Bangladesh.

Muhammad Yunus studied economics in college and worked for the newly independent government of Bangladesh in the 1970s, but when the famine of 1974 killed more than one million of his fellow citizens, he felt the system had to change. While visiting a poor village near the University of Chittagong, Yunus learned of the usurious interest rates local women were forced to pay on loans they had to take out to buy the raw materials to make bamboo furniture. After a whole day's work, these women were often left with little to show for it. Unable to borrow from banks, these poor women were virtual indentured servants to local loan sharks. As Tolstoy famously pointed out, "Money is a new form of slavery, and distinguishable from the old simply by the fact that it is impersonal—that there is no human relation between master and slave."

So starting with just $27 of his own money, Yunus made microloans to forty-two women in the village. As the program expanded, he created groups of borrowers who could guarantee that all members of the group would repay—women helping other women. Crowdsourcing the guarantee provided security in numbers. This was true community-based lending. Understanding the concern these women felt for their families, Yunus did something unheard of in the Muslim world: he gave small loans directly to working women rather than to their husbands, fathers, or brothers. By 2007, Yunus's Grameen Bank ("Village Bank") had issued over $6 billion in microcredit to some 9.4 million of his country's poorest workers.[20] The loans were both a good investment and transformative for millions of women and their families.

While he gave millions a hand to help lift them out of poverty, Muhammad Yunus was not without critics. Some Muslim clerics even went so far as to tell the women that if they borrowed money from Yunus, they would be denied a proper Muslim burial and not go to heaven. Disruption, even when achieving positive results, is still a threat to those who benefit from established market inequalities. For his work in disrupting the cycle of usury and poverty that gripped his nation and revolutionizing how aid is delivered in the developing world, Muhammad Yunus was awarded the Nobel Peace Prize in 2006. The committee cited his "efforts through microcredit to create economic and social development from below."[21]

Yunus has inspired the next generation of disruptors who are incorporating technology to expand the reach of microbanking to populations all across the developing world. For example, MobiCash combines mobile phones and biometrics to provide fingerprint-based banking to villages in over a dozen African countries that previously relied on a cash economy.[22] Anyone with access to a mobile device now has access to secure banking.

A broken banking system that doesn't serve the needs of consumers is not a concept limited to the emerging world. According to a 2011 survey by the Federal Deposit Insurance Corporation (FDIC), 28.3 percent of Americans are either unbanked or underbanked.[23] With sixty-eight million U.S. adults not participating in the existing banking system, the market void has been filled by a range of alternative financial services. The most popular is the prepaid debit card, with its high fees and limited protections. The unbanked and underbanked aren't just low-income households; it's also been a growing trend with millennials. In fact, 51.3 percent of American households headed by someone under twenty-four years of age are considered unbanked or underbanked.[24]

Entrepreneur Josh Reich saw a huge opportunity to serve a growing population that was both computer literate and unserved by traditional banks. Reich realized that many young adults needed to have up-to-the-minute real-time access to their account balance to help them manage their spending and avoid traditional bank overdraft fees. By operating a virtual bank with no physical branches or paper checks, he could keep overhead low and pass the savings on to his users. The result was Simple, which offers free online checking accounts and debit cards tied to a mobile app. The advantage to his clientele, according to the thirty-four-year-old CEO, is that Simple will do "the mental math you try and do when you log in at traditional banks."[25]

With no fees and no minimum required balances, Simple proved so popular that when it launched, there was a two-week waiting list to get an account. The company makes its money from the interest it earns on consumers' capital and transaction fees, not from the hidden fees and charges so common with the big banks. "We never want to profit from customers not understanding their finances," Reich told reporters when launching—and that is what has allowed him to disrupt a market owned by the largest financial institutions in the world.[26]

The founders of Lending Club looked at the massive consumer credit card debt and saw the opportunity to disintermediate the banks and disrupt their lock on consumer credit. Their platform leveraged the crowd to provide microloans. Those paying high credit card interest rates could pay lower fees, while investors could make greater returns than they would if their money was sitting in a traditional bank. Lending Club removed the bank as the middleman and connected the human borrower with the human lending the money directly. Efficiency powered by the network effect. In just a few years, Lending Club has grown to a $5 billion company.[27]

DISRUPTIVE IDEAS IN TRANSPORTATION, TRAVEL, AND ENERGY
Elon Musk is a serial entrepreneur and über-disruptor who made his first fortune taking on the world of banking. His first startup was the

financial services company X.com, which merged with Confinity in 2000 to become PayPal. PayPal changed Internet commerce by streamlining the process of making auction payments and money transfers through the Internet. Two years after its founding, PayPal was acquired by eBay for $1.5 billion.[28] With that success as his base, Musk has amassed a fortune estimated at over $6.7 billion by tackling some of the planet's biggest issues.[29] Actually, Musk's vision for disruption goes beyond the planet.

Musk took on the big automotive giants with Tesla Motors in his quest to make a green vehicle that could reduce global warming. To disrupt the automotive industry, Musk not only reengineered how an electric vehicle was built; he also set out to disrupt the entire financial structure of automotive retailing. Unbeknownst to the average consumer, most states have laws that require cars to be sold through local dealers, part of an inefficient system that grew out of the pioneering days of the twentieth-century motor industry. Musk wanted to bring transparency to automotive retailing and faced myriad lawsuits. But by breaking the dealership link of the automotive value chain, Musk could reduce costs and build a more affordable vehicle for consumers. To be successful, he would have to take on Big Government, Big Oil, and Big Auto all at the same time. As with the ideas of most radical visionaries, Musk's Tesla was scoffed at and written off by the automotive establishment as a rich man's hobby. But in the first quarter of 2012, the Tesla Model S achieved the unthinkable: it outsold Mercedes-Benz, BMW, and Audi in the full-size luxury category.[30] Not only did Tesla smash its earnings report, but *Consumer Reports* gave the electric car its highest score ever—a 99 out of 100—making it the best car they had ever reviewed.[31] No one is laughing at the fearless entrepreneur today as he prepares to launch a new category of Teslas aimed at the middle-class consumer. In 2014, Musk announced that his Tesla Model 3 would retail at $35,000, around half the price of previous models.[32]

Elon is a big-picture thinker and one of the most visionary people I've ever known. He cares passionately about the environment and the future of our planet. When I first met him, in 2008, I got a glimpse of his true commitment to addressing our environmental challenges when he quipped, "I have enough money to cure cancer, but what good would that do when life on this planet is over?"

Musk was serious. He is on a personal mission to colonize Mars, and I would not bet against him. Using $100 million from his sale of PayPal, Musk founded Space Exploration Technologies, better known as SpaceX, with the goal of bringing entrepreneurial rigor to space travel. The first successful private space company, SpaceX designs and manufactures commercial rockets. With the retirement of the government's space shuttle program, SpaceX was awarded a $1.6 billion contract from NASA to bring cargo to the international space station.[33] On May 25, 2012, Musk made history when his privately owned SpaceX *Dragon* rocket became the first commercial vehicle to dock in space.[34] Disruption truly has no limits.

"Being an entrepreneur is like eating glass and staring into the abyss of death," Musk famously said. Still in his forties, he has the time, money, and vision to disrupt many more industries. "I think that's the single best piece of advice: constantly think about how you could be doing things better and questioning yourself."[35]

Solving the world's need for clean, green, renewable energy is perhaps the biggest financial opportunity available today. In addition to building a green car company, Musk has launched SolarCity, already the largest provider of solar power systems in the United States.[36] The opportunities for green energy are enormous. A trillion-dollar ecosystem has been built on harvesting fossil fuels that are currently being used in every country on the planet. The world consumes over eighty-seven million barrels of petroleum products per day, and supplies of crude are getting harder and harder to extract. An innovation that saved just 1 percent of this spending would generate revenues of over $75 million per day.[37] In the quest to save energy, scientists have studied wind, solar, and geothermal for producing energy, but few new methods have been developed for storing this energy. Battery technology can fuel a host of new disruptions. Nuclear energy, into which France invested heavily, didn't look like the best solution to fossil fuels after the disaster in Fukushima, Japan. But not all innovation requires millions of dollars of research and development. Sometimes it just takes some out-of-the-box disruptive thinking. My personal award for most innovative approach to reducing energy consumption goes to the French conglomerate Groupe Casino, for what I like to call the chicken battery. Yes, an efficient energy-storing battery made 100 percent from chickens.

Casino is a major international retailer with over twelve thousand stores in eight countries. An operation on that scale consumes massive amounts of electricity. With an aggressive plan to reduce consumption, the company began installing solar panels on its buildings. This was great for capturing free energy during the day, but without sunlight at night, the frozen foods would slowly thaw out and the food would be spoiled by morning, so Casino was still pulling electricity from the power grid at night to run its stores' freezers. As with most disruptive thinking, the problem was actually the solution.

The problem wasn't really a lack of sunshine at night; it was a problem of where it could store excess solar energy before the sun set. Casino realized that if it could shift its power consumption pattern, millions of dollars could be saved, and its reduced carbon footprint would benefit the entire community.

The solution was as simple and counterintuitive as turning their freezers' thermostat dial. All that the Casino stores had to do was lower the temperature of their poultry freezers to far below freezing during the day, when there was an ample supply of free power coming from the sun. Then, overnight, the frozen chickens would slowly thaw down to a normal freezer temperature. Since no one was opening the freezer doors at night, it just took some simple math to determine the right temperature to get to in the evening so that everything would stay safely frozen until morning. When the sun rose, the entire process would cycle again. Casino effectively found a way for its frozen chickens to act as batteries for storing extra energy without suffering any negative effect in their edibility or taste. While "chicken batteries" like this are now used all around the world, from Brazil to Vietnam, when food does spoil for other reasons, clever grocers have discovered how to turn today's garbage into tomorrow's electricity.

Kroger, America's largest grocery store chain, with over $90 billion in annual sales, decided to do something about the 40 percent of its food that was going unsold and spoiling at retail each year.[38] This waste was not just a financial drain but also a costly environmental issue. Organic waste in America's landfills presently accounts for 25 percent of the nation's methane emissions, according to the Natural Resources Defense Council.[39] Kroger realized that instead of sending all the rotten fruit and other organic waste to landfills, it could build an anaerobic digester system to convert moldy bread and rancid meat into electricity. A fifty-nine-acre facility on the outskirts of Los Angeles takes the organic waste from 359 of the company's Southern California stores and pumps the sludge into a system that generates thirteen million kilowatt-hours of electricity per year (enough energy to power over two thousand homes for a year). As a bonus, the only by-product of this process is a nutrient-rich sludge that can be used for fertilizer. The fertilizer is profitably sold to California produce farmers, and the whole process repeats itself. The cycle is a completely efficient, eco-friendly ecosystem for agriculture. Kroger estimates that it saves $110 million with the digester, and communities save on landfill space and air pollution.[40]

Some disruptive energy solutions are literally out of this world. Using fuel cell technology originally developed for NASA's Mars missions, Bloom Energy generates clean electricity from its Bloom Boxes, which actually remove CO_2 from the environment. Companies like Walmart, FedEx, and Coca-Cola are using Bloom Boxes to save money and reduce their carbon footprints. But if Bloom CEO Dr. K. R. Sridhar's predictions are correct, within a decade the boxes, which now cost $750,000, will run only $3,000 and will be used everywhere to produce clean, renewable energy.[41]

Around the globe, small disruptors are partnering with governments and NGOs to tackle some of the most pressing issues facing mankind, including access to clean drinking water. More than 3.4 million people die each year from water and sanitation issues. Over 780 million people lack access to clean drinking water.[42] With large-scale water treatment facilities being too costly for many rural communities, Chile's Alfredo Zolezzi set his sights on building a solution. His $500 Plasma Water Sanitation System kills 100 percent of the bacteria and viruses in water and has the potential to change the lives of billions.[43]

My friend Akon is taking his celebrity status as one of the world's most famous recording artists and using it to bring electricity to rural communities, without building a costly electric grid. With over fifty million Facebook followers, Akon is using his business skills and his fame to shine a light on one of Africa's biggest problems: a lack of infrastructure. Akon has partnered with leading technology companies and nine African governments to bring solar electricity to Africa. The Akon Lighting Africa project provides an off-grid solution that will give millions of people access to lighting, the Internet, and a larger community than they ever imagined.[44]

With the right people, networks, or chickens, any societal construct can be disrupted and improved. Even better, industries are born from solving the problems of others and by creating efficiencies that were not previously possible. Innovative disruptors can unlock value in the waste of other industries and create new sectors of employment.

> *Innovative disruptors can unlock value in the waste of other industries.*

DISRUPTION IN MATTERS OF STATE

Disrupting the corporate world may take drive and initiative to succeed, but the worst thing that can happen to you if you fail is that you go broke and have to start all over again. Transforming governments in many parts of the world means risking one's life and the lives of one's family. Yet the same tools that work to disrupt businesses and social enterprises apply to disrupting ineffective governments. As Margaret Mead said, "Never doubt that a small group of thoughtful, committed citizens can change the world. Indeed, it is the only thing that ever has." From Bill Gates's global war on polio to those working to reduce carbon emissions, the United States government is built on a foundation of people empowered to change what they don't like.

But to be a disruptor in the world of totalitarian dictators and drug cartels elevates disruption to a matter of life and death. Can the same principles behind breaking the value chains of industry be applied to corruption and criminal enterprises? Can the power (the value that is created by authoritarian regimes) be disrupted by emerging technologies and redistributed to a new generation of social entrepreneurs? Can smartphones and Twitter do for other nations what Benjamin Franklin's print shop and Paul Revere's midnight ride did for our founding fathers? To the U.S. State Department's Alec Ross, the answer to these questions is yes.

In 2009, Secretary of State Hillary Clinton created a new position, senior adviser for innovation, assigning Alec Ross to the post and giving him a wide mandate to utilize advances in technology to change how the State Department conducted "21st Century Statecraft."[45] Prior to his appointment, most governments had only two blunt tools in their toolbox for settling differences: diplomacy and war.

Transforming how a $50 billion-a-year government department with nearly forty-eight thousand employees worldwide approaches and deals with global crises is a daunting task. But in our increasingly interconnected world, looking at issues from a technological disruptor's point of view yields astonishing results.

Ross implemented a two-pronged approach. First was getting the department and its diplomats using social media, and second was assembling the best techies to work on specific problems.

"If Paul Revere had been a modern-day citizen, he wouldn't have ridden down Main Street. He would have tweeted," Ross said in an interview.[46] Whereas the State Department traditionally met behind closed doors with established leaders all around the globe, Twitter and the Web enable the department to go beyond the corridors of power to reach millions of people directly. Knowledge and the network effect are an unstoppable duo. As part of this effort, the State Department now tweets in nine languages and fights against Internet censorship.

"We support technologies and train activists so they can exercise their universal rights, including freedom of expression," Ross told *Time* magazine, which named him one of the world's best Twitter feeds in 2012.[47]

As recently as 2014, Turkey's prime minister, Recep Tayyip Erdogan, tried to shut down Twitter for allowing people to share true but damaging information just before national elections.[48] As with most attempts at censorship, his efforts were futile and actually galvanized the citizenry. The people took to the street. But instead of protesting, they spray-painted posters of Erdogan's governing party with the code DNS 8.8.8.8. This was the Internet protocol address of non-Turkish

DNS servers that allowed everyone to still get on Twitter. The government's attempt to block Twitter backfired. A people's press that can't be blocked or shut down is a truly free press.

When the pro-democracy protesters in Hong Kong had their cell tower access to the Internet cut by authorities in 2014, Chinese students created a mesh network using FireChat, Open Garden, and other tools that connect mobile phones together to form a temporary Internet. Student protesters from Tehran to Taiwan continue to share their digital innovations in order to overcome government censorship.

When the governed don't feel that governments are doing enough to fight crime or corruption, technology can also be leveraged to disrupt criminal power. The United States' costly war on drugs and its foreign policy for dealing with international drug cartels have failed for decades. Nowhere on earth are the effects of this felt more than in Ciudad Juárez, Mexico, just across the border from El Paso, Texas.

Juárez is known as the deadliest city on earth. Between 2007 and 2011, warring gangs fighting for control of the drug trade murdered more than nine thousand people in and around the city.[49] If it was left unchecked, U.S. government leaders feared that the violence would spread across the border. Corruption within the Mexican federal and local authorities made prosecuting criminals nearly impossible. The citizens of Juárez didn't know where to turn for help.

Alec Ross's team at the State Department had a plan. What if they hacked together a technology that enabled people to anonymously text in tips to the proper authorities? If the texts could be encrypted and the sender protected, more people would come forward, and order could be restored.

The State Department worked with the Mexican government to make sure the cyber tip line went to a noncorrupt enforcement squad and Ross's hackers. As successful prosecutions increased, the murder rate decreased, and 2012 saw a 64 percent decrease in murders.[50] While much work still needs to be done, according to the president of the bureau of public safety, Arturo Valenzuela, people now feel safe enough to walk down the streets again. "There is no superman, or one person that did all the changes," reflects Valenzuela. "It was a multifunctional process."[51]

Much has been written about the State Department's and social media's roles in the Arab Spring, but behind the scenes, Ross's team contributed by creating custom technology solutions to thwart dictators and protect those seeking a free society. When Syrian dictator Bashar al-Assad allegedly used GPS to locate journalists' mobile phones in order to target and assassinate them, Ross's team trained rebels and NGOs on how to avoid cyber snooping. To Ross, a free and open Internet is a despot's worst enemy.

🐦 *A free and open Internet is a despot's worst enemy.*

"There have been strongly negative reactions from Belarus, Iran and China and other nations that are not as open as our own," Ross said in the *Time* interview. "The Chinese are grappling with the implications of a networked citizenry. Ultimately, the future of the Internet in China will be determined by citizens under 25 who are growing up digitally."[52] Thanks to disruptors like Alec Ross, people empowered are learning that they have more authority than people in power.

Not all solutions to governmental issues and societal problems require complex technology or established organizations. Sometimes it is as simple as looking for a business solution to a nonbusiness problem. In business, the easiest way to change someone's point of view is to show them how they can profit from your viewpoint. This same idea can help move legislation forward in government.

When I was still in my teens, I had the opportunity to intern for Ralph Nader in Washington. At the time, Nader was the most famous disruptor in the United States. A lawyer by training, he'd become nationally known by taking on General Motors with his book *Unsafe at Any Speed,* which for the first time showed that car accidents could be the result of poor design and not just driver error. The attention Nader brought to this issue resulted in Congress's unanimously passing the National Traffic and Motor Vehicle Safety Act, the first act of its kind. With that early success and prominence, Nader attracted dozens of young college students to come work for him and take on issues ranging from water pollution to pension rights to nuclear power safety. I joined the group of young idealists that the press later came to call

Nader's Raiders. I was surrounded by other college students committed to changing the world and saving our environment, and it was an amazing experience. But that summer, the best lesson I learned in disruption was how Nader's Raiders got recycling to go mainstream. It is a methodology that can easily be replicated, and it shows that understanding how to create value in a corporate business chain is also the key to achieving disruption in government.

Today we take for granted that newspapers, bottles, and cans are gathered and recycled. But in the 1970s, recycling didn't exist. Supermarkets didn't want to have to store dirty containers that would attract bugs and rodents. Beverage companies that sold a can or a bottle of soda for a dime didn't want the negative attention of making billions of single-use containers. And politicians didn't want to legislate requirements that would alienate large corporate donors. Early efforts to set up recycling boxes at stores and shopping centers went nowhere. It was a classic case of the tragedy of the commons: if everyone benefited equally from recycling, no single group had an incentive to make it happen.

That all changed when a profit motive was added to the equation. The first bottle bill, which was enacted in Oregon, came up with the idea of requiring a five-cent deposit for each can or bottle. If consumers returned their containers, they received their deposit back. If a consumer didn't recycle, the local bottler kept the nickel. Bottlers' profit margins would skyrocket if, as anticipated, most people didn't recycle. Bottle bills would generate billions of dollars for the beverage companies. Overnight, the industry supported recycling, and the concept spread from coast to coast.

Understanding that a business approach may be needed to fix a dysfunctional Washington, tech superstars Sean Parker, Ron Conway, and Marc Benioff launched Brigade in 2014. The company's mandate is to raise political engagement and involvement in all levels of government all across the United States. Their goal is to use the tools of social media to combat voter apathy and build a more participatory government.[53] Whether or not this venture ends up being successful, clearly twenty-first-century technologies will radically change how people engage with one another and their government to address global issues. Other social entrepreneurs, such as AllSay's Geoff Campbell, are focused on creating a more informed and activated citizenry through app participation. AllSay seeks to match citizens with the issues that have the biggest impact on their lives, the way that Pandora utilizes collaborative filtering to recommend music you care about.

The promise of social media to better connect the world in new ways provides hope that those with novel ideas about how to improve our world can find one another and collaborate more easily. Just as each disruptor looks internally at which assets they can leverage from their personal value chain, the global crowd can now operate across barriers of distance, time, and language. By pooling their talents, capital, and open-source code, the next generation of disruptors can tackle massive issues, from global warming to water access, from energy issues to famine. With greater international access to capital, human capital, and cloud computing, nothing that can be imagined by humanity is outside the scope of possibility. Disrupting large institutions and systems requires a healthy dose of pragmatism, but through analyzing the value chain and finding new ways to capture value, virtually any system can and will be improved. The real challenge is for each of us to determine where we feel we can make the most impact.

> *The real challenge is for each of us to determine where we feel we can make the most impact.*

Epilogue: The Self-Disruptor's Manifesto

"I wonder if I've been changed in the night. Let me think: was I the same when I got up this morning? I almost think I can remember feeling a little different. But if I'm not the same, the next question is, Who in the world am I? Ah, that's the great puzzle!"
—Alice in Lewis Carroll's
Alice's Adventures in Wonderland

One of my favorite stories is about the CEO of a very large and successful tech company who realized that it had been years since he toured the halls of the giant corporation he had built. Walking the floors of its Silicon Valley campus unannounced, he stumbled upon a young man staring out the window. Ten minutes went by and the young man continued to stare out the window, not realizing that the CEO was watching him. Another ten minutes, then an hour, and the young man still just lazily stared out the window. The CEO, who had built the company working eighty-hour weeks for fifteen years, was starting to get livid. With his blood pressure rising by the minute, the founder glared at the young man for two hours, until he couldn't take it any longer. The boss angrily raced up to the boardroom, ready to fire the company's management. He demanded that all his senior executives explain what kind of company they were running, where an employee could sit idly for hours doing nothing. "Who is that young man? Who does he work for? What does he do?" the enraged CEO shouted.

Nervously, an executive VP with an Ivy League M.B.A. explained that the engineer in question was the one who had thought up the company's hit product that year and their bestseller from the year before.

This appeared to appease the CEO and save their jobs. Everyone went back to work as normal. The next morning, the daydreaming young man returned to his office, where he discovered that he had been given a bigger window.

We all start out life filled with big dreams and ambitions. The stories recounted and the process described in this book are designed to rekindle that childlike sense that anything is possible. Your future—our world's future—is far more malleable and controllable than most people realize. If we take the time to study how our business and social institutions are constructed, it is possible to determine how they can be disrupted.

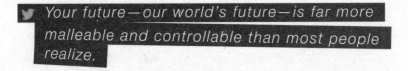

Your future—our world's future—is far more malleable and controllable than most people realize.

No one writes books about those who failed to take risks. History doesn't remember those who maintained the status quo. The glory comes from being a disruptor. Every man and woman would like to leave their mark—some evidence of their existence—on this world. This is the self-disruptor's manifesto: to transform yourself, your business, and the world.

History doesn't remember those who maintained the status quo.

We are all born into an imperfect world filled with opportunities for improvement. For some, the improvement is to build a business that provides products that make life better for their customers. For others, the improvement comes from working to create a more just and verdant society. Still others are driven to connect people in ways never before possible or even imaginable. But anyone setting out to change the world will follow the same path. First, they will have to transform themselves to maximize the opportunities in their lives. According to *Forbes*, only 13 percent of the world's billionaires were born into money.[1] The vast majority of today's most successful individuals changed themselves in such a way as to make becoming a billionaire possible.

JAY SAMIT

"My interest in life comes from setting myself huge, apparently un-achievable challenges and trying to rise above them," Sir Richard Branson said. Branson's first business experience was modest: he sold Christmas trees when he was just twelve years old. He had no formal business training and didn't even go to college.[2] But he is a genius when it comes to just putting his mind to overcoming obstacles. Mary Kay Ash, Simon Cowell, Michael Dell, Barry Diller, Haim Saban, John Paul DeJoria, Steve Jobs, and dozens of other business icons achieved their goals by deciding that nothing would stop them.

All of these business disruptors also looked for where their efforts could make the biggest impact and change the status quo. Innovation is merely problem solving, and problems are merely opportunities waiting to be seized. No obstacle is so big that one person with determination can't make a difference.

> No obstacle is so big that one person with determination can't make a difference.

The more world leaders I have the privilege of meeting, the more I realize that they are no different from you or me. They are simply men and women determined to make the greatest impact they can in the time they have. No one who ever led a nation got there by following in the path of another. Isn't it better to walk alone than to follow a crowd going in the wrong direction? Disruptors just set higher, loftier goals for themselves and those around them.

> No leader got there by following another's path. Better to walk alone than follow a crowd going in the wrong direction.

Lack of access to capital is no longer an excuse for today's disruptors. When Larry Page and Sergey Brin founded Google, back in 1998, the search engine needed the processing power of a $1 million DEC AlphaServer 8400 and a server farm with racks of hard disk storage.[3] Today, an iPad is more powerful than that AlphaServer, and storage in the cloud is a cheap, universally accessible commodity. Researchers spent over $1 billion sequencing the first full human genome at the turn of the twenty-first century, and now software can do it for less than $3,000—and that process may soon cost only $100.[4] The latest technology is waiting for disruptors with big zombie ideas. Low-cost smartphones will bring another one billion people into the digital age and greatly enhance interconnectivity among billions around the globe. The Internet of Things will connect some fifty billion Internet Protocol (IP) devices by the year 2022.[5] Just as barcodes changed how products communicated in retail, IP devices in the home will be able to do everything from monitoring the health of loved ones far away to knowing when the eggs in the refrigerator spoil. In 2016, IP traffic will grow to more than 1.3 zettabytes—ten times all the global IP traffic in 2008.[6] Online connections are now 180 times faster than they were at the turn of the twenty-first century.[7] The actual cost to start a globally disruptive business is much lower than it was just a decade ago.[8] These developments have given all of us the same knowledge and computing power that was limited to very elite institutions just a generation ago. What will we create, and what challenges will we be able to overcome? This is my true purpose in writing this book. I want to help foster a new generation of disruptors: visionaries unfettered by the limitations of the past, who will solve the issues other generations thought impossible.

Even our greatest accomplishments are destined to be disrupted. In 1492, Christopher Columbus was granted a lifetime pension from Spain's Ferdinand and Isabella for making it across the Atlantic. Today, there are over seven hundred transatlantic flights a day, and no one thinks twice about it. People don't drive Model T Fords or use Microsoft DOS computers. Each of these revolutionary advancements was merely a moment in the never-ending cycle of disruption, and they are made all the more special because of how quickly they empowered the next generation of disruptors. The joy of disruption comes from accepting that we all live in a temporal state. In this era of endless innovation, each of us has the power to seek out new problems to solve, to look inside and reexamine our strengths, and to develop a disruptor's mind-set. Our purpose is to contribute to the time we live in by reinventing ourselves and our world.

Daydreams and role models continue to foster my sense of wonder. I feel a deep sense of gratitude for all those who have inspired me and who, by their example, have proved that anything can be disrupted for the betterment of others. By exposing in this book the process for unlocking and creating value, my hope is to inspire the next wave of innovation and disruption. Disruptors benefit society by bringing positive change to all aspects of life.

"You cannot teach a man anything; you can only help him to find it within himself," Galileo wrote. If the insights and stories shared in this book have in any way inspired you to disrupt your life or the world for positive change, please let me know about it. What lessons have you learned? What challenges have you overcome? And what impact are you having on our world?

I very much want to hear from you, my readers, and to share your knowledge. Your personal successes can and will inspire others to write their own disruptor's maps and set a course for positive growth. You can pay it forward by sharing the knowledge and wisdom that you gain from your experience. I have made a place where disruptors can share their stories at jaysamit.com. I hope that by gathering readers' collected wisdom and sharing it online, we can inspire more people to think about how they can change their lives and the lives of others. Take notes. Post pictures. Reach out to me through social media. I would love to share in your joy, your achievements, and your insights. I want to crowdsource the best examples and advice for disruption so that all may benefit. "There are no problems we cannot solve together, and very few that we can solve by ourselves," President Lyndon Johnson wrote.

Disrupt You! is only the beginning of the process. *Disrupt You!* is a call to action, a cry for positive change. I hope it has inspired you to transform yourself, your industry, and the world.

Acknowledgments

Writing a book is a humbling experience. While I did not use a ghost-writer or researchers in writing this book, I also did not come to these insights on my own. My approach to self-disruption was honed over a thirty-year career. The seeds of my philosophy were planted even earlier, during my undergraduate days studying Machiavelli, Schumpeter, Marx, and Engels at the University of California, Los Angeles.

If Marx and Engels had lived in our era and seen the impact of technology broadly disseminated to the masses, how different their writings would have been. While I am the antithesis of a Marxist, I will be the first to admit that his writings point out inherent weaknesses of a capitalistic system that can be easily disrupted through innovation. Today's capitalism is not just disrupted by innovation; market value that is unlocked can easily be lost. Marx drew from Hegel's concept of *Aufheben*, or sublation, which states that something can be preserved only by being destroyed. Sublation is at the core of each cycle of technology and disruption. Faster, more powerful computers destroy the old way of doing things by enabling more data to be processed more quickly and more cheaply. "Change in all things is sweet," Aristotle wrote over two millennia ago.

The insights I've shared in this book are the amalgamation of principles gleaned from every disruptor I have had the pleasure of interacting with over the years. The impact Bill Gates, Paul Allen, David Geffen, Steven Spielberg, Sir Richard Branson, Pierre Omidyar, Steve Jobs, Reid Hoffman, Edgar Bronfman, President Bill Clinton, and Vice President Al Gore have had on my career is immeasurable. I only hope that in some small manner, this book is a way of paying it forward.

I wish I had the space to thank all who have influenced me. To my grandfather Jack Samit, who asked only that I get a story published in my college newspaper: without that one request, I might never have learned how to write. To my college editors, Terry Lee Jones and Tamara Manjikian, who patiently taught me the fundamentals of journalism. To my students of ITP-466: Building the High Tech Startup, the USC Stevens Center for Innovation team, and USC president C. L. Max Nikias: thank you for being the inspiration for this book and for creating such a supportive structure for teaching disruption. (And please continue to forgive me when my students drop out of school to launch their businesses.)

To Ken Berry, Andy Lack, and Sir Howard Stringer, three of the most empowering bosses any disruptor could ever have hoped to work for: I thank you all for having my back and allowing me the latitude to achieve success by breaking the corporate rules again and again.

I owe a huge amount of gratitude to the eighty-plus startup teams I've worked with over the years. I have learned and grown through your actions and your genius. To our investors, big and small: all of these accomplishments were possible only because you risked your capital on the improbable. And to Larry Lieberman and Jack O'Halloran, who taught me that a positive attitude is more valuable than a positive balance sheet.

An immeasurable amount of gratitude goes to Ken Rutkowski and the men of METaL. I have met so many accomplished and inspiring disruptors through this organization. Gabby Stern, Andy Regal, and the entire team at *The Wall Street Journal*: thanks for letting me be a part of your Startup of the Year series and introducing me to the next generation of innovators from around the nation.

Special thanks go out to my poker game buddies, Brad, Rob, Bob, Paul, Mike, Adam, Hank, Randy, and Randal, for decades of weekly free therapy. To Eric Rice, Harrison Painter, Kristin Campbell, and everyone who keep the bytes buzzing at jaysamit.com: thanks for always going above and beyond.

I want to give a big thanks to Tim Sanders for decoding the book publishing business and pointing me in the right direction at the start of this journey. To my literary agent, Richard Pine, Eliza Rothstein, and everyone at InkWell Management who helped me find the perfect publisher. A huge thanks to Bob Miller and Flatiron Books for believing in this project, and to my editor, Whitney Frick, for working with me to get it right. I need to thank my amazing sons, Benji and Danny, who suffered through their father's earliest drafts and who challenged me to make the book better. Boys, you continue to inspire me that the future is so much brighter than the past.

I am grateful to every elementary school teacher who noted on my report card that I "march to the beat of a different drummer," and I'm grateful to my parents for eventually accepting that fact. And last, I dedicate this book to my muse, Dava. Every day, you inspire me to take on the world and make a difference.

Notes

Introduction

1. I would later learn that the California state senator Alan Robbins accepted over $13,500 in bribes from GTECH in exchange for awarding them the lucrative lottery contract—a crime for which Robbins was later sentenced to five years in prison. For more information, see Paul Jacobs and Mark Gladstone, "Robbins Quits Senate, Admits to Corruption: Probe: The San Fernando Valley Democrat Will Be Sentenced to 5 Years in Prison," *Los Angeles Times,* November 20, 1991.

Chapter One: In Defense of Disruption

1. McKinsey Global Institute, *Disruptive Technologies: Advances That Will Transform Life, Business, and the Global Economy,* May 2013, 5.

2. Ibid.

3. Ibid., 9.

4. Hayley Peterson, "America's Shopping Malls Are Dying a Slow, Ugly Death," *Business Insider,* January 31, 2014.

5. James C. Cooper, "3 Million High Paying Jobs (or More) Lost Forever," *The Fiscal Times,* May 16, 2011.

6. Ronald Grover, "L.A.'s Richest Man Ups the Ante for City, Cancer Fight," Reuters, October 3, 2012, accessed October 9, 2014, http://www.reuters.com/article /2012/10/03/us-soon-shiong-idUSBRE89205320121003.

7. Jeff Rubin, *The End of Growth* (Toronto: Random House Canada, 2012), https:// books.google.com/books?id=y40CqP_yY4EC&pg=PT46&lpg=PT46&dq=$2.5 +trillion+oil+consumption&source=bl&ots=r7trVbBjy7&sig=CvZVqDUJapz THDRDhgGWdHrlEiw&hl=en&sa=X&ei=gsegVJrtKcHToAT1tYDABw&

ved=0CB0Q6AEwADgK≠v=onepage&q=%242.5%20trillion%20oil%20con-
sumption&f=false.

8. "Fortune 500 2014," *Fortune,* January 1, 2014, accessed October 9, 2014, http://
fortune.com/fortune500.

9. Christian G. Sandström, "A Revised Perspective on Disruptive Innovation—
Exploring Value, Networks and Business Models," Ph.D. diss., Chalmers University
of Technology, Göteborg, Sweden, 2010.

10. Ibid.

11. Ibid.

12. Richard Foster, *Innovation: The Attacker's Advantage* (New York: Summit Books,
1986).

13. Jeff Leeds, "EMI Accepts $4.7 Billion Buyout Offer," *New York Times,* May
22, 2007, accessed October 9, 2014, http://www.nytimes.com/2007/05/22/business
/22music-web.html.

14. Alex Pham, "EMI Group Sold as Two Separate Pieces to Universal Music
and Sony," *Los Angeles Times,* November 12, 2011, accessed October 9, 2014,
http://articles.latimes.com/2011/nov/12/business/la-fi-ct-emi-sold
-20111112-68.

15. Naoko Fujimura, "Sony's Shopping Spree Is 'Wrong Direction' in Apple Battle,"
Bloomberg, December 13, 2011, accessed October 9, 2014, http://www.bloomberg
.com/news/2011-12-13/stringer-s-shopping-spree-wrong-direction-for
-sony-in-apple-battle-tech.html.

16. "Economic Security for Seniors," fact sheet, National Council on Aging, 2014,
accessed August 30, 2014, http://www.ncoa.org/press-room/fact-sheets/economic
-security-for.html.

17. Dane Stangler and Sam Arbesman, "What Does Fortune 500 Turnover
Mean?" Ewing Marion Kauffman Foundation, June 2012, 4.

18. Antonio Regalado, "Technology Is Wiping Out Companies Faster Than Ever,"
MIT Technology Review, September 10, 2013.

19. Laura Baverman, "Colleges Help Budding Entrepreneurs Get Started," *USA Today,* June 10, 2013, accessed October 9, 2014, http://www.usatoday.com/story /money/columnist/2013/06/09/baverman-columnist-startups-entrepreneurs /2400073.

20. National Business Incubation Association, Resource Library, accessed October 9, 2014, http://www.nbia.org/resource_library.

21. Alan Hall, "'I'm Outta Here!' Why 2 Million Americans Quit Every Month (and 5 Steps to Turn the Epidemic Around)," *Forbes,* March 11, 2013, accessed October 9, 2014, http://www.forbes.com/sites/alanhall/2013/03/11/im-outta-here-why -2-million-americans-quit-every-month-and-5-steps-to-turn-the-epidemic-around.

Chapter Two: Become a Disruptor

1. Caroline Howard, "The 12 Most Disruptive Names in Business: The Full List," *Forbes,* March 27, 2013, accessed October 9, 2014, http://www.forbes.com/sites/caro linehoward/2013/03/27/the-12-most-disruptive-names-in-business-the-full-list.

2. Steven Bertoni, "How Mixing Data and Fashion Can Make Rent the Runway Tech's Next Billion Dollar Star," *Forbes,* September 8, 2014.

3. Chris Denhart, "How the $1.2 Trillion College Debt Crisis Is Crippling Students, Parents and the Economy," *Forbes,* August 7, 2013, accessed August 30, 2014, http://www.forbes.com/sites/specialfeatures/2013/08/07/how-the-college-debt-is -crippling-students-parents-and-the-economy.

4. Howard, "The 12 Most Disruptive Names."

5. Anya Kamenetz, "For Profit and People: UniversityNow Rides a Low-Cost Wave," *New York Times,* November 1, 2013.

6. Bertram Forer, "The Fallacy of Personal Validation: A Classroom Demonstration of Gullibility," *Journal of Abnormal and Social Psychology* 44, no. 1 (January 1949): 118–23.

7. Davis Dyslexia Association International, "Famous People with the Gift of Dyslexia," accessed August 30, 2014, http://www.dyslexia.com/famous.htm.

8. Steve Jobs, commencement address, Stanford University, June 15, 2005, accessed November 11, 2014, http://news.stanford.edu/news/2005/june15/jobs-061505 .html.

9. Jon Hamilton, "How Can Identical Twins Turn Out So Different?" *Shots* blog, NPR, May 9, 2013, accessed October 9, 2014, http://www.npr.org/blogs /health/2013/05/14/182633402/how-can-identical-twins-turn-out-so-different.

10. Reid Hoffman and Ben Casnocha, *The Start-up of You* (New York: Crown Business, 2012), 35.

11. Matt. 25:29 (King James Version).

12. Malcolm Gladwell, *Outliers: The Story of Success* (New York: Little, Brown, 2010), 6.

13. Sheryl Sandberg, "Sheryl Sandberg Leans In," *Cosmopolitan*, March 8, 2013, http:// www.cosmopolitan.com/career/advice/14255/sheryl-sandberg-lean-in-book-excerpt.

14. Sally E. Shaywitz, MD, and Bennett A. Shaywitz, MD, "The Neurobiology of Reading and Dyslexia," *Focus on Basics* 5, issue A (August 2001): 11–15.

15. Emily K. Schwartz, "Richard Branson and the Dyslexia Advantage," *Washington Post*, November 7, 2012.

16. Julie Logan, "Dyslexic Entrepreneurs: The Incidence; Their Coping Strategies and Their Business Skills," Wiley InterScience, 2009, accessed November 11, 2014, doi: 10.1002/dys.388.

17. Brent Bowers, "Tracing Business Acumen to Dyslexia," *New York Times*, December 6, 2007.

18. Gerd Kempermann, "Experience Leads to the Growth of New Brain Cells," Max Planck Institute for Human Development, *Science*, May 10, 2013.

19. Jim Montgomery and Mo Chamber, *Mastering Swimming* (Champaign, Ill.: Human Kinetics, 2009), 3.

20. Antti Revonsuo, "The Reinterpretation of Dreams: An Evolutionary Hypothesis of the Function of Dreaming," *Behavioral and Brain Sciences* 23, no. 6 (2000): 877–901.

21. Brett Henning, *7 Pre-Game Habits of Pro Hockey Players* (Irvine, Calif.: Score 100goals, 2008), 20.

22. Ryan Holiday, "A Leadership Lesson from Eisenhower's Stoic Reversal at D-Day," *Entrepreneur*, June 6, 2014.

23. *Murderball,* directed by Henry Alex Rubin and Dana Adam Shapiro (EAT Films, 2005).

24. Stacy Perman, "How Failure Molded Spanx's Founder," *Bloomberg Businessweek,* November 21, 2007, accessed October 9, 2014, http://www.businessweek.com /stories/2007-11-21/how-failure-molded-spanxs-founderbusinessweek-business -news-stock-market-and-financial-advice.

25. Ibid.

26. Michael Goldberg, *Knock-Out Networking* (Orange, Tex.: Building Blocks Consulting, 2011), 12.

Chapter Three: The Disruptor's Map

1. W. D. Wattles, *The Science of Getting Rich: The Secret to Getting What You Want: Three Prosperity Classics* (New York: Sterling, 2007), 19.

2. Norman Vincent Peale, *The Power of Positive Thinking* (New York: Simon & Schuster, 1952), 13.

3. "Suze Orman's The 9 Steps to Financial Freedom," Random House, accessed October 9, 2014, http://www.randomhouse.com/features/suzeorman.

4. Robert Byrne, *1,911 Best Things Anybody Ever Said* (New York: Fawcett Columbine, 1988), 274.

5. Catherine New, "5 Moms Who Launched a Business After Having a Kid," *Huffington Post,* May 11, 2013, accessed November 11, 2014, http://www.huffington post.com/2013/05/11/moms-who-started-their-own-successful-businesses_n _3253397.html.

6. Reid Hoffman and Ben Casnocha, *The Start-up of You* (New York: Crown Business, 2012), 85.

7. Bronnie Ware, "Top 5 Regrets of the Dying," *Huffington Post,* January 21, 2012, accessed August 30, 2014, http://www.huffingtonpost.com/bronnie-ware/top-5 -regrets-of-the-dyin_b_1220965.html.

8. Clayton J. Moore, *Your Money Puzzle* (Clayton J. Moore Ltd., 2009), 34.

9. Mary Eule Scarborough and David A. Scarborough, *The Procrastinator's Guide to Marketing* (Toronto: Entrepreneur Media, 2008), 27.

Chapter Four: Building a Brand of One

1. Lauren Indvik, "How To: Land Your Dream Job Using Google AdWords," *Mashable,* May 13, 2010, accessed August 31, 2014, http://mashable.com/2010/05/13/job-google-ad-words.

2. David Goldman, "Music's Lost Decade: Sales Cut in Half," *CNN Money,* February 3, 2010, accessed August 31, 2014, http://money.cnn.com/2010/02/02/news/companies/napster_music_industry.

3. Ibid.

4. "Global Wireless Accessories Market to Grow to $50.2 Billion by 2015," CTIA, Resource Library, accessed August 31, 2014, http://www.ctia.org/resource-library/facts-and-infographics/archive/global-market-wireless-accessories.

5. Janet Ong and Naoko Fujimura, "HTC to Acquire Control of Dr. Dre's Beats Headphone Maker for $300 Million," Bloomberg, August 11, 2011, accessed August 31, 2014, http://www.bloomberg.com/news/2011-08-11/htc-to-acquire-control-of-dr-dre-s-beats-headphone-maker-for-300-million.html.

6. Megan Brooks, "Top 100 Most Prescribed, Top-Selling Drugs," *Medscape Medical News,* May 13, 2014, accessed November 11, 2014, http://www.medscape.com/viewarticle/829246.

7. Helen Thompson, "The Boomer Touch," *Advisor Today,* NAIFA, accessed August 31, 2014, http://www.advisortoday.com/archives/article.cfm?articleID=868.

8. "One-Stop Career Transition Services," NOVA, accessed October 9, 2014, http://www.novaworks.org.

9. Calvin Reid, "Blurb: Making Books in Real Time," *Publishers Weekly* 260, no. 34 (August 26, 2013).

10. Christina Austin, "THE BILLIONAIRES' CLUB: Only 36 Companies Have $1,000 Million-Plus Ad Budgets," *Business Insider,* November 11, 2012, accessed October 9, 2014, http://www.businessinsider.com/the-35-companies-that-spent-1-billion-on-ads-in-2011-2012-11.

11. Seth Godin, *Linchpin: Are You Indispensable?* (New York: Portfolio, 2010), 56.

12. Don Power, "Twitter Success Story: Stacey Ferreira Lands a Million Dollar Tweet," *Sprout,* January 22, 2013, accessed August 31, 2014, http://sproutsocial .com/insights/richard-branson-twitter/

Chapter Five: Disruptors at Work and the Value of Intrapreneurship

1. David Goldman, "Music's Lost Decade: Sales Cut in Half," *CNN Money,* February 3, 2010, accessed August 31, 2014, http://money.cnn.com/2010/02/02/news /companies/napster_music_industry.

2. Joseph Menn, *All the Rave: The Rise and Fall of Shawn Fanning's Napster* (New York: Crown Business, 2003), 158–61.

3. Shawn Tully, "Big Man Against Big Music: Think the Record Companies Will Bury Napster? John Hummer Is Betting You're Wrong—and He's Hired David Boies to Prove It," *Fortune,* August 14, 2000.

4. Brian Hiatt and Evan Serpick, "The Record Industry's Decline," *Rolling Stone,* June 19, 2007.

5. Goldman, "Music's Lost Decade."

6. John Paczkowski, "The iPhone Doesn't Appeal to Business Customers at All?" *All Things D,* December 2, 2008, accessed August 31, 2014, http://allthingsd .com/20081202/no-the-iphone-doesnt-appeal-to-business-customers-at-all.

7. Vijay Govindarajan and Chris Trimble, *The Other Side of Innovation: Solving the Executive Challenge* (Cambridge, Mass.: Harvard Business Review, 2010), ix.

8. "Kodak Cuts over the Years," RochesterHomepage.net, January 29, 2009, accessed August 31, 2014, http://www.rochesterhomepage.net/story/web-extra-kodak -cuts-over-the-years/d/story/yEnvA-84rke582S4aRor0w.

9. Michael J. de la Merced, "Eastman Kodak Files for Bankruptcy," *New York Times,* January 19, 2012, accessed August 31, 2014, http://dealbook.nytimes .com/2012/01/19/eastman-kodak-files-for-bankruptcy.

10. Govindarajan and Trimble, *Other Side of Innovation.*

11. Gordon Moore, "Cramming More Components onto Integrated Circuits," *Electronics Magazine,* January 1, 1998.

12. "2014 January: CEO Turnover Soars 32 Percent as Year Starts," Challenger, Gray & Christmas, accessed August 20, 2014, http://www.challengergray.com /press/press-release/2014-january-ceo-turnover-soars-32-percent-year-stats.

13. Jennifer Rooney, "CMO Tenure Hits 43-Month Mark," *Forbes,* June 14, 2012.

14. "'Managerial Myopia': How CEOs Pump Up Earnings for Their Own Gain," Knowledge@Wharton, Wharton School of the University of Pennsylvania, accessed August 30, 2014, http://knowledge.wharton.upenn.edu/article/managerial-myopia -ceos-pump-earnings-gain.

15. http://www.thefreelibrary.com/Simutronics+Inks+Game+Development+Pact +with+Universal+Studios-a019734718.

16. Kenneth Wong and Dina Bass, "SAP to Acquire Ariba for $4.3 Billion in Push into Cloud," Bloomberg, May 23, 2012, accessed October 9, 2014, http:// www.bloomberg.com/news/2012-05-22/sap-agrees-to-buy-ariba.html.

17. Jessi Hempel, "Will Marissa Mayer Save Yahoo?" *Fortune,* May 1, 2014, accessed October 9, 2014, http://fortune.com/2014/05/01/will-marissa-mayer-save -yahoo.

18. David Karp, news post, Tumblr, May 20, 2013, accessed August 30, 2014, staff.tumblr.com/post/50902268806/news.

Chapter Six: In Search of the Zombie Idea

1. Dana Canedy, "Procter & Gamble Is Buying Maker of Premium Pet Food," *New York Times,* August 12, 1999.

2. Amir Efrati, "Google Confirms Waze Maps App Purchase," *Wall Street Journal,* June 11, 2013, accessed October 9, 2014, http://online.wsj.com/news/articles/SB1 0001424127887323499045785393709800686106.

3. Martha Barlette, *Marketing to Women: How to Understand, Reach, and Increase Your Share of the World's Largest Market Segment* (Chicago: Dearborn Trade, 2003), https://books.google.com/books?id=yXwW25rY1VcC&pg=PR7&lpg=PR7&dq =women+83%25+of+all+consumer+purchases&source=bl&ots=plaXtM0Xfc& sig=2ODgiKW_Ih3ycODE-BH78hBeN5w&hl=en&sa=Xei=C8ygVL6Y A8nsoAS7k4LgDA&ved=0CCwQ6AEwAw≠v=onepage&q=women%20 83%25%20of%20all%20consumer%20purchases&f=false.

4. Mary-Catherine Lader, "Axon Sleep Research Laboratories," *Brown Daily Herald,* March 23, 2005, accessed October 9, 2014, http://www.browndailyherald .com/2005/03/23/axon-sleep-research-laboratories.

5. Kimberly Kuizon, "Google Science Fair Winner, Sarasota's Brittany Wenger, Created Program to Help Detect Breast Cancer," *ABC Action News,* July 27, 2012, accessed November 11, 2014, http://www.abcactionnews.com/news/region-sara sota-manatee/google-science-fair-winner-sarasotas-brittany-wenger-created-pro gram-to-help-detect-breast-cancer.

6. Adeo Ressi, "No One Is Going to Steal Your Stupid Startup Idea, by Adeo Ressi," Founder Institute, February 1, 2013, accessed August 31, 2014, http:// fi.co/posts/937.

7. About the Founder Institute, Founder Institute, accessed October 9, 2014, http:// fi.co/about.

8. John Greathouse, "Steve Jobs: 5 (More) Motivational Business Tips," *Forbes,* May 18, 2013, accessed October 9, 2014, http://www.forbes.com/sites/johngreat house/2013/05/18/steve-jobs-5-more-motivational-business-tips.

9. Duke Lee, "Your Job Is to Kill Your Stupid Idea," Founder Institute, February 18, 2014, accessed August 31, 2014, http://fi.co/posts/4471.

10. Raffaele Mauro, "The Y-Combinator Model: High-Potential Accelerators and Innovative Ecosystems," *Rafstart,* December 2013, accessed August 31, 2014, http://rafstart.blogspot.com/2014/01/the-y-combinator-model-high-potential .html.

11. John Furrier, "Entrepreneurial 'Red Meat'—Calling All Entrepreneurs—Paul Graham Throws Chum in the Water," SiliconAngle.com, July 20, 2008, accessed August 31, 2014, http://siliconangle.com/furrier/2008/07/20/entrepreurial-red -meat-calling-all-entrepreneurs-paul-graham-throws-chum-in-the-water.

12. Paul Graham, "Startup Ideas We'd Like to Fund," Y Combinator, July 1, 2008, accessed October 9, 2014, http://old.ycombinator.com/ideas.html.

13. "Steal This Start-Up! No Longer Content to Write Checks, VCs Are Giving Away Their Best Ideas," *Observer,* June 30, 2011, accessed February 7, 2015,

http://observer.com/2011/06/steal-this-start-up-no-longer-content-to-write
-checks-vcs-are-giving-away-their-best-ideas.

14. Anthony Ha, "Angel Investor Ron Conway: Every Entrepreneur Should Get Funded," *VB News,* July 29, 2010, accessed February 7, 2015, http://venturebeat .com/2010/07/29/angelconfron-conway-michael-arrington.

15. "Overture Services (GoTo.com)," IdeaLab, accessed August 31, 2014, http:// www.idealab.com/our_companies/show/all/overture.

16. Seth Weintraub, "Excite Passes Up Buying Google for $750,000 in 1999," *Fortune,* September 29, 2010, accessed November 11, 2014, http://fortune.com /2010/09/29/excite-passed-up-buying-google-for-750000-in-1999.

Chapter Seven: Pivoting Your Energies

1. Bill Gates to Executive Staff and Direct Reports, email message, May 26, 1995, available at Letters of Note, accessed August 31, 2014, http://www.lettersof note.com/2011/07/internet-tidal-wave.html.

2. Robert Jordan, "How to Make One Better Decision Each Day," *Forbes,* September 21, 2012, accessed October 9, 2014, http://www.forbes.com/sites/robert jordan/2012/09/21/how-to-make-one-better-decision-each-day.

3. Randall Smith and Geoffrey Fowler, "Yelp IPO Targets $2 Billion," *Wall Street Journal,* November 9, 2011, accessed October 9, 2014, http://online.wsj.com/arti cles/SB10001424052970204190704577026140347386380.

4. Evelyn Rusli, "Facebook Buys Instagram for $1 Billion," *New York Times*, April 9, 2012, accessed November 11, 2014, http://dealbook.nytimes.com/2012/04/09 /facebook-buys-instagram-for-1-billion.

5. Michael Arrington, "Google Has Acquired YouTube," *TechCrunch,* October 9, 2006, accessed August 31, 2014, http://techcrunch.com/2006/10/09/google-has -acquired-youtube.

6. "Twitter, Inc.," finance market cap as of August 31, 2014, Yahoo! Finance, http://finance.yahoo.com/q?s=TWTR&ql=1.

7. Allison Canty, "The Early Failures of Famous Entrepreneurs (and What They Learned)," *Entrepreneurship,* November 17, 2011, accessed August 31, 2014, http://

grasshopper.com/blog/the-early-failures-of-famous-entrepreneurs-and-what
-they-learned-3.

8. "Bill Gates, "Entrepreneurship Hall of Fame," accessed August 31, 2014, http://
www.theehalloffame.com/gates.html.

9. "Jessica Simpson's Net Worth Rises, Empire Makes $1 Billion," Lalate.com,
December 7, 2010, accessed August 31, 2014, http://news.lalate.com/2010/12/07
/jessica-simpson-net-worth-rises-empire-worth-1-billion.

10. Sapna Maheshwari, "The Numbers Behind Victoria's Secret and Its Iconic Fashion Show," *Buzzfeed News,* November 13, 2013, accessed August 31, 2014, http://
www.buzzfeed.com/sapna/the-numbers-behind-victorias-secret-and-its-iconic
-fashion-s#3l7oddq.

11. Sam Shead, "Ubuntu Edge Sets Crowdfunding Record, Beating Pebble
Smartwatch," *Techworld,* August 16, 2013, accessed August 31, 2014, http://news
.techworld.com/mobile-wireless/3464373/ubuntu-edge-sets-crowdfunding-record
-beating-pebble-smartwatch.

12. Ian Harvey, "Richard Branson Doesn't Mind Being a 'Crazy One,'" *Globe and
Mail,* August 22, 2014, accessed August 31, 2014, http://www.theglobeandmail
.com/report-on-business/innovators-at-work/richard-branson-doesnt-mind
-being-a-crazy-one/article20172565.

13. Zack Epstein, "Amazon's Secret Weapon (No, It's Not Drones)," BGR.com,
December 17, 2013, accessed August 31, 2014, http://bgr.com/2013/12/17/amazon
-prime-spending-study-cirp.

14. Adrienne Jane Burke, "Startup Creativity Flourishes at NY Tech Day," *Techonomy,*
April 29, 2013, accessed August 31, 2014, http://techonomy.com/2013/04/startup
-creativity-flourishes-at-ny-tech-day.

Chapter Eight: Unlocking the Value Chain

1. Michael E. Porter, *Competitive Advantage: Creating and Sustaining Superior
Performance* (New York: Free Press, 1985).

2. Franziska Bieri, *From Blood Diamonds to the Kimberley Process: How NGOs
Cleaned Up the Global Diamond Industry* (Burlington: Ashgate Publishing, 2010),
https://books.google.com/books?id=liq6NrDcm5UC&pg=PA5&dq=$9+billion

+diamonds+mined+annually&hl=en&sa=X&ei=g82gVPfMNYKloQTQ
8IKIBA&ved=0CCsQ6AEwAg#v=onepage&q=%249%20billion%20
diamonds%20mined%20annually&f=false.

3. Bain & Company, *The Global Diamond Industry—Lifting the Veil of Mystery* (Antwerp: Antwerp World Diamond Centre, 2011), http://www.bain.com/Images /PR_BAIN_REPORT_The_global_diamond_industry.pdf.

4. Mike Spector, Douglas MacMillan, and Evelyn M. Rusli, "TPG-Led Group Closes $450 Million Investment in Airbnb," *Wall Street Journal,* April 18, 2014, accessed August 31, 2014, http://online.wsj.com/news/articles/SB1000142405270 2304626304579509800267341652.

Chapter Nine: Research and Development: Unlocking the Value of Waste

1. Drew Armstrong and Susan Decker, "Pfizer's Deal on Generic Viagra Shows Treatment Changes," Bloomberg, December 18, 2013, accessed October 9, 2014, http://www.bloomberg.com/news/2013-12-18/pfizer-s-deal-on-generic -viagra-shows-treatment-changes.html.

2. "Peter C. L. Hodgson Obituary (*New York Times*)," *Silly Putty—Early History— This Is What I Know* blog, January 1, 2011, accessed August 31, 2014, http://silly puttyhistory.blogspot.com/2011/01/blog-post.html.

3. Ann Thayer, "What's That Stuff? Silly Putty," *Chemical and Engineering News* 78, no. 48 (2000): 27.

4. "Play-Doh FAQ & Tips," Hasbro, accessed October 9, 2014, http://www.has bro.com/playdoh/en_US/discover/faq.cfm.

5. Bethanne Kelly Patrick and John M. Thompson, *An Uncommon History of Common Things* (Washington, D.C.: National Geographic, 2009).

6. "Million Dollar Baby—Businesses Designing and Selling Open Source Hardware, Making Millions," *Adafruit* blog, May 3, 2010, accessed August 31, 2014, www.adafruit.com/blog/2010/05/03/million-dollar-baby-businesses-designing -and-selling-open-source-hardware-making-millions.

7. Chris Anderson, "How I Accidentally Kickstarted the Domestic Drone Boom," *Wired,* June 22, 2012, accessed October 9, 2014, http://www.wired.com/2012/06 /ff_drones/all.

8. "Million Dollar Baby."

9. "New Beer Uses Pre-Launch Viral Email Vote to Turn Consumers into Evangelists," MarketingSherpa, June 24, 2003, accessed October 9, 2014, http://www.marketingsherpa.com/article/case-study/new-beer-uses-prelaunch-viral.

10. "Spinoff Benefits: By the Numbers," fact sheet, NASA.gov, 2013, accessed August 31, 2014, http://spinoff.nasa.gov/Spinoff2012/pdf/by_numbers.pdf.

11. Ibid.

12. "NASA Engages the Public to Discover New Uses for Out-of-this-World Technologies," NASA.gov, October 23, 2013, accessed February 7, 2015, http://www.nasa.gov/content/nasa-engages-the-public-to-discover-new-uses-for-out-of-this-world-technologies/#.VNZ4PLDF-5I.

13. Molly Wood, "Samsung Stakes Claim in Wearable Tech That Monitors Health," *New York Times*, May 29, 2014.

14. Fiona Graham, "Crowdsourcing: Inventing the Question to Fit Your Answer," BBC.com, June 10, 2013, accessed August 31, 2014, http://www.bbc.com/news/business-22847802.

15. Ibid.

16. "30 Under 30," *Inc.*, 2007, accessed August 31, 2014, http://www.inc.com/30under30/2007/1-kaufman.html.

17. Graham, "Crowdsourcing."

Chapter Ten: Design: Disruption Through Aesthetics

1. Jack Hope, "A Better Mousetrap," *American Heritage*, October 1, 1996.

2. Seth Stevenson, "Why Are Poland Spring Bottles So Crinkly?" *Slate*, June 19, 2012, accessed August 31, 2014, www.slate.com/articles/business/operations/2012/06/poland_spring_s_new_bottles_why_are_they_so_thin_and_flimsy_.html.

3. Allen Myerson, "Pennzoil and Quaker State Plan a Two Stage Merger," *New York Times*, April 16, 1998, accessed August 31, 2014, http://www.nytimes.com/1998/04/16/business/pennzoil-and-quaker-state-plan-a-two-stage-merger.html.

4. Peter M. Senge, *The Fifth Discipline: The Art and Practice of the Learning Organization* (New York: Doubleday/Currency, 1990).

5. "Quotebank: Brands," Warc.com, accessed August 31, 2014, http://www.warc
.com/Pages/NewsAndOpinion/Quotebank.aspx?Category=Brands.

6. "U.S. Travel Market Tops $300 Billion as Fiscal Cliff Looms," Yahoo! Finance,
http://finance.yahoo.com/news/u-travel-market-tops-300-225659240.html.

7. Harry McCracken, "The 50 Best Websites of 2011," *Time,* August 16, 2011.

8. "Beyond the Rack Doubles Mobile Sales After Launching Dedicated Mobile
Site," Google case study, accessed August 31, 2014, http://static.googleusercontent
.com/media/www.google.com/en/us/think/multiscreen/pdf/beyond-the-rack
-multi-screen-resources_case-studies.pdf.

Chapter Eleven: Production: Reuse, Repurpose, Re-create

1. "Population of Germany," Tacitus.nu, accessed August 31, 2014, http://www.taci
tus.nu/historical-atlas/population/germany.html.

2. Terry Breverton, *Breverton's Encyclopedia of Inventions: A Compendium of
Technological Leaps, Groundbreaking Discoveries and Scientific Breakthroughs* (London:
Quercus, 2012), chapter 3.

3. Francis Bacon, *Novum Organum* (1620), as quoted on HistoryGallery.com, accessed
August 31, 2014, http://historygallery.com/books/1740bacon/1740bacon.htm.

4. McKinsey Global Institute, *Disruptive Technologies: Advances That Will Transform Life, Business, and the Global Economy,* May 2013.

5. T. J. McCue, "3D Printing Industry Will Reach $3.1 Billion Worldwide by
2016," *Forbes,* March 27, 2012, accessed August 31, 2014, http://www.forbes.com
/sites/tjmccue/2012/03/27/3d-printing-industry-will-reach-3-1-billion-world
wide-by-2016.

6. Neal Ungerleider, "This African Inventor Created a $100 3-D Printer from E-
Waste," *Fast Company,* October 11, 2013, accessed August 31, 2014, http://www
.fastcompany.com/3019880/this-african-inventor-created-a-100-3-d-printer
-from-e-waste.

7. Nathan Laliberte, "No Time for Car Shopping? Click 'Print' to Make Your

Own," *New York Times,* September 26, 2014, accessed October 8, 2014, http://www
.nytimes.com/2014/09/28/automobiles/no-time-for-car-shopping-click-print
-to-make-your-own.html.

8. Andy Greenberg, "$25 Gun Created with Cheap 3D Printer Fires Nine Shots,"
Forbes, May 20, 2013, accessed August 31, 2014, http://www.forbes.com/sites
/andygreenberg/2013/05/20/25-gun-created-with-cheap-3d-printer-fires-nine
-shots-video.

9. Lorenzo Franceschi-Bicchierai, "Officials: Stopping 3D Printed Guns Could
Be Impossible," *Mashable,* May 24, 2013, accessed August 31, 2014, http://mashable
.com/2013/05/24/stopping-3d-printed-guns.

10. "3D Printing Is 'Bringing the Factory Back to the Individual,'" *Dezeen,* October 19, 2012, accessed August 31, 2014, http://www.dezeen.com/2012/10/19/3d
-printing-is-bringing-the-factory-back-to-the-individual.

11. "Staples First Major US Retailer to Announce 3D Printers," Staples.com, May
3, 2013, accessed August 31, 2014, http://investor.staples.com/phoenix.zhtml?c=9
6244&p=RssLanding&cat=news&id=1814995.

12. Vivek Wadhwa, "Anyone Anywhere Can Build the Next Google—There Are
No Barriers," *Forbes,* November 21, 2013, accessed August 31, 2014, http://www
.forbes.com/sites/singularity/2013/11/21/anyone-anywhere-can-build-the-next
-google-there-are-no-barriers.

13. Barack Obama, State of the Union Address, February 12, 2013, WhiteHouse
.gov, accessed August 31, 2014, http://www.whitehouse.gov/the-press-office
/2013/02/12/remarks-president-state-union-address.

14. Jarrett Murphy, "One Billion Live in Slums," CBSNews.com, October 8,
2003, accessed August 31, 2014, http://www.cbsnews.com/news/1-billion-live-
in-slums.

Chapter Twelve: Marketing and Sales: Finding the Problem to
Fit Your Solution

1. Robert Litan, "What Priceline.com Learned from Economists," *Fortune,* September 29, 2014, accessed October 10, 2014, http://fortune.com/2014/09/29
/what-priceline-learned-from-economists.

2. "The Idea: Continuous Magazine Subscriptions," Walker Digital, accessed

August 31, 2014, http://www.walkerdigital.com/innovations_ideas-in-action
-continuous.html.

3. John Brownlee, "Why Printer Ink Should Be Packaged like Chanel No. 5,"
Fast Company, December 12, 2013, accessed August 31, 2014, http://www.fast
codesign.com/3021290/why-printer-ink-should-be-packaged-like-chanel-no-5.

4. Peter Drucker, *Innovation and Entrepreneurship* (London: Routledge, 2007), 223.

5. Geraldine Fabrikant, "Lowell Paxson Has a Dream: To Start Yet Another
Television Network," *New York Times,* June 30, 1997, accessed October 1, 2014,
http://www.nytimes.com/1997/06/30/business/lowell-paxson-has-a-dream-to
-start-yet-another-television-network.html.

6. "Corporate Profile," HSN, accessed October 10, 2014, http://www.hsni.com/in
vestors.cfm.

7. "Bud Paxson Net Worth," TheRichest.com, accessed August 31, 2014, http://www
.therichest.com/celebnetworth/celebrity-business/men/bud-paxson-net-worth.

8. Eszter Hargittai, "Amazon's Price Discrimination," *Crooked Timber* blog, December 22, 2008, accessed August 31, 2014, http://crookedtimber.org/2008/12/22
/amazons-price-discrimination.

9. Asad Madni, "Cost Benefit Analysis of RFID Implementations in Retail Stores,"
IEEE Systems Journal 1, no. 2 (January 2008), doi: 10.1109/JSYST.2007.909788.

10. Rebecca Clancy, "Red Bull 'Worth £5bn' After Felix Baumgartner Skydive,"
Telegraph, October 15, 2012, accessed August 31, 2014, http://www.telegraph.co.uk
/finance/newsbysector/retailandconsumer/leisure/9609231/Red-Bull-worth-5bn
-after-Felix-Baumgartner-skydive.html.

11. Verse, "Trey Songz Scores 1st UK Top Ten Single with 'Simply Amazing,'"
Soul Culture, August 19, 2012, accessed August 31, 2014, http://soulculture.com
/music -blog/trey-songz-scores-1st-uk-top-ten-single-with-simply-amazing-music
-news.

12. "Jeffrey P. Bezos," Academy of Achievement, accessed February 7, 2015, http://
www.achievement.org/autodoc/page/bez0int-5.

13. Wayne Neimi, "Zappos Milestone: Q&A with Tony Hsieh," Zappos.com,

May 4, 2009, accessed August 31, 2014, http://about.zappos.com/press-center /media-coverage/zappos-milestone-qa-tony-hsieh.

14. Michael Bush, "Virgin America on Why Twitter, Facebook Are More Important Than TV," *Advertising Age,* February 9, 2011, accessed August 31, 2014, http:// adage.com/article/digital/virgin-america-values-twitter-facebook-tv/148795.

15. "40 Eye-Opening Customer Services Quotes," *Forbes,* March 3, 2014, accessed August 31, 2014, http://www.forbes.com/sites/ekaterinawalter/2014/03/04/40 -eye-opening-customer-service-quotes.

16. "CD-ROME: Pope Blesses PBS Disc," *Variety,* May 29, 1995, accessed August 31, 2014, http://variety.com/1995/scene/markets-festivals/cd-rome-pope-blesses -pbs-disc-99127196.

Chapter Thirteen: Distribution: Unlocking Unattained Value and the Challenge of Unlimited Shelf Space

1. Nilay Patel, "Kindle Sells Out in 5.5 Hours," engadget.com, November 21, 2007, accessed March 2, 2015, www.engadget.com/2007/11/21/kindle-sells-out-in -two-days.

2. Peter Diamandis, "Why Billion-Dollar, 100-Year-Old Companies Die," *Peter's Blog,* Peter H. Diamandis, April 19, 2013, accessed October 10, 2014, http://www .diamandis.com/the-launch-pad/why-billion-dollar-100-year-old-companies -die/1743.

3. Claire Cain Miller and Julie Bosman, "E-Books Outsell Print Books at Amazon," *New York Times,* May 19, 2011, accessed August 31, 2014, http://www.nytimes .com/2011/05/20/technology/20amazon.html.

4. Jeff Jordan, "Why Malls Are Getting Mauled," *Jeff Jordan* blog, December 21, 2012, accessed August 31, 2014, http://jeff.a16z.com/2012/12/21/why-malls-are -getting-mauled.

5. Polly Curtis, "Is Cyber Monday Just PR Spin?" *Guardian,* December 5, 2011, accessed October 10, 2014, http://www.theguardian.com/politics/reality-check -with-polly-curtis/2011/dec/05/retail-internet.

6. Daniel Lyons, "A Decade of Destruction," *Newsweek,* July 19, 2009, accessed August 31, 2014, http://2010.newsweek.com/essay/a-decade-of-destruction.html.

7. Douglas A. McIntyre, Samuel Weigley, Alexander E. M. Hess, and Michael B. Sauter, "Retailers That Will Close the Most Stores," *USA Today*, February 3, 2013, accessed August 31, 2014, http://www.usatoday.com/story/money/business /2013/02/01/retailers-close-stores-24-7/1873745.

8. Ibid.

9. Ibid.

10. Steven Levy, "In Conversation with Jeff Bezos: CEO of the Internet," Wired .co.uk, December 12, 2011, accessed August 31, 2014, http://www.wired.co.uk/mag azine/archive/2012/01/features/ceo-of-the-internet/viewall.

11. Marie Cabural, "Market News: Apple Inc., Archer Midland Daniels, Amazon, eBay," *ValueWalk*, November 29, 2013, accessed August 31, 2014, http://www.value walk.com/2013/11/market-news-apple-inc-archer-midland-daniels-amazon-ebay.

12. "Apple's App Store Marks Historic 50 Billionth Download," Apple.com, May 16, 2013, accessed August 31, 2014, http://www.apple.com/pr/library/2013 /05/16Apples-App-Store-Marks-Historic-50-Billionth-Download.html.

13. George Anders, "Jeff Bezos's Top 10 Leadership Lessons," *Forbes*, April 4, 2012, accessed October 10, 2014, http://www.forbes.com/sites/georgeanders/2012 /04/04/bezos-tips.

14. Pierre Omidyar, "From Self to Society: Citizenship to Community for a World of Change," commencement address, Tufts University, May 2002, *Tufts Journal*, accessed November 11, 2014, http://tuftsjournal.tufts.edu/archive/2002/august /features/commencement_2002.shtml.

15. "eBay and U.S. Postal Service Drive Shipping Innovation for Millions of Entrepreneurs, Small Businesses and Retailers," USPS.gov, April 5, 2012, accessed August 31, 2014, http://about.usps.com/news/national-releases/2012 /pr12_042.htm.

16. "About Ellusionist," Ellusionist.com, accessed August 31, 2014, http://www.el lusionist.com/about-us.

17. L. Gordon Crovitz, "Justice Department Bites Apple," *All Things D*, April 23, 2012, accessed August 31, 2014, http://allthingsd.com/20120423/justice-depart ment-bites-apple.

18. Romain Dillet, "Apple's Pile of Cash Is Still Growing, Up 6% to $145 Billion," *TechCrunch,* April 23, 2013, accessed August 31, 2014, http://techcrunch.com/2013/04/23/apple-cash-q2-2013.

19. John Koetsier, "Apple's Cash Hoard Reaches $137 Billion," *VentureBeat,* January 23, 2013, accessed August 31, 2014, http://venturebeat.com/2013/01/23/apples-cash-hoard-reaches-137-billion.

20. Megan Geuss, "On Average, Americans Get 189 Cable TV Channels and Only Watch 17," *Ars Technica,* May 6, 2014, accessed August 31, 2014, http://arstechnica.com/business/2014/05/on-average-americans-get-189-cable-tv-channels-and-only-watch-17.

21. Robin Wauters, "TiVo Research Claims Only 38 Percent of Users Watch Live TV," *TechCrunch,* January 11, 2012, accessed August 31, 2014, http://techcrunch.com/2012/01/11/tivo-research-claims-only-38-percent-of-users-watch-live-tv.

22. "Ad Forecasts: Reaching the Half Trillion Mark," Magna Global, June 16, 2014, accessed October 10, 2014, http://news.magnaglobal.com/article_display.cfm?article_id=1578.

23. "Are Young People Watching Less TV? (Updated—Q1 2014 Data)," *MarketingCharts,* July 7, 2014, accessed August 31, 2014, http://www.marketingcharts.com/television/are-young-people-watching-less-tv-24817.

24. Gordon Smith, "Opinion: Compromise Benefits TV Viewers," *Politico,* November 16, 2010, accessed October 10, 2014, http://www.politico.com/news/stories/1110/45152.html.

25. Paul Tassi, "Always On: Microsoft Xbox Live Subscriptions Up to 46M, Will Never Be Free," *Forbes,* April 20, 2013, accessed August 31, 2014, http://www.forbes.com/sites/insertcoin/2013/04/20/always-on-microsoft-xbox-live-subscriptions-up-to-46m-will-never-be-free.

26. "The U.S. Digital Consumer Report," Nielsen, February 10, 2014, accessed October 10, 2014, http://www.nielsen.com/content/corporate/us/en/insights/reports/2014/the-us-digital-consumer-report.html.

27. Tim Bajarin, "How Twitter Is Impacting the World of Television," *PC Magazine,* February 3, 2014, accessed August 31, 2014, http://www.pcmag.com/article2/0,2817,2430128,00.asp.

28. David Goldman, "Music's Lost Decade: Sales Cut in Half," *CNN Money*, February 3, 2010, accessed August 31, 2014, http://money.cnn.com/2010/02/02/news /companies/napster_music_industry.

29. Zoe Fox, "85% of the World Will Have High-Speed Mobile Internet by 2017," *Mashable*, June 5, 2012, accessed October 10, 2014, http://mashable.com /2012/06/05/mobile-internet-global-reach.

30. Sven Grundberg, "'Candy Crush Saga' Maker Files for an IPO," *Wall Street Journal*, February 18, 2014, accessed October 10, 2014, http://online.wsj.com/news /articles/SB10001424052702304675504579390580.

31. Clay Shirky, "It's Not Information Overload. It's Filter Failure," keynote presentation, Web 2.0 Expo, New York, October 18, 2008, http://www.web2expo .com/webexny2008/public/schedule/detail/4817.

32. "Statistics," YouTube.com, accessed August 31, 2014, https://www.youtube .com/yt/press/statistics.html.

33. Suzanne Vranica, "TV Ad Dollars Slowly Shifting to Web Video," *Wall Street Journal*, May 12, 2014, accessed August 31, 2014, http://online.wsj.com/news /articles/SB10001424052702303851804579558091795473048.

Chapter Fourteen: Capital Revisited: Other People's Money

1. Diane Mulcahy, Bill Weeks, and Harold S. Bradley, "We Have Met the Enemy . . . and He Is Us," Ewing Marion Kauffman Foundation, May 2012, accessed August 31, 2014, http://www.kauffman.org/~/media/kauffman_org/research%20 reports%20and%20covers/2012/05/we%20have%20met%20the%20enemy%20 and%20he%20is%20us(1).pdf.

2. Ibid.

3. Pamela G. Hollie, "Advertising; Big Mac's Olympic Giveaway," *New York Times*, August 10, 1984, accessed August 31, 2014, http://www.nytimes.com /1984/08/10/business/advertising-big-mac-s-olympic-giveaway.html.

4. "Electronic Commerce," *Reference for Business: Encyclopedia of Business,* accessed October 10, 2014, http://www.referenceforbusiness.com/encyclopedia/Eco-Ent /Electronic-Commerce.html.

Chapter Fifteen: Disruption in the Era of the Crowd

1. "Wikipedia Founder Jimmy Wales Responds," *Slashdot,* July 28, 2004, accessed October 10, 2014, http://interviews.slashdot.org/story/04/07/28/1351230/Wikipedia -Founder-Jimmy-Wales-Responds.

2. "Wikipedia:Statistics," Wikipedia, accessed August 31, 2014, http://en.wikipedia .org/wiki/Wikipedia:Statistics.

3. Ted Dziuba, "Sphinx—Text Search the Pirate Bay Way," *Register,* May 8, 2009, accessed August 31, 2014, http://www.theregister.co.uk/Print/2009/05/08/dziuba _sphinx.

4. Interview with Craig Newmark, *News War, Frontline,* PBS, February 27, 2007.

5. "Craigslist," *TechCrunch,* accessed August 31, 2014, http://techcrunch.com/topic /company/craigslist.

6. Daniel Lyons, "A Decade of Destruction," *Newsweek,* July 19, 2009, accessed August 31, 2014, http://2010.newsweek.com/essay/a-decade-of-destruction.html.

7. Mark Bao, "Creative Destruction: How Entrepreneurs and the Internet Disrupt Old Industries," *Mark Bao's Journal,* November 18, 2009, accessed August 31, 2014, http://journal.markbao.com/category/startups.

8. Thomas L. Friedman, "Welcome to the 'Sharing Economy,'" *New York Times,* July 20, 2013, accessed August 31, 2014, http://www.nytimes.com/2013/07/21 /opinion/sunday/friedman-welcome-to-the-sharing-economy.html.

9. Eric Markowitz, "Airbnb Is Changing Travel," *Inc.,* November 29, 2012, accessed August 31, 2014, http://www.inc.com/eric-markowitz/airbnb/company-of -the-year-2012-runner-up.html.

10. Evelyn Rusli, "Facebook Buys Instagram for $1 Billion," *New York Times,* April 9, 2012, accessed November 11, 2014, http://dealbook.nytimes.com/2012 /04/09/facebook-buys-instagram-for-1-billion.

11. Parmy Olson, "Facebook Closes $19 Billion WhatsApp Deal," *Forbes,* October 6, 2014, accessed October 10, 2014, http://www.forbes.com/sites/parmyolson /2014/10/06/facebook-closes-19-billion-whatsapp-deal.

12. Tero Kuittinen, "As iPhone Mobile Data Usage Soars, Voice Calls Dive," *Forbes,* October 15, 2012, accessed August 31, 2014, http://www.forbes.com/sites /terokuittinen/2012/10/15/as-iphone-mobile-data-usage-soars-voice-calls-dive.

13. Colleen Taylor and Ingrid Lunden, "With $1.2 Billion Yammer Buy, Microsoft's Social Enterprise Strategy Takes Shape," *TechCrunch,* June 25, 2012, accessed August 31, 2014, http://techcrunch.com/2012/06/25/its-official-microsoft-con firms-it-has-acquired-yammer-for-1-2-billion-in-cash.

Chapter Sixteen: Disrupt the World

1. Jeff Suess, "Libraries Are Carnegie's Legacy 106 Years Later," Cincinnati.com, October 29, 2012, accessed August 31, 2014, http://www2.cincinnati.com/blogs /ourhistory/2012/10/29/libraries-are-carnegies-legacy-106-years-later.

2. Susannah Fox and Lee Rainie, "How the Internet Has Woven Itself into American Life," *Pew Research Internet Project,* Pew Research Center, February 7, 2014, accessed October 10, 2014, http://www.pewinternet.org/2014/02/27/part-1 -how-the-internet-has-woven-itself-into-american-life.

3. With an eBay fortune in excess of $8 billion, Pierre and his wife, Pam, have dedicated the years since to philanthropic work around the world. Their Omidyar Network investment firm has given hundreds of millions of dollars to for-profit and nonprofit organizations that foster economic advancement and government transparency. "Who We Are," Omidyar Network, accessed August 31, 2014, http:// www.omidyar.com/who-we-are.

4. "President Clinton's Plans for Education in America," *Phi Delta Kappan* 78, no. 2 (October 1996), available at Questia, accessed August 31, 2014, http://www.questia .com/library/journal/1G1-18850899/president-clinton-s-plans-for-education-in -america.

5. "Universal Service Program for Schools and Libraries (E-Rate)," Federal Communications Commission, accessed August 31, 2014, http://www.fcc.gov/guides /universal-service-program-schools-and-libraries.

6. Diana Sanglab, "Flipped Learning: Online Academy Spreads Education," *Caring Magazine,* accessed August 31, 2014, http://www.caringmagazine.org/flipped -learning.

7. Jerry Useem, "Business School, Disrupted," *New York Times,* May 31, 2014, ac-

cessed October 10, 2014, http://www.nytimes.com/2014/06/01/business/business
-school-disrupted.html.

8. Susan Adams, "Starbucks Announces It Will Give a Free College Education to
Thousands of Workers," *Forbes,* June 16, 2014, accessed October 10, 2014, http://
www.forbes.com/sites/susanadams/2014/06/16/starbucks-announces-it-will-give
-a-free-college-education-to-thousands-of-workers.

9. "Higher Education in Science and Engineering," in *Science and Engineering In-
dicators 2012,* National Science Foundation, January 1, 2012, accessed October 10,
2014, http://www.nsf.gov/statistics/seind12/c2/c2s4.htm.

10. David L. Chandler, "MIT Launches Student-Produced Educational Video
Initiative," *MIT News,* April 25, 2012, accessed August 31, 2014, http://newsoffice
.mit.edu/2012/k-12-education-video-initiative-0425.

11. Idit Harel, telephone interview with author, September 22, 2014.

12. "The Official Source of Literacy Data," UNESCO Institute for Statistics, accessed August 31, 2014, http://www.uis.unesco.org/literacy/Pages/default.aspx.

13. Reid Hoffman, "LinkedIn Turns 10: Celebrating 10 Years of Relationships
That Matter," *LinkedIn Official Blog,* May 5, 2013, accessed August 31, 2014, http://
blog.linkedin.com/2013/05/05/linkedin-turns-10.

14. Salvador Rodriguez, "LinkedIn Reaches 225 Million Users as It Marks Its
10th Birthday," *Los Angeles Times,* May 6, 2013, accessed August 31, 2014, http://
articles.latimes.com/2013/may/06/business/la-fi-tn-linkedin-turns-10-20130506.

15. Ibid.

16. Julie Bort, "Reid Hoffman: Founding a Startup Is like 'Throwing Yourself Off
a Cliff,'" *Business Insider,* May 9, 2013, accessed August 31, 2014, http://www.busi
nessinsider.com/hoffman-linkedin-nearly-failed-2013-5#ixzz3CPD13T7v.

17. "Disruptive Digital and Social Technology Transforms Hiring in Staffing,
Recruiting, and HR Industry," white paper, OpenReq, accessed August 31,
2014, http://public.cdn.openreq.com/OpenreqWhitePaper1-V2.pdf.

18. "Top Banks in the World 2014," RELBanks.com, http://www.relbanks.com
/worlds-top-banks/assets.

19. Henry C. K. Liu, "The Crisis of Wealth Destruction," Roosevelt Institute, accessed August 15, 2014, http://www.rooseveltinstitute.org/new-roosevelt/crisis -wealth-destruction.

20. The Grameen Foundation, http://grameenfoundation.org/our-impact/numbers.

21. "The Nobel Peace Prize for 2006," Nobelprize.org, 2006, accessed October 10, 2014, http://www.nobelprize.org/nobel_prizes/peace/laureates/2006/press.html.

22. Adam Vrankull, "MobiCash and KCB Bank Launch Fingerprint Banking in Rwanda," BiometricUpdate.com, January 4, 2013, accessed August 31, 2014, http://www.biometricupdate.com/201301/mobicash-and-kcb-bank-launch -fingerprint-banking-in-rwanda.

23. Susan Burhouse and Yazmin Osaki, *2011 FDIC National Survey of Unbanked and Underbanked Households,* Federal Deposit Insurance Corporation, September 2012, accessed August 31, 2014, https://www.fdic.gov/householdsurvey/2012 _unbankedreport.pdf.

24. Ibid.

25. Catherine New, "Simple's Free Checking Accounts Are So Popular, There's a Waiting List to Get One," *Huffington Post,* May 24, 2013, accessed August 31, 2014, http://www.huffingtonpost.com/2013/05/22/simple-bank_n_3314373.html.

26. Ibid.

27. "From Zero to $5 Billion: The Lending Club Story," Lending Club, 2014, accessed August 31, 2014, https://www.lendingclub.com/public/zero-to-5b.action.

28. Margaret Kane, "eBay Picks Up PayPal for $1.5 Billion," *CNET News,* July 8, 2002, accessed August 31, 2014, http://news.cnet.com/2100-1017-941964.html.

29. Brian Solomon, "The Youngest Billionaires on the Forbes 400: 20 Under 45," *Forbes,* September 16, 2013, accessed October 10, 2014, http://www.forbes.com /sites/briansolomon/2013/09/16/the-youngest-billionaires-on-the-forbes-400-20 -under-45.

30. "Tesla Model S Review: An Electric Sports Car Earns Our Top Test Score," *Consumer Reports,* July 2013, accessed August 31, 2014, http://consumerreports .org/cro/magazine/2013/07/tesla-model-s-review/index.htm.

31. Ibid.

32. Richard Lawler, "Tesla's $35,000 Car Will Be Called the Model 3," *Engadget,* July 15, 2014, accessed August 31, 2014, http://www.engadget.com/2014/07/15 /tesla-model-iii.

33. "Mission Summary: SpaceX Dragon Becomes First Private Spacecraft to Visit the Space Station," SpaceX.com, June 1, 2012, accessed August 31, 2014, http:// www.spacex.com/news/2013/02/08/mission-summary.

34. Ibid.

35. Elon Musk, interview with Sarah Lacy, 4th Founder Showcase, Mountain View, Calif., August 5, 2010, accessed November 12, 2014, http://foundershowcase .com/videos.

36. Lucas Mearian, "SolarCity Plans Largest Solar Panel Plant in Upstate N.Y.," *Computerworld,* June 17, 2014, accessed August 31, 2014, http://www.computer world.com/article/2490889/sustainable-it/solarcity-plans-world-s-largest-solar -panel-plant-in-upstate-n-y.html.

37. "World Oil Transit Chokepoints," U.S. Energy Information Administration (EIA), August 22, 2012, accessed August 31, 2014, http://www.eia.gov/countries /regions-topics.cfm?fips=wotc&trk=p3.

38. Brad Plumer, "How the US Manages to Waste $165 Billion in Food Each Year," *Washington Post,* August 22, 2012, accessed August 31, 2014, http://www .washingtonpost.com/blogs/wonkblog/wp/2012/08/22/how-food-actually-gets -wasted-in-the-united-states.

39. "Wasted: How America Is Losing Up to 40 Percent of Its Food from Farm to Fork to Landfill," Natural Resources Defense Council, accessed August 31, 2014, http://www.nrdc.org/food/wasted-food.asp.

40. Tiffany Hsu, "A Powerful Use for Spoiled Food," *Los Angeles Times,* May 15, 2013, accessed August 31, 2014, http://articles.latimes.com/2013/may/15/busi ness/la-fi-ralphs-energy-20130516.

41. Ryan Bushey, "11 Billion Dollar Startups You Never Heard Of," *Business Insider,* February 3, 2014, accessed August 31, 2014, http://www.inc.com/ryan -bushey/billion-dollar-startups.html.

42. "Billions Daily Affected by Water Crisis," Water.org, accessed August 31, 2014, http://water.org/water-crisis/one-billion-affected.

43. Vivek Wadhwa, "Anyone Anywhere Can Build the Next Google—There Are No Barriers," *Forbes,* November 21, 2013, accessed August 31, 2014, http://www .forbes.com/sites/singularity/2013/11/21/anyone-anywhere-can-build-the-next -google-there-are-no-barriers.

44. Clare Foran, "Akon Is Pushing Solar Power in Africa," *National Journal,* August 4, 2014, accessed August 31, 2014, http://www.nationaljournal.com/energy /akon-is-pushing-solar-power-in-africa-20140804.

45. Alexander Howard, "Exit Interview: Alec Ross on Internet Freedom, Innovation and Digital Diplomacy," *Huffington Post,* March 12, 2013, accessed August 31, 2014, http://www.huffingtonpost.com/alexander-howard/exit-inter view-alec-ross-_b_2860211.html.

46. Alec Ross, panel discussion, "Twiplomacy: The Rise of Ediplomacy and the Future of Communications," Washington, D.C., October 22, 2012.

47. Sam Gustin, "Digital Diplomacy," *Time,* September 2, 2011, accessed August 31, 2014, http://content.time.com/time/specials/packages/printout/0,29239, 2091589_2091591_2091592,00.html.

48. Karl Vick, "Turkey's Erdogan Turns Off Twitter, Turns Up the Nationalism," *Time,* March 21, 2014, http://time.com/33393/turkey-recep-tayyip-erdogan-twitter.

49. Chivis Martinez, "Juarez No Longer World Homicide King as It Drops to Second Place," *Borderland Beat,* January 14, 2012, accessed August 31, 2014, http:// www.borderlandbeat.com/2012/01/juarez-no-longer-world-homicide-king-as .html.

50. Ibid.

51. Nick Valencia and Arturo Chacon, "Juarez Shedding Violent Image, Statistics Show," CNN.com, January 5, 2013, accessed August 31, 2014, http://www .cnn.com/2013/01/05/world/americas/mexico-juarez-killings-drop.

52. Gustin, "Digital Diplomacy."

53. Alex Byers, "Napster Co-founder Sean Parker to Lead Civic Start-up," *Politico,* April 14, 2014, accessed August 31, 2014, http://www.politico.com/story/2014/04 /napster-co-founder-sean-parker-startup-brigade-105673.html.

Epilogue: The Self-Disruptor's Manifesto

1. Luisa Kroll, "Inside the 2014 Billionaires List: Facts and Figures," *Forbes,* March 3, 2014, accessed August 31, 2014, http://www.forbes.com/sites/luisakroll/2014/03/03/inside-the-2014-forbes-billionaires-list-facts-and-figures.

2. Cal Fussman, "What I've Learned: Richard Branson," *Esquire,* January 2002, accessed August 31, 2014, http://www.esquire.com/features/what-ive-learned/ESQ0102-JAN_BRANSON.

3. Vivek Wadhwa, "Anyone Anywhere Can Build the Next Google—There Are No Barriers," *Forbes,* November 21, 2013, accessed October 10, 2014, http://www.forbes.com/sites/singularity/2013/11/21/anyone-anywhere-can-build-the-next-google-there-are-no-barriers.

4. Eilene Zimmerman, "The Race to the $100 Genome," CNN.com, June 25, 2013, accessed August 31, 2014, http://money.cnn.com/2013/06/25/technology/enterprise/low-cost-genome-sequencing.

5. "The Internet of Things," Cisco Systems, accessed August 31, 2014, http://share.cisco.com/internet-of-things.html.

6. Grant Gross, "Cisco: Global 'Net Traffic to Surpass 1 Zettabyte in 2016," *PC World,* May 30, 2012, accessed August 31, 2014, http://www.pcworld.com/article/256522/cisco_global_net_traffic_to_surpass_1_zettabyte_in_2016.html.

7. "New to Broadband Guide," ThinkBroadband.com, http://www.thinkbroadband.com/guide/beginners-guide-to-broadband.html.

8. "Demystifying the Tech Startup Bubble," Bizbrain.org, http://www.bizbrain.org/startup-bubble. The cost of launching a new startup has dropped from the millions to $50,000, making them easier to fund. The actual cost to start a globally disruptive business is 95 percent lower than it was just a decade ago.

Index

Hawthorne Court Apartments, 171
HBO Go, 191
headhunters, 222
HealthAddress, 57
Hearst, William Randolph, 48
Hearst Castle, 48
Heinz, 149
Heinz, Henry, 122
Hendrix, Jimi, 155
Hepburn, Katharine, 44
Hercules & Xena: Alliance of Heroes, 91
Hewlett-Packard (HP), 112, 170, 172
Hipmunk, 156
hitRECord, 212
hockey, 35
Hodgson, Peter, 137–38, 139
Hoffer, Jeff, 213
Hoffman, Reid, xi–xii, 34, 53, 222–24
Holiday, Ryan, 39
Hollywood Reporter, 59–60
home building, 165–66
Home Shopping Network (HSN), 6, 171
Honda, 102
Hong Kong, 234
hotels, 172, 187, 209, 210
Houdini, Harry, 5
How to Get Control of Your Time and Your Life (Lakein), 56
Hsieh, Tony, 175, 176
Hu, George, 54
Huffington Post, 75
Huffman, Steve, 156
Hulu, 191
human genome, 241–42
Hummer, John, 81
Hurley, Chad, 6, 121
Hyman, Becky, 28
Hyman, Jenn, 28, 29
Hyundai, 94

Iams, 104–5
IBM, 12, 24, 65, 100, 118
    Jasmine Productions and, 19–21
    Kaypro II, 99–100
IdeaLab, 115
ideas:
    big, 104–9, 113, 242
    "eureka" moments and, 105

fear of theft of, 112
focus groups and, 126–27
killing, 101, 113
as team effort, 114–16
testing of, 123–25
at work, 110–11
zombie, 99–116, 214, 242
zombie, creation of, 112–13
"I Hope I Get It," 57
iMall, 94
Inc., 144
Indiegogo, 212
Industrial Light & Magic, 100
Infoseek, 115
Ingoldsby, Arthur, 138
Ingoldsby, James, 138
Innocent IV, Pope, 178
innovation, 10, 11, 15–16, 22, 24, 83, 133,
    145, 147, 159, 160, 163, 241, 242
Innovation Arts, 37
Innovator's Dilemma, The (Christensen),
    15
Inside the Vatican, 178
inspirations, 46–49
Instagram, 120, 125, 128, 211
intellectual property, 167–68
Internet, 21, 23, 91, 118, 164, 167, 205,
    214, 220, 242
    in classrooms, 215–19
    cyber crime and, 72
    ecommerce and, 10, 182, 184–85
    music and, 14, 23, 53, 79, 81
    Napster and, 14, 23, 62, 80–81,
        167–68, 207, 208, 209
    newspapers and, 207
    research and development and, 139–43
    social media, *see* social media
    travel agencies on, 155–56
    video games for, 90–91
    World Wide Web, 21, 23, 88, 89,
        90–92, 118
Internet Protocol (IP) devices, 242
internships, 54
Interpublic Group, 190
intrapreneurship, 23, 77–97
    Animalhouse.com and, 92–95
introspection, 5
Iovine, Jimmy, 63